SOUL EXPLORER

SOUL EXPLORER

Healing through Past Life Regression

PATRICIA S. McGIVERN

ISBN-13: 9780692814178
ISBN-10: 0692814175
Library of Congress Control Number: 2016920143
Soul Key, Tarpon Springs, FL

Dedicated to

My love, Timothy D. McGivern,
who has traveled with me through many lifetimes

You cannot teach a man anything,
you can only help him discover it himself.

—Galileo

CONTENTS

ACKNOWLEDGMENTS

To my always supportive husband, Tim, and our daughters Kylie and Meghan. I'm so happy we chose to do this lifetime together!

To my dearest friend and confidant, Alice Cockrell, who was the first person to ever speak the word *reincarnation* to me and who has been in my life ever since. Thank you for always believing me and believing in me. I have no doubt we've been together before.

To Bev Coe, who encouraged me to write about my clients' experiences and supported me along the way. I value your friendship and insight more than I can say.

A very special thanks to Ginny and Martha*, who inspired me to write *Soul Explorer.* Your willingness to explore your souls' journeys and allow me to witness your insight and healing was a beautiful gift.

To all my clients who have allowed me to share their powerful and poignant experiences of healing through past life regression so that others can learn: Alexandra*, Bill, Bobbie, Diane*, Ginny, Linda, Martha, Pat, Sarah, and Sunny*. I am honored to have been part of your journey.

And to Linda Farr and Marcella Zinner, gifted spiritual mediums, who demonstrated their gifts powerfully in their reading of Bobbie.

---

*Some names have been changed in this book for the sake of privacy. These names are marked with an asterisk the first time they appear.

PREFACE

You never know where life is going to take you. At least not consciously. I assure you I would have never thought I would aspire to be a hypnotist/hypnotherapist specializing in past life regression at twenty, thirty, or even forty years of age, but the unexpected twists and turns of life can lead us to something better than we ever could have imagined. Sometimes those turns are due to a tragedy in our lives, as it was for me. The miscarried loss of my second baby, then learning he was my father reincarnated shifted my spiritual belief paradigm so completely I knew I could never go back to my old way of thinking. The path behind me had disappeared.

Reincarnation was not part of my belief system growing up, nor was it a topic I had learned in any of the churches I had attended as a child. The first time I recall hearing about reincarnation, at least in a meaningful way, was on a business trip to Miami where I shared a hotel room with a colleague. Exhausted after a long day of work, we lounged on our beds, talking about the day's events. For reasons I no longer recall, the topic of our conversation shifted, and I found myself telling her about experiences of communication from my mother—after she had died. It was something I did with few people, as the experiences were precious to me, and I was fearful the communication would be ridiculed or simply dismissed. And yet, I felt safe enough to share them with my new friend, Alice.

Alice listened attentively as I told her the different accounts of communication from my mom and then waited with my stomach in a tight knot for an eye roll, a shocked look, or a cryptic response that never came.

Alice looked at me, took a deep breath, and calmly told me, "I died on the *Titanic*. I was a gypsy stowed away on the lower deck where I drowned. I haven't wanted to put my head underwater in this life."

Riveted to her every word, I listened intently as she spoke, my mouth no doubt agape. She believed my experiences of communication with my mother, so I believed her. It was that simple. I was twenty-three years old. Belief in reincarnation, however, was a leap of faith I wouldn't fully take for another two decades.

Thirteen years after my conversation with Alice, in the lobby of my doctor's hospital office, I discovered I was pregnant with my second child. When I was told the baby's due date was close to my deceased father's birthday, I had the thought that the baby would be born on that day, as I'd heard often happens. I then had what I now call an uncensored thought: a thought that seemed to come into my mind that was not my own. *The baby would be born on my dad's birthday because the baby was my dad returning to me.*

My eyes widened. *What? Where had that thought come from?* I stood momentarily dazed. I was surprised at the information but more so that the thought resonated with me in some odd way. *Why would I have such a bizarre thought?* I questioned silently. Just as suddenly, another thought came to my mind in the form of an answer: *the baby would bring me great emotional pain.* I gasped, and then a wave of sadness enveloped me. I stood paralyzed, staring into nothingness, and tried to discern the information until my nearly two-year-old daughter, Kylie, tugged on my leg and broke my trance. I scooped her up and began walking to the elevator as I tried to shake the sadness away. Where did this all too real sense of foreboding come from? This was a baby we had planned for and wanted. Why wasn't I excited?

I now believe my soul was preparing me for what would happen next. Five and a half weeks later, I lost our precious baby. As I look back on my pregnancy, there were many situations where my soul knew of the impending loss. There were times when I would sob uncontrollably over a situation that didn't warrant such an outburst, whether it was not getting a loan for a room addition to our house or being scolded by someone for announcing my pregnancy too early. In fact, it happened so many times that now, as I write about it, I'm surprised I didn't understand it more at the time. My soul tried to prepare me through a deep knowing within me, a knowing, an instinct, or an intuition that I hadn't learned to recognize or understand yet. A knowing I simply dismissed as pregnancy hormones.

Four and a half years after the miscarriage, days away from what would have been the baby's estimated birthday, the course of my life would change. As I was waking up from a nap, in that in-between state (which I now understand is an altered state in which we can hear the other side), I heard a small child's voice next to me clearly and emphatically state, "I'm right here. I'm right *here!*" My eyes flew wide open, expecting to see my three-year-old daughter, Meghan, who was born fourteen months after the miscarriage, standing next to me. But I was alone in the room. A spontaneous answer came to me that was not my own: I learned the voice I heard was that of the baby I had lost. To say it was shocking would be an understatement. I questioned my sanity.

Later that week, during a massage, a little boy appeared to my masseuse, Maryanne, looking to be about four years old, who said, "That's my mommy on the table. She wanted to know what sex I am." Maryanne later told me she wasn't sure if she should tell me what she was seeing, as she knew I wasn't metaphysical and thought it might risk her losing me as a client. I learned his name was Dillon, and I was able to speak with him directly, mind to mind. Although I didn't see him, I felt his presence next to me. I also sensed an older man present, whom today I would describe as a guide, although I didn't have that word or understanding at the time.

"What about Meghan?" the guide asked.

I felt annoyed. Who was he, and why was he getting in the way of me talking to my miscarried baby? Dillon answered the guide's question, telling me they had come together. While he had fulfilled his mission, she wanted me to be her mommy so much, she had returned to me. My mind reeled with the realization that I had been pregnant with twins. His words brought me out of that in-between state, and in an instant he, too, was gone.

I couldn't wait to get home to tell my husband, Tim, about what had happened. He was always so supportive, but on that day, his lack of a response made me think he didn't believe me. Today, of course, I realize he was as stunned as I. Whether it was his reaction or the fact that the experience was just too big to accept, for reasons I don't understand, I either completely forgot or consciously suppressed this amazing experience. I wonder now what might have happened if I'd never gone back to see Maryanne.

~

When I returned a few months later for another massage with Maryanne, I was completely confused when she asked me what Tim had thought of my massage with her.

Thinking she was fishing for a compliment, I told her it was relaxing and wonderful.

She looked at me, puzzled, and exclaimed, "I talked to your miscarried baby!" Her comment broke my amnesia, and I remembered that I had talked to my baby. Yet oddly and quite shockingly, I could not recall his name. This brought Dillon forward again to Maryanne and made it perfectly clear that he was unhappy with my forgetfulness. On that day, I promised him I'd never forget anything he ever said again.

Through Maryanne, Dillon told me that one of my life missions was to write a book entitled "Angel Babies to help heal the mommies who've lost their babies." At the time, I did not easily or readily accept the mission. In fact, my initial thought about the mission was quite clear: "wrong mommy, wrong life mission." First, I wasn't a writer. Also, what would people think? They would think I was crazy! For the next few years, Dillon continued to nudge me along with many signs of communication.

I began voraciously reading every book I could find on angel encounters, near-death experiences, and reincarnation. The first book I read was Dr. Brian Weiss's *Many Lives, Many Masters*—a book about reincarnation and past life regression. Although my eyes were wide and filled with wonder as I read his book, it felt as though I had found an ancient truth. A truth that made more sense than anything I'd been taught or rather what I *hadn't* been taught through organized religion.

Perhaps it was too early for me when Alice shared her life and death on the *Titanic* nearly two decades earlier. The teacher was there, but the student wasn't ready. A seed had been planted, but it would take a great loss for me to be jarred awake.

Once I had read and researched so much about reincarnation and past life regression I no longer doubted their possibility, I decided to experience a past life regression myself.

I was excited and felt as though I was about to take an exciting trip. What I didn't expect was how profound and moving the experience would be for me. In my past life session, I was amazed but not surprised to recognize Tim, although he looked completely different. As I stood at the entrance of our ancient mud abode, tears fell gently upon my cheeks with his return to our village. He had survived a bloody war.

The regression was an immensely powerful experience, and yet upon emerging, I was relieved it was over. I didn't think I could imagine anything more of that life. Although I believed in reincarnation, I questioned if I had imagined it all. Many years have passed since then, and I have had numerous confirmations of that particular lifetime—too many to doubt or question their authenticity. It explained my early relationship with Tim, why we were drawn to live in a small Greek community, and why we nearly went to the Greek Islands on our honeymoon. I knew my nickname, but while daydreaming remembered my full name, which I'd never heard. I even discovered the name of the island where we lived. To this day, I can still describe that lifetime in great detail.

I continued exploring my past lives and became interested in becoming a hypnotist in order to help others. While attending a workshop, I met Carole Bowman, author of *Children's Past Lives*. I discussed my interest in becoming a hypnotist, and she introduced me to past life regressionist Carolene Heart, who was also at the workshop. I set up an appointment with her to find out who I should train with and to experience a session with her. I decided to discover if I could heal from a physical symptom through a past life regression.

Specifically, I wanted to find the source of my sinus infections and ultimately heal. I didn't expect nor was I prepared for where the regression would take me.

While hypnotized, I learned that Dillon *was* my father returning to me. I tried to ignore the information as it came through, as for some reason, I wanted a different answer. I learned he had *chosen* not to come, because in his not coming, he could help me the most. It would be through his not coming and my receiving messages from him that I would be catapulted on my spiritual journey. I felt the power of his intention and his deep, unconditional love for me as he expressed it as the greatest gift he could give me.

There aren't words that can adequately express the depth of emotions I felt in the regression. The experience touched my very soul, and somewhere deep within me, I understood its truth. I realized the uncensored thought I had in the hospital lobby when I learned I was pregnant had been right. My dad was returning to me as the baby!

Four years passed before I accepted the mission to write *Angel Babies*. Fear had blocked me, and in an insightful, poignant moment, I realized that by not writing it, I would lose an opportunity for my soul's growth. I questioned what I knew about babies on the other side until a colleague suggested I write about my own experiences of communication with Dillon. The words flew effortlessly on the pages as I handwrote each remembrance of Dillon contacting me.

I knew I couldn't be the only one having such experiences, but at the time, few people acknowledged an early-loss baby, let alone talked about receiving signs of communication from the baby. I began my search for others, and found them through advertisements I had placed in the back of parenting magazines as well as in a letter to the editor of *Venture Inward*, a magazine published by the Association of Research Enlightenment (ARE).

Parents wrote to me from around the world with their powerful experiences of communication with their lost babies. After more than four years of research and compilation, *Angel Babies: Messages from Miscarried and Other Lost Babies* was published in May of 2009, the same month in which Dillon would have been born eighteen years earlier.

I became interested in guiding others to their past lives and trained with Gerald Kein at the Omni Hypnosis Center as a hypnotist and hypnotherapist. His technique was different from that of most other hypnosis trainers, as he focused on regression work and discovering the emotional root cause of a problem. He is a gifted instructor I feel fortunate to have studied under. Six months later, I trained with Dr. Brian Weiss for more in-depth past life regression. His was the first book I'd read on reincarnation, so to train with him felt as though somehow I'd come full circle. I continued my training through the International Board for Regression Therapy and opened my practice in the office of a local psychiatrist—a very open-minded one—who understood the power of the subconscious mind and the depth of the soul.

My sinus infections disappeared after my regression. When my clients discovered where their issues first began, they, too, experienced emotional and physical healing. Although I am well trained and have conducted thousands of sessions, it is still exciting work, and I continue to be astounded by how effective hypnosis and regression are for healing. There is a part in each of us that subconsciously knows why we have a physical or emotional issue and in revealing that knowing we can heal; we just haven't been made aware of how to access that information. I'm still puzzled as to why medical training touches on hypnosis so briefly when it has proved to be so effective.

It wasn't until I worked with Ginny that I began to think of writing about the healing experiences she and others were having through their past life regressions with me. Ginny came to me for a fear of heights, and through our conversation, I knew she grew up in the Catholic faith and was not metaphysical in her beliefs. I regressed her to when her feeling of a fear of heights first began. She went back to early childhood and seemed to find the source of her fear of small heights, such as getting on a ladder, but her fear of driving in the mountains remained.

Several sessions later, Ginny spontaneously regressed to a past life. She was so fascinated, she wanted to explore more, and so we did over the next two years. Ginny healed from her fear of heights, but more importantly, she also healed a deep emotional wound with her abusive mother. You'll read about her regression and those of other clients later on.

This book isn't about proving the existence of reincarnation, although I feel there is compelling evidence to consider the possibility. It's about people experiencing emotional and physical healing through revisiting past lives and understanding themselves better. Hopefully, those who are interested in reincarnation and past life regression will find my clients' experiences as fascinating as they have been for me.

The title of this book came to me during a drive from Saint Louis to mid-Missouri, when I saw a road sign that read Lewis and Clark. I recalled my cousin telling me our ancestry traced back to Meriwether Lewis. I wondered if the exploration gene was nestled within me and what, if anything, I had explored in my life. It was then that I realized my passion wasn't in discovering new lands, but in exploring old frontiers—those of the soul, the frontiers of undiscovered past lives. It was in that moment that I realized I am a soul explorer.

REINCARNATION, HISTORY OF REINCARNATION, HYPNOSIS, AND PAST LIFE REGRESSION

From the moment I began seeing clients as a hypnotist and regressionist, I have been nothing less than astounded at the results of their sessions. That sense of awe and total amazement of the healing that occurs from regressions continues with me nearly twenty years later with each new client. I never know where the deeper wisdom in a client will take us, but I know to trust it. The soul *always* knows where to go to heal.

Within the first months of opening my practice, clients who came to me for clinical hypnosis (smoking, weight loss, etc.) began to spontaneously regress to other lifetimes. I knew they were getting to the core issues to resolve their problems, even when reincarnation was not part of their belief system, and I was always excited to hear of the healing that occurred for them as a result of their regressions.

In one case, a young woman came to me to help her to sleep through the night. She said she would wake up in the middle of the night and not be able to go back to sleep. Once she was in hypnosis, I asked her to go back to when this feeling first began. When she spoke, her voice dropped to a lower tone as she said in a deep Southern drawl, "I'm a *man*! I'm about to be hung [sic]. I did it all right. I stole the horses...and I'd do it again!"

I knew from our initial conversation that she did not believe in reincarnation, so after I emerged her from hypnosis, I explained to her that some people look at an experience such as hers as a metaphor or a psychodrama of the mind. "This was *not* a metaphor of the mind!" she practically screamed. "I *was* that man! I *am* that man!" We then talked about reincarnation and past lives. I did not know why she went to that lifetime or what it had to do with her sleep issue until she returned several weeks later and said, "My husband reminded me that I wake up because I get a pain in my neck." I quickly looked at her intake form to see if I had missed something. I hadn't. I looked at her, puzzled. "I didn't mention I was in a car accident four years ago," she explained. "I hurt my neck in the exact same spot the rope was on my, or his, neck. I've been going to a chiropractor twice a week for all these years to help me. When I went for my next appointment after our session, my chiropractor told me I was in complete alignment and asked me incredulously, 'What did you do?' Patricia, I am so sorry, but there was no way I was going to tell him what I'd done." I knew she was still trying to understand the concept of reincarnation and past lives. "I'm sleeping through the night now and riding my bike."

Her neck and sleeping issues were resolved. The soul remembers everything.

Another of my first clients had a fear of swallowing—even swallowing his own saliva. Regression brought us back to when he was a newborn, and his mother put soda in his baby bottle. The carbonation of the drink had made him choke. Regression led us to many more subsequent events, such as sucking on a pacifier and having too much saliva accumulate in his mouth, causing him to choke. Each event anchored the feeling of fear deeper and deeper within him as we discovered and then healed each event. Afterward, his fear greatly subsided, and he was pleased and relieved. But I have always been curious to know, if he had returned, whether we might have discovered he had died from choking in some way in a past life.

I was content that my clients were greatly improved, if not healed, from re-experiencing a previous life, but when they began researching their past life names, time periods, or regions of the world and actually found themselves (or some type of validation) on the Internet, I found it just as exciting as they did. Much of the time during regressions, clients find themselves living very simple lives in the distant past that are so nondescript, they are impossible to research for validation. Researchable or not, the outcomes are powerful in terms of healing to the client, which is always the ultimate goal. Those who are able to find themselves through research are always thrilled because it validates their experience; they often say, "It really happened!" However, even when they discover who they were, most people, themselves included, would not recognize their names, a specific war, or a regional issue without a vast knowledge of world history. For example, most of us are not familiar with the Battle of Worringen or the War of the Spanish Succession; we can't even recall the name of the first rebellion in our own early American colonies, let alone the dates or leaders of those battles.

I have had clients regress to lifetimes as far back as 6000 to 8000 BC and others as recent as the 1980s. They have died by jumping off a New York City building during the stock market crash in 1929, in the atomic bomb at Hiroshima, in the gas chambers of Auschwitz-Birkenau, in the American Civil War, in a Viking war, and at the Battle of Wounded Knee. Some clients died of diseases, by drowning, from drug overdoses, or from smoke inhalation, while others were human sacrifices. Some committed suicide or were murdered, while others passed peacefully in their sleep.

They have been African American, Native American, Eskimo, Japanese, Egyptian, Norwegian, French, Belgian, English, German, and early American, to name just a few. They have had every skin color possible and been both male and female, child and adult. They have been homosexual and heterosexual. They have been blind and had Down Syndrome. They have been fathers, mothers, sisters and brothers, orphans, warriors, prostitutes, street urchins, priests, mistresses, politicians, poor and wealthy. We take on many different types of human bodies and circumstances to accumulate the experiences we need on the Earth plane for our soul's growth. And here is some good news: sometimes we have easy lives, too.

REINCARNATION

Reincarnation is simply when the soul returns to a new body for the purpose of learning and growing. We have all had hints of past lives, through different experiences when we might ask ourselves, "How did I know that?" "Where do I know that person from?" or "Why did I react that way?"

For example, have you ever been somewhere that you've never visited before and yet known your way around the streets or felt comfortable there? Have you ever been drawn to a certain time period, a specific war, or a country and not known why? Have you ever read everything you possibly could on a certain topic, time period, or person or been in a situation or event in which you've overreacted emotionally and not understood why? Have you had reoccurring dreams of being in another time period? Have you met someone and had the distinct feeling of knowing that person? Perhaps you have even asked the person where he or she grew up, went to school, or work, trying to find the connection but just not able to put it together. You feel like you already *know* this person. He or she feels familiar to you. Conversely, you might meet someone and have the feeling *I don't know what it is about this person, but I just don't like or trust him or her.* This is a soul recognition. These are all hints or indicators that you've been here before. You can't consciously put it together, but your soul remembers.

Before returning to Earth, we plan our next life, and we see how our human life will unfold, so when we have the feeling of déjà vu, it can be that we are remembering our blueprint for this life. Who plays what role is decided during the planning stage. The pre-birth planning includes choosing our parents, who choose us as well. We may choose our parents for karmic reasons or for their genes, which will enable us, for the purpose of our soul's growth, to have a physical trait, intellect, or talent.

We travel in soul groups. Many of the people in your life today have been with you before. Your mother today may have been your brother, best friend, child, or father in another life. We volunteer to play different roles for one another for the purpose of our soul's growth, for the growth of another person, or for an entire soul group. Nearly every regression I've facilitated has resulted in the client recognizing someone in his or her current life.

Some talents or gifts we may bring forward from other lifetimes. A good example of this is Mozart, who began playing the piano flawlessly at three years of age, composing at six, and writing symphonies at eight. It can also be evident when we learn another language or a new skill easily and effortlessly, often to the amazement of our instructor.

The challenges we experience are planned to help us grow through karma. Karma is simply a balance of experience. I view it not as punishment, but as an opportunity for the soul's growth. We choose the challenges. Our lives are filled with challenges, pain, and disappointment, a framework of possibilities, but all are designed as opportunities for our soul's growth. We have a good idea during the planning stage of how our lives can unfold to accomplish everything we want, but once here, we have free will, and we can make whatever decisions we choose.

Whatever our life theme is currently, we have probably experienced it before in other lives. If we want to learn the theme of compassion, we would need opportunities to feel compassion. If our theme is abandonment, perhaps we were abandoned in another life, and we are experiencing it again so that we might learn to understand and forgive. Or perhaps we abandoned someone, so we are now experiencing how abandonment feels. The purpose is to learn and grow.

What if we looked at struggles that keep repeating themselves as opportunities to grow that, once learned, won't repeat themselves? If we knew that every struggle that ever happened to us was designed for the purpose of our spiritual growth, could we look at them differently? If we were able to look at our life challenges from a higher perspective, what we once saw as negative situations, we might now look at as gifts. Because we decide our challenges, we are not victims. From the soul's perspective, all experiences are simply opportunities for growth. If you looked at your experiences from this viewpoint, how would you look at your life today? Could you see the experiences differently?

What if you chose to be blind in this life, so you wouldn't have to see terrible things in the world? Or you chose to be unable to speak because you wanted to learn to listen in this life. In *A Child of Eternity: An Extraordinary Young Girl's Message from the World Beyond*, Kristi Jorde is the mother of Adriana Rocha, a low-functioning autistic who did not speak. In 1991, at nine years old, Adriana began speaking to her mother through picking out keys on a specialized computer. It was then that her parents learned she was a very bright little girl in a body she was unable to control. She told her mother she hurt herself when she was in the womb by not eating. She told her she *chose* to have autism. She chose it to learn patience and humility. She typed messages to her mother about her past lives, about Jesus, about choosing her to be her mother, and about the guides available to help her mother on her own path to enlightenment.

Most of us were taught that, as babies, we come as blank slates, but deep within us is a higher wisdom and remembrance of our other lives. How we died in another life can affect us in this life. It may be brought forward when something happens that reminds the soul. There may be phobias, emotional issues, or physical issues with our bodies that we bring forward, including birthmarks where past trauma occurred.

Some children remember their past lives and will talk about them until the age of five or so. In *Children's Past Lives*, author Carol Bowman writes about her own son's regression to a life as an African American soldier in the Civil War. Once this life was remembered (through hypnosis), his fear of loud noises and eczema (located on his body where he was shot in the war) disappeared.

Many children speak spontaneously about their past lives and give detailed stories of people, places, and events that they would have no way of knowing about. Sometimes this can happen riding in a car's back seat while falling asleep in that in-between state or when doing something that reminds them of a different time. The child may say something startling such as, "My other mommy had blond hair" or "When *I* was the mommy..."

Psychiatrist Dr. Ian Stevenson is the former chairman of the department of psychiatry at the University of Virginia and author of *Twenty Cases Suggestive of Reincarnation*. In his book he focuses on twenty cases of children he investigated and writes about the phenomenon of young children between the ages of two to four having spontaneous recall of a previous life. Over a period of forty years, Dr. Stevenson investigated three thousand cases of children around the world who recalled previous lives. Approximately one-third of the cases he investigated in which phobias developed were linked to how the child had died in a previous life. For example, a fear of the water developed if he or she had drowned. Most interesting is when a child can speak a language he or she has never heard or been exposed to. This is called xenoglossy. Dr. Stevenson also did further studies showing how birthmarks can correlate with how a child died in an earlier life.

Our last thoughts before dying in a previous life can come forward as a residue energy that can influence this life. Rabbi Yonassan Gershom shares compelling evidence through many examples in his book *Beyond the Ashes: Cases of Reincarnation from the Holocaust*. Gershom said, "I am now convinced that the vast majority of Jews born into the baby boom generation are Holocaust victims returned." Many had recurring nightmares of the Holocaust and found their way to Rabbi Gershom. Some of the last thoughts from those who perished included "If only I had been born with blond hair and blue eyes." In their current lives, they have blond hair and blue eyes.

In a case you will read about later on, moments before passing in an Auschwitz/Birkenau gas chamber, Ginny had the thought that if only she had been unloved or had not loved, it wouldn't hurt so much. You will also read how her present life unfolded as a result of that thought.

HISTORY OF REINCARNATION

Most Christians aren't aware that reincarnation isn't new to Christianity. During the first three decades after Christ, some Christian sects taught reincarnation. Among the believers in reincarnation were the Gnostics, whose practice spoke of having a personal experience of God. Belief in reincarnation traces back to the earliest of times: Greek pre-Socratics and Celtic Druids are reported to have taught the doctrine of reincarnation.

It is a belief that was held by Pythagoras (570–495 BC), Socrates (470–399 BC), and Plato (428/427–348/347 BC) and carried through to Biblical times.

In 325 AD the Roman emperor Constantine deleted references to reincarnation contained in the New Testament at the Council of Nicaea. Then in 553 AD, during the Second Council of Constantinople, the concept of reincarnation was declared heresy.

Perhaps they felt it would weaken the growing power of the Church. Yet the early Church fathers had accepted reincarnation as part of their beliefs. Many of the early Gnostics (from the ancient Greek word meaning *having knowledge*), including Origen, Clement of Alexandria, and Saint Jerome, all believed they had lived before and would return to live again.

Belief in reincarnation traveled to medieval France, where it survived in the Languedoc (meaning *language of the Occ* [Occitan]) region of southern France. It was a central part of the Cathar (from the Greek word meaning *the pure* [ones]) sect until the Roman Catholic church brutally exterminated Cathars and Catharism in the thirteenth century.

The Albigensian Crusade, also known as the Cathar Crusade, was initiated by Pope Innocent III to eliminate Catharism in Languedoc. The first attack was on the town of Béziers. When a soldier asked Arnaud Amalric (also known as Arnaud-Amaury), the Cistercian abbot-commander in the town of Béziers, how to distinguish the difference between the Catholics and the Cathars, he supposedly answered to kill them all. God will recognize his own. They then slaughtered the entire population of Béziers. Arnaud-Amaury wrote to Pope Innocent III telling him twenty thousand heretics were put to the sword, regardless of rank, age, or sex.

The castle of Montsegur (meaning *safe/secure mountain*) was one of the last strongholds of the Cathars who, as pacifists, would not fight back. The castle withstood a nine-month siege of ten thousand troops. Ultimately, the Cathars surrendered, and more than two hundred *perfecti* (seen by the Catholic Church as the perfect heretics) were burned en masse in a bonfire at the base of the mountain on March 16, 1244. The last known Cathar burning occurred in 1321.

The Inquisition was formed to extinguish religious sectarianism as a response to the growing Cathar movement in southern France. It lasted roughly seven hundred years. An estimated one million were annihilated. Inquisitors required sympathizers of heretics to sew a yellow cross onto their clothes. But belief in reincarnation survived through the nineteenth century in Kabbalists,

Rosicrucians, Alchemists, Hermeticists, and Freemasons. Those who accepted reincarnation read like a *Who's Who* list and include French philosopher Voltaire, Ralph Waldo Emerson, and Henry Wadsworth Longfellow, as well as W. B. Yeats, Rudyard Kipling, Salvador Dali, Victor Hugo, Carl Yung, and Benjamin Franklin.

According to a 2013 Harris Poll, 24 percent of Americans believe in reincarnation and another 13 percent aren't sure. Globally those numbers are much higher at 51 percent according to a survey conducted by the Global Research Society and the Institute for Social Research in 2016. European beliefs have been steadily increasing in the acceptance of reincarnation. The concept is widely accepted in South America, India, and Asia.

HYPNOSIS

Hypnosis has been around since ancient times. Egyptian sleep temples or dream temples may be examples of ways in which hypnosis was used more than four thousand years ago, under the influence of Imhotep. Imhotep, (2650-2600 BC), was one of the most revered people of his time and after. He was a healer, architect, high priest, sage, and advisor to King Djoser.

The sleep temples were considered hospitals, as they healed a variety of physical and perhaps emotional problems. In ancient Greece, there were healing temples of Asclepios, named for the Greek god of medicine. In 2600 BC, Wong Tai, considered the father of Chinese medicine, wrote about healing techniques that involved using words to heal people. In 1550 BC, *Ebers Papyrus*, one of oldest known medical works, described trance procedures that are similar to modern-day hypnotherapy. Hippocrates (460–377 BC), the father of medicine, said, "The affliction suffered by the body and soul sees quite well with the eyes shut."

Hypnosis (from the Greek god of sleep, Hypnos) is a term coined by Dr. James Braid (1795–1860), a Scottish surgeon who used it to perform painless surgical procedures. He is considered the father of modern hypnotism.

James Esdaile, MD (1808–1859), another Scottish doctor, used hypnosis in surgery while stationed in India, with astounding results. He performed several thousand minor operations and three hundred major ones, including nineteen amputations, all painlessly. It is also reported that he cut the 50 percent mortality rate to less than 8 percent. Yet neither the Indian nor the English medical societies were impressed with his success. He was ridiculed, belittled, and expelled from the British Medical Society with charges his patients were pretending to have no pain so they could get free operations.

During the American Civil War, hypnosis was used by field doctors until anesthetics were introduced in 1846 (ether) and 1847 (chloroform). The British Medical Association and the American Medical Association approved the use of hypnosis in 1955 and 1958, respectively, yet it is little used today. Doctors work with the conscious mind; hypnotists work with the subconscious mind.

Hypnosis was largely kept alive by stage magicians, who unfortunately also tainted the word. It has been poorly understood, due to misrepresentations in film, television, and literature, and as a result, most people have preconceived and incorrect ideas of hypnosis. Let me dispel some of those myths and misconceptions.

For a moment, I'd like you to think about stage hypnotists, whom many have seen or heard are able to "make" someone cluck like a chicken. If you watch, they will do some exercises with the audience that are fun, such as having audience members close their eyes and put their arms straight in front of them. Then they will have the audience members imagine that their right arms have helium balloons attached to them and feel the arms with the balloons begin to rise. Audience members are then told to open their eyes.

Those people with their right arms raised will be good candidates to bring onstage later. Why? Because they followed directions and allowed themselves to accept the suggestion. When they are selected to come onstage, they often know they are going to be asked to do something silly, whether it's sing off key, cluck like a chicken, or be a ballerina. They willingly accept the suggestion.

All hypnosis is self-hypnosis. If you don't want to be hypnotized, you won't be. Anyone of average intelligence can be hypnotized if they allow themselves to be. Hypnosis is simply a state of focused concentration. When you are relaxed and your concentration is so focused that you are not distracted by outside noises, you are in a light state of hypnosis. It's is a state you go into and out of throughout the day without realizing it. It's that state right before you fall asleep at night or as you are waking. It can happen when you are driving and are so focused in thought about something that you arrive at your destination wondering how you got there. It happens when you are absorbed into a good book or movie. It can happen when you daydream, for example, or during a massage.

Hypnosis feels natural because it is natural. You might think you are not hypnotized because you expect it to feel weird. Unlike what movies have portrayed, you are not asleep, unconscious, or a zombie. You hear every word the hypnotist says. The conscious mind is aware of everything that is going on and is always keeping an eye on things, while the subconscious mind takes a front seat. The subconscious mind is not limited by time, space, or logic.

A hypnotist is simply guiding you into a state where you can access your subconscious mind. You are always in control while hypnotized, and if at any time you want to stop the process, you can. Think of it like this: you are driving the car, and the hypnotist is simply suggesting you take a right at the next road. If you don't want to, you won't. In fact, you can pull over and stop driving. You are in control. Not the hypnotist. However, if you want to go into the beautiful state of hypnosis, it's important to let go and allow your hypnotist to guide you.

You will not do things against your will or do whatever your hypnotist tells you to do. If that were true, everyone who went to a hypnotist to stop smoking would quit. You have to want to make the change and accept the change to being a nonsmoker, not be there just because your spouse or doctor wants you to. You aren't put under hypnosis. You are simply guided into the beautiful state of hypnosis, where you can access a level deeper than your conscious state. This deeper level is where your intuition and creativity lie.

Hypnosis is not a truth serum. You can comment, criticize, and censor yourself while in hypnosis. If you find yourself in a lifetime doing something you are embarrassed by or uncomfortable with, you may not want to reveal that until you are ready to do so.

You won't do anything against your moral or ethical values while hypnotized. You also won't get stuck anywhere. It's like a book that you can close anytime you want.

You can talk while hypnotized. Some people become so relaxed that they speak in a whisper when they answer a question the hypnotist asks. Others speak as loudly and clearly as they do while in the conscious state.

You may experience the scene in which you find yourself with sights, smells, tastes, hearing, and emotions. You may be in the scene in a different body or looking at a scene as an observer. Or you may not see but rather sense or somehow know what is happening. If you meditate, you will find you can get to this state effortlessly. If your conscious mind is too active, you can't access the information of your past lives.

The conscious mind is where you analyze, rationalize, and have temporary memory. It is where willpower is located. The subconscious mind remembers everything. Every taste, smell, habit, emotion, and event you have experienced is recorded in a deep part of you. As you experience another lifetime, there is a part of you that is always watching and keeping an eye on things, so to speak. However, if that part of you becomes too analytical, it will bring you up to your conscious state, the state you are in every day after waking, where the remembrance of another time is forgotten.

In hypnosis you can access your deeper wisdom, where you can find all of your answers. But if you aren't truly ready for a change, even once you know the cause, you won't change. This can happen when someone has a secondary gain by having an issue or problem, likes the way they are, or is somehow benefitting from a problem. An example of this is when an elderly client smiled broadly as she said to me, "This is the first time my husband has paid attention to me during our nearly fifty-year marriage." Her issue was resolved 90 percent, but she had to hold on to the rest because the attention she was receiving from her husband benefitted her.

During a past life regression, you may see everything clearly. If you are visual, you see your feet, the clothing you are wearing, your body type, your gender, and your age. The only way you see what you look like is by looking at a reflection of yourself in a mirror, glass, or water, as is the case in your current body. Also, you may not "see" a scene or situation in your mind's eye but somehow know or sense what is happening. Just as we have different learning styles, such as being visual, auditory, or kinesthetic, there is no right or wrong; we can obtain this information in different ways, and there can be deep emotion involved as you experience the lifetime firsthand.

While hypnotized, you may get an immediate answer to questions regarding the year, the town, or your name. Sometimes you won't get an answer. It's OK. Maybe that piece of information isn't important in the big scheme of things. Perhaps not all the information you experience is 100 percent accurate. An example of this is a client who researched the name and address of the person she was in 1938. She later learned she didn't live at 15 Patrick Street, but at 15 Mission Street—above a building called Patrick and Company. Remember, you are still going through the human mind, and what you remember is based on your perception of what happened.

However, when you are researching your lifetime and you find enough facts that are correct, it is, at the very least, extremely interesting and thought provoking. And if you gain an insight into a situation while removing a block or healing in some way, isn't that all that really matters?

There is a part of you that is always watching over you when you are hypnotized. It's that part of you that can begin to analyze the information coming to you. When this happens, it brings you up to the conscious state. I remind my clients that they can analyze all they want after the session, but during the regression, they should let their imaginations soar. Don't worry about what is right or wrong. Imagination is the gateway to the soul and the memories.

PAST LIFE REGRESSION

Past life regression is exploring your soul's history. It can be experienced in various ways, but the easiest and most direct method is through hypnosis. Mediums can tell you about your past lives with accuracy, but in a past life regression, you relive the experience. You aren't hearing someone tell you of a lifetime in Egypt, you are *in* Egypt.

Some suggest these past life memories are carried in the genes. Yes, we can and do reincarnate with our own families, and we can do so quickly, but that doesn't mean we stay within that specific bloodline forever. There are some lifetimes in which a genetic pool has ended, as with the Holocaust. We have lived in both male and female bodies with different skin colors and in different cultures around the globe. We have lived at different socioeconomic levels and have had different academic backgrounds so that we see ourselves and the world from different perspectives.

Why does remembering a previous life help? Because in re-membering, you remind the soul of what happened. Just the remembering can be enough to neutralize a fear or phobia. By recalling past lives, you can understand yourself better and overcome present problems, including phobias and fears; we *can* heal ourselves.

Most major life events are preplanned, including your birth, family, relationships, and career, as well as accidents, illnesses, and death. However, no plan is set in stone, as once you're here, your free will and free choice are in effect. Choice overrides destiny, which brings me to karma. Some people say karma is punishment. I prefer to look at karma as an opportunity for balance and growth. Difficult life experiences never feel good while you are in the midst of them, but reflect on them later and ask yourself, "What did I learn from the experience?"

Sometimes, the answer to an issue can be found in one lifetime. Other times, the issue may repeat itself over many lifetimes. Whatever pattern you have in your current life, it is there for a reason. You've probably had it before and either didn't work out the karma of it or didn't learn what you needed to from it, so you are experiencing it again. It was your choice. You have another opportunity to grow. When we understand where a problem or issue originated, we are then in a position to let it go.

In a regression, you can go through a death scene from a previous life and know how you died without your physical body dying. The knowledge of how you died often releases any energy residue you've carried forward that manifests as physical issues, fears, or phobias. For instance, learning that a chronic clearing of your throat is due to your dying from smoke inhalation can resolve the issue, as you will read about in Pat's lifetime as Carly.

Souls tend to reincarnate together again and again over the span of many lifetimes. We are always with our soul group. We decide who will play what role. We choose when we come into this life and when we leave, and we have a mission plan.

We come to learn lessons to spiritually evolve, and we choose the experiences and circumstances that will enable us to do so. If we want to learn about compassion, we will need experiences that will allow us an opportunity to learn compassion. We may come to help a loved one learn that lesson, as you will read about in one of Ginny's experiences.

Belief in reincarnation isn't a criterion to experience a past life. It is not uncommon for a client to come to me for clinical hypnosis and, while looking for the root cause of an issue, spontaneously regress to another life. When I instruct clients to go a deeper wisdom inside of them, their deep wisdom knows exactly where to go. It is the wisdom and the understanding brought to the current life that make past life regressions so profoundly moving.

If guilt has been brought forward into a client's current life, I make sure the client speaks to the person or persons the client has hurt in the in-between state as well. I have seen guilt dissolve as a client learns guilt is unnecessary and all is forgiven by that person's spirit.

What action heals the most? Forgiveness. Simply put, forgiveness is letting go of pain. It is a gift from you to you. It's not saying what the other person did to you was OK; it's saying, "I will no longer allow this experience to affect my life."

When I facilitate a group past life regression, individuals are silent as they find answers in their minds to the questions I ask. I don't know who is in a past life until afterward, but I pay close attention to body language, facial expressions, and those who have tears running down their cheeks. After the regression, I like to allow time for those who want to discuss their past lives with the group do so. It's a safe place to share their experiences where others' dogma, beliefs, and criticism don't undermine their experience. I've noticed that some people don't emote during the regression, but as they begin to talk about their past life, the emotion comes up and they cry, as reliving the experience was so powerful. I encourage them to let it all out. They are ancient tears that have been bottled up for a long time. That alone can be very healing.

Not long ago, I facilitated a past life regression workshop in a local metaphysical store, where I watched as two attractive college age girls walked through the door. Following them like puppy dogs were two good-looking boys. I was happy to see young people interested. All were dressed for the nearby beach, and I wondered if the girls had coerced the boys into coming to the workshop. One boy sat opposite me in the circle, as far away as he could, crossed his arms, and looked at me intently. His body language stated his "I've got my eye on you" message very clearly. After the regression, as we were going around the room listening to everyone's experiences, he remained silent until the last moments, when I asked him if he'd like to share his own experience… and waited to get blasted by him.

I was surprised as I watched his eyes well with tears, as he shared his experience of finding himself in a World War II scene. He knew his name was John Jacob*, but everyone called him JJ. In the war scene, he was with his best friend, whom he recognized as his grandfather in his current life. As they were advancing in the field, JJ saw a wire on the ground and quickly yanked his friend back, saving his life. However, the land mine exploded, and JJ himself was killed.

He was now sobbing as he continued with his story. He told us how he and his grandfather had been very close in his present life before his grandfather passed. There were few dry eyes as we listened to his moving story. He told us how he had heard about JJ from time to time growing up and knew he had saved his grandfather's life, but he never knew JJ's full name, as it was never used. He quickly called his mom and asked her JJ's full name. She told him it was John Jacob. Still crying, he sputtered, "And do you know who that is?" as he pointed to the other boy who came with him. "He's my best friend. His name…" He struggled to get the words out as he sobbed, "…is JJ."

SARAH

Elizabeth Grey, England

One of my first experiences of witnessing a physical healing from a past life regression came soon after I became a hypnotist/hypnotherapist in 1998. A colleague's daughter was in high school, and she was having difficulty forming close relationships with boys. She wondered if it had to do with her daughter possibly being molested by her father at an early age.

"She's a natural athlete, whether in golf, tennis, soccer, or swimming, but she frequently bails out because of illness or doesn't practice in her off hours," her mother told me. Although Sarah had been raised by her mother in an open-minded, spiritual home where reincarnation was accepted, I thought our session would simply be about healing from an early childhood event. But her soul knew exactly where to go to heal.

Sarah was a beautiful seventeen-year-old girl with a bubbly personality, gorgeous red hair, and an openness to healing. She went into hypnosis easily, as most young people do.

"There's a feeling inside you that you don't like. It has everything to do with why you are here today. I'd like you to go back to first grade to see if the feeling is there," I instructed. "At the count of one you will be there. Three, two, one. Be there now. Notice if you are wearing shoes, and if so, what they look like."

"Blue shoes...overalls with a red shirt," she responded.

"Let the scene unfold."

"There's a woman at the desk. There's a book fair going on. Jenny is here!"

"Notice the feeling inside you. Is this a new feeling or an old feeling?"

"Old."

"At the snap of my fingers, I'd like you to go back to when you were four years old. Three, two, one." *Snap.* "Is it dark or light?"

"Light," she whispered.

"Are you inside or outside?"

"Outside. In the carport...on a little bike," she answered.

"Is this a new feeling or an old feeling?"

"Old."

"Go back as far as you need to go to when this feeling first began," I instructed.

"I'm in the courtroom. I don't want to get my daddy in trouble. I just want to be with my mom. I'm afraid."

"Notice your hands. Your hands will tell you how old you are. How old are you?"

"I'm three." She paused. "I don't understand what's going on," she said quietly, as she began to cry. "Where's my mom?" she asked, sounding like a scared three-year-old.

"It's OK to have all your feelings," I said gently and encouraged her to get all her tears out. When her crying subsided, I continued, "Let the scene fade, Sarah, and be back in my office. I'd like you now to take your grown-up self back to the courtroom as a third party with the three-year-old you. At the count of one you are there. Three, two, one. Be there now. Pick up little Sarah and tell her how much you love her and that you are there for her now."

"She's calmer," Sarah said. "I feel tired. I don't want to be here."

"Now take Sarah out of the courtroom," I instructed. Sarah began sobbing. "Get all those tears out. They've been in there for a very long time, and you are going to feel a whole lot better when they are all out. Take all the time you need."

A few minutes passed before Sarah spoke. "She's scared and tired," she explained, referring to her younger self. Then, sounding exasperated as her younger self, she said, "I have to keep telling the same story over and over again. I don't want to talk about it anymore!" Sarah exclaimed. She paused before adding, "She looks happy."

"How are you feeling now?" I asked.

"OK."

"Only OK?" I asked. OK wasn't good enough for me, and I wanted to be certain we got to the root cause. "Go back now to moments before this feeling first began."

Sarah began speaking immediately. "Gonna get dark soon."

"Notice your feet and what you are wearing on them."

"Pointed black boots that lace up. They're big."

I wondered if she was playing dress up as the three-year-old. "What else is happening?" I asked.

"I'm in the back of a carriage looking out the left side."

I wondered if she'd crawled up into a baby carriage until she began describing the landscape she was seeing from the carriage. I then realized she had spontaneously regressed to another lifetime. "Move time ahead," I instructed.

"I'm in a room...with lots of people. Everyone is talking. I feel out of place, but I'm talking to someone. It's a meeting to talk about the town."

"Spell the name of the town," I instructed.

"A-B-E-T...Abets...ville? England."

"I'm going to snap my fingers, and you'll know what year it is." *Snap.* "What year is it?"

"1879."

"Someone calls out your name." *Snap.* "What's your name?"

"Elizabeth."

"Tell me about yourself, Elizabeth."

"I'm not married," she said before pausing. "No children," she said before pausing again, as though she was getting more information. "Life is OK."

I wondered if it was the same "OK" as she had said when she was outside the courtroom.

I wanted to find out more about the lifetime she was experiencing. "I'd like you to go to your next meal and tell me what you notice."

"My father...my little brother is there," she responded.

"Where are you?"

"At Father's home." Her response was very proper and unlike her usual self. "Mother's not there. She died a few years ago. Not that long…" Sarah said as her voice trailed off.

"Tell me about your father."

"We're not that close. He makes me nervous. He's so…he yells. So loud. He's just mean ever since my mom died."

"Go now to a time before your mother died."

"I'm running up to her. We're walking. We laugh. Her hands hurt her. She gets dizzy sometimes and just sits and rests." She paused before continuing. "She's very nice. I walk with her."

"Look deep into her eyes, deeper than you've ever looked before. Do you recognize her as someone from your lifetime as Sarah?"

"I don't recognize her."

"Now go to her death."

"She's lying in bed. We don't know what is wrong with her. I want her to get up. I hold her hand." She began to sob and sputtered, "She's…all…I…have."

I waited for her crying to subside. "Go now to a time after she passes, to the next significant event."

"I'm sitting next to my brother. There are lots of flowers. We're talking about life. About stuff we did as kids." She smiled.

"What's his name?"

"John…Grey. Father was nice before. He couldn't forgive her for dying. (Referring to her mother.) He takes it out on John. It's not his fault. I feel loneliness over my mom (passing). I never married."

"Did you ever love anyone?"

"Yes, Eric. I was twenty-four. He found someone else, and he left and moved away. Everyone *I* like doesn't like me. It just doesn't work. There's nobody there for me. I don't have any friends because they think I'm weird because I'm not married. I like to do boy things. The girls look at me weird."

"What do you mean by boy things?"

"I play with the boys. There's a stick and a ball and then we run. I can play with them."

"You do this as an adult?

"No, when I was young, sixteen, seventeen. They would pick on me. The girls are just mean and stupid!" she said, sounding hurt.

"Go to the next significant event at the count of one. Three, two, one. Be there now."

"I'm sitting in a room in a red chair. My brother is next to me. A man sits behind a desk in a chair. It doesn't feel good. He's telling us the house has burned down, and our father was inside." I noticed there were no tears or emotion as she told me this. "We don't know where to go. We might have to stay with John's friend and wife."

"Is John not married?"

"He sports around. He likes Lydia a lot, though."

Sports around was a common phrase used in Victorian England when referencing liking the ladies, but not one Sarah knew. "Now go to the morning of the last day of your life, Elizabeth."

"We're standing in front of the house on an open field. There's a war... something bad. We need to move on. I'm confused. I don't know what's going on. John's not there. I'm standing there. A man on a horse is trying to help me...tells me where to go. There's fighting. He tells me to go so I don't get hurt from the fighting, but my mom's buried there. I can't leave her!" she said, raising her voice urgently. "I'm lying on her grave. I won't leave her! I won't!" She paused and then exclaimed, "Oh! They shot me!" She sounded shocked that she had been shot. "My chest." She winced.

"Float above your body and look down. Where were you shot?"

"In chest...died."

"Time passes, and you have all the knowledge and all the wisdom. What were you to learn in your lifetime as Elizabeth?"

"Even if you're hurt, there's help. You help others. That's good. They need help."

"Who needs help?"

"People who are lost."

"What didn't you learn?"

"I didn't go on with my life after Mother died. I just stayed back. I couldn't let go and live. I felt sad forever. I was only thirty-five."

"In this place that you find yourself, watch or sense now as your mother comes to you, Elizabeth. You can ask her anything and then listen for her answer."

Sarah repeated her mother's words to me. "You didn't need me. You are strong. You can do anything you want. You could have had so much. You made yourself sick. Made yourself stay back."

"How much does that apply to your life as Sarah?" I asked.

"I feel like there's so much holding me back. I need to live as life comes to me. Not to worry. She's always there. My mother is telling me to believe. Just believe. Don't hold back. Just go."

I emerged her from hypnosis. Sarah was as surprised as I was that she had not only gone back to the courtroom scene but to another lifetime. I received an e-mail from Sarah the next day:

I cannot thank you enough for what you have done for me! I have felt a lot calmer since our session. My mom even noticed my calmness and mentioned it to me. I do feel a lot better about my future now. I know not to give up or let things get me down, I have to just keep going and to try my hardest to go on in life. I feel like a small weight has been lifted off of me somehow too, not a huge one or like I am fine now, but I find myself not thinking as negative, and I am not feeling as badly as I was. I am glad that I got to cry about that whole court scene, because I had blocked out that memory, or maybe I was just too little. But I didn't remember that ever happening consciously. I also felt that I was scared and I just wanted my mom to hug me and be there. I told my mom about that and she said that I probably felt like that because they didn't allow her to be in the courtroom. She told me that she always hugged me and held me, and that may be why I felt like that.

One week later I received another e-mail from Sarah:

Thank you again. I guess I can't really say that enough. These last few days I have been calmer and happier. I am doing a lot better in soccer, and my breathing is better too. I also haven't gossiped about anyone and people are coming to me to tell me their problems too. I feel more at peace. Just thought I would tell you.

Sarah's mother wrote to me as well, saying that Sarah told her it felt so great to cry in the regression when she was outside the courtroom and that Sarah now felt that *she* was the mother in that life and that's why they were so close in this life. She recounted the time in the courtroom when Sarah told a completely different story than the one she'd told so many times before. When she asked her then three-year-old daughter, "Sarah, why didn't you tell the story?" Sarah looked at her mother and said, "I just couldn't tell that story *one more time!*" Sarah became open to having relationships with boys, and she no longer held back when playing sports.

Sarah is happily married today with two small children. I contacted her, asking permission to use her regression in this book. She wrote back to me:

I remember well the sadness I felt about my mother's grave being trampled on by men riding horses. That was the time of my death and being shot so it is one of the few things I recall vividly. It was a small battle. It felt like they were passing through, preparing people for something, but were in a hurry. I'm not sure if it was just a stray bullet from firing in the air, shooting toward someone else, range practice, etc., but I remember very well gasping for air and having pain in my chest. (The same symptoms one has with asthma) It was sad. Also, in my research, I found a brother and sister named John and Elizabeth Grey from England. If you look at the attached link, John and his parents are the first on the list, and Elizabeth is the ninth person down and has the same parents listed. The ages are off though. She is older, and he is younger. But it is interesting. It seems like there is some information missing, so perhaps dates are wrong or there was more than one child by the name of John? Who knows.

I went to the link Sarah had sent me (www.gray-ons.org/secondsite/p123) and found a John and Elizabeth Grey born to John Grey and Jane Nixon. Elizabeth was born in 1854 at Gateshead, County Durham, England. When I had asked Sarah what year it was during the regression, she had said 1879. The time seemed to be accurate, and the information on the document showed that neither of the children married. Although I could not find a town called Abetsville in England, I found a town called Abbotsford, a settlement in West Sussex, England. Today, the town name is rarely used to describe the area.

What I found fascinating, however, was Sarah's physical healing. Sarah's mother told me she had asthma from an early age, and after her regression, it had completely disappeared. As of this writing, nearly two decades later, her asthma has not returned.

PAT

Civil War Soldier;
Elizabeth Rothton, Pilgrim Girl;
Carly, Prairie Girl; and African American Man

Pat had moved home to Florida after years of living in Texas. Since returning, she felt her spiritual side had opened, prompting her to read Dr. Brian Weiss's books on past life regression. Born and raised Catholic, she had lived in what she referred to as the Bible Belt. As she began researching the Bible, she learned that parts of it were left out in the fifth century, and she discovered that Jesus had talked about reincarnation. Pat referred to Emperor Justinian who, in 545 AD, applied with his authority the full power of Rome to stop the belief in reincarnation. He forced the ruling cardinals to draft a papal decree, stating that anyone who believed in reincarnation would be punished by death.

She also told me she had read the Bible many times, and a verse always came to mind when Jesus said, "Do you not recognize me?" She had attended many Bible classes when they would discuss reincarnation references in the Bible.

Pat said she was able to see and feel things and also had visions and premonitions. Pat told me that, as a four-year-old child, she had tea with Mother Mary, whom she knew as Bessa Mommy. She would tell her mother, who never believed her. Bessa Mommy told her she would live in Texas when she grew up. Pat spent most of her life in Ohio, but when she grew up, Pat did indeed live in Texas for fourteen years.

"In Texas I put God in this tiny box. I moved here (Florida), and wow, things opened up," she exclaimed as she smiled broadly.

I first met Pat when she attended one of my group past life regression workshops, where she discovered she had been a soldier in the Civil War, and in another life, she was a thirteen-year-old Pilgrim girl astounded to be in America.

After attending the workshop, Pat sent me the following e-mail:

Hi Patricia, Thank you so much for your workshop Saturday. Wow! So much was put in place after the workshop. I was a soldier in the Civil War. I was wearing a blue coat holding a rifle in my hands. I was missing my wife and two children so much. They needed me. I looked down at my boots and I was walking on green grass having a sense it was summer. I looked down at my boots again and I saw snow feeling very sad that I am away too long from my family. I saw blood in the snow and then I died. As I died I was very sad that I missed my family. I saw my wife looking out of the window looking for me.

Years ago, I lived near Kennesaw Mountain, Georgia (where a Civil War battle was fought in 1864). I was walking the battlefields very early in the morning and it was very foggy. I walked past a cannon and I heard marching feet. I looked around to see who in the world was marching this early in the morning it was so foggy. I could feel a battle was about to begin near me. I could smell the gunpowder from the battlefield and the smell of death as men cried out. I could hear the wheels of the cannons and men marching. There were many men.

Patricia, I always loved being married and I have such yearning to be married again.

WOW. This has opened my eyes so much. I was a good husband and a good father then. Could you please give me more information about exploring my journey with you?

When Pat arrived for her private session, she told me once again about her lifetime as a soldier in the Civil War and her brief visit to a life in which she was a Pilgrim girl. Pat cleared her throat on and off throughout our conversation.

She apologized for needing to clear her throat so often and said, "It feels like something is in my throat. The doctors say it's allergies, but nothing they've given me has helped."

I wondered if the constant clearing would get in the way of her going into hypnosis, but she went easily into the state. "Notice your feet," I began.

"I have on brown shoes...standing on grass. I have a long dress on with an apron. My hair is yellow and it's back. I'm fourteen. I'm looking at the land. It's *beautiful!*" she said enthusiastically. "It's new! It's all *new!*" she gushed in excited awe, sounding like a young girl. I sensed she was the Pilgrim girl again. "Daddy said it would be new." Her tone intonated her father was correct. "He's a big man. He takes good care of me. He looks down at me... smiling. He has on dark pants with a big belt...long hair. Big hands...smiling at me."

"Look deep into his eyes, deeper than you've ever looked. Do you recognize him from your lifetime as Pat? Is there a soul recognition?"

"It's my uncle!" Pat said, sounding surprised. "Momma's at the table making something to eat. It's a sunny day. Momma's at a big wood bench. The ocean is on the side. My little sister is playing with a stick." She smiled and paused before adding, "I love her. Oh, it's my sister!" She had recognized her from her current life. "We have corn...vegetables. A little house. Everything is new! It's *America!*" she exclaimed in awe and excitement. "We came from a boat far away. My little sister was born here. The trees are green...and it's all *new.*"

"Are there others?" I inquired.

"They live down the hill. Sally and I play a lot. We're friends. We get together on a Saturday, Sunday, and we dance. We see rabbits and deer."

"What is the name of your town?"

"Douglasville," she said without hesitating.

"What year is it?"

She paused before saying, "I don't know."

"What country do you come from?"

"England. It always rains there."

"What is your name?

"Elizabeth. I like my name. Rothton," she said assuredly.

"Go to the next significant event, Elizabeth."

"I'm getting married," she said, smiling. "I'm nineteen. Becky, my sister, is here. We're laughing."

"Who are you marrying?"

"Thomas. He'll be a good husband." She smiled before adding, "I met him at church." She paused. "Thomas Brooken. I have flowers around my hair. Becky picked them for me...Preacher's there. Everyone from town is there. It's a beautiful day. I'm a schoolteacher."

"What does Thomas do?"

"He cuts wood and works with horses."

"Move time ahead again," I instructed.

"I have a son and a daughter. I'm twenty-four...twenty-five. They are little. I love them. We have our own house. I tend to the garden and the children. He farms. He shoes the horses for the town."

"What year is it now?"

"1724."

"What state do you live in?" I inquired.

"Pennsylvania."

Go now to the next significant event, Elizabeth."

"My son is all grown up...and my daughter. I'm much older. It's wintertime. I'm bundled up by the fireplace. I'm watching the grandbabies play. It's wonderful. I'm blessed," she said with a big smile.

"Go to the morning of the last day of your life, Elizabeth."

"I have a pain in my chest. I'm not feeling too good...eighty-two. I have a lot of wrinkles and I'm cold...and my chest is hurting on my right side. I think it's time. I feel my chest. My heart stops. I'm in my rocking chair. I put my head down. I'm alone."

"Time passes, and you have a full understanding of that lifetime. What did you want to learn?" I asked.

"Happiness," she responded with a broad smile.

"A wise and loving Being comes to you who has loved you through all of time." Pat had a wonderful personal conversation with this Being. Nothing had been unveiled regarding her throat issue. When her conversation ended, I asked Pat, "Would you like to ask your Being about your throat?"

She paused before answering. "I was in a fire…the smoke. I can't breathe." Pat was in another lifetime.

"Where are you?"

"I'm in a barn. Smoke is getting bad. I can't get out. The smoke is so bad. I fall to the ground. The barn is on fire. I can't move. I can't breathe. My eyes… it's hot, it hurts. The horses are burning. The hay…alone. I don't know where Momma's at…I die," she said as her voice trailed off.

"Float above the scene and move time backward half an hour or so. Tell me what happened."

"It's sunny…daffodils…up on a hill. The whole town comes running up. They didn't know I was in there. Momma's running around calling for me." Pat began crying. "She's holding my daddy," she muttered between heaving sobs, "And beating his chest. He's crying…they fall to the ground yelling, 'Carly! Carly, where are you?'"

Tears filled my eyes as I listened to her parents frantically calling out to her. It was a powerful scene. She paused, and I allowed her a few moments to let the scene she was in unfold. "I see them burying me, and they're crying so hard," she said quietly. "It broke their hearts. I see my little brother…the whole town is crying."

"Let go of any negativity from that lifetime into the light for healing," I said, before I emerged her from hypnosis.

"Wow!" Pat blurted out, "That was awesome!"

~

Three days later, I received an e-mail from her.

OMG (oh my gosh) my clearing of my throat is GONE!!!! I am so excited. The third day I noticed it was gone.

When you experience another lifetime, you see or sense a lot more than what you share with the hypnotist during the regression, so I asked Pat to tell me more about what she saw and experienced. This was her reply:

I have been clearing my throat for three or four years. It might have been longer. It was really bad the last two years. It always seemed there was something in my throat.

I went to a doctor and was told it was allergies draining, but it felt like something was stuck in my throat. Regarding the regression: As I looked back at my mother I saw the back of the house. The house and the roof were made of dark brown wood. My father had built the house. The house was small. The clothesline was at the back of the house. The land was rolling hills with grass. It looked like the prairie out West. It was a sunny day. The wind was blowing softly enough to move the sheet on the line. I felt it was out west. I loved the horses and they were in the barn. The barn was up on a small rolling hill in the back of the house. I got away from my mother to go and see the horses. I looked back to see if she was watching. As I walked in the barn it was so big to me. Then the fire started. The horses were trying to get out but the fire was big.

I could not breathe because of the smoke and my eyes were burning. I started to cry because the horses were burning. Then I laid down on the barn floor and died. I did not know how the fire had started. My mother was calling out for me frantic. Then I was floating over the barn. I saw my mother screaming and running toward the barn and my father grabbed her. My mother was trying to get away from him and she was screaming, "My baby! My baby! My Carly!" Mother turned to my father and started to beat on his chest. Daddy held on to her and they both fell to the ground on their knees crying. I saw my grave. The dirt was a light brown color mounded with a little wooden cross on it. It was a small grave. My mother, father and brother were standing near the grave crying. My brother was a little older than me. People from town came to the grave as well. I could not read the cross for a date. Darn it. I feel that it was the time of the old West like Little House on the Prairie. *Carly was four-years-old. I know I went to the barn to see the horses. I loved horses. I can still see me looking back at my mother hanging up sheets on the line. They were moving in the wind.*

OH MY GOD THERE REALLY IS A DOUGLASSVILLE IN PENNSYLVANIA! I have cold chills...I am so excited. In this life I have never been to Pennsylvania. I was born and raised in Ohio. My father then is my uncle now and my sister then is my sister today.

~

Curious, I researched the history of Douglassville, Pennsylvania, and discovered that the earliest pioneers to the area were Swedish pilgrims (she had said she was a Pilgrim) who had decided to move from Sweden to Holland where religious freedom was practiced, and they would be allowed to worship God as they chose. Pilgrims lived in Holland until 1620. They became unhappy with their situation and decided to move back to England to leave for the New World, where once again, they could practice religious freedom.

Nearly a year passed before I saw Pat again, when she attended another group past life regression workshop I facilitated. Soon afterward, I received an e-mail from her.

Hi Patricia, I had to e-mail you on my new discovery. May 10th, 2013 I took your regression workshop. I should start by telling you that several weeks before my regression I had a vision. I closed my eyes and I saw through my third eye three pictures." (The third eye is an esoteric or mystical concept, also known as the inner eye, which provides perception beyond ordinary sight. It can offer mental images having deeply personal or spiritual significance. It is usually thought to be located between and slightly above the eyebrows.)

The frames of the pictures I saw were oval shaped and looked like the frames and pictures from the Victorian period. The two top pictures were of two black women, and the bottom picture was of a black man. I looked closely to see if I knew them. At the time, I did not know them. I asked God to tell me who these people were and what it meant to see this. As I have learned in the past, asking God for something, I must be patient and He will give me the answer. Sure enough through the regression I saw the people in this picture. One of the women in the framed photo was that of my wife and the other was my mistress. The picture on the bottom was ME! As a man! I was a black man in the Victorian days. I was a psychoanalyst with my practice in my home. I was standing in the hall entrance looking at a beautiful dark wooden staircase. Very happy in my home and with my practice. I was married and loved my wife very much but my wife was always very unhappy. No matter what I did it was not good enough and I tried so very hard to show her I loved her and to make her life grand for her. I looked into my wife's eyes and it is my mother today! I died as a very old man but I was so sad that I could not make my wife happy. A very deep sadness. My life today with my mother has always been very hard on me. Through the many years of abuse from my mother, as a little girl I would bite my nails until my fingers would bleed. And this had carried well into my adulthood. May 17th (one week after the regression) I looked down at my hands and realized that for the first time in my life I have nails and I have not had my hands in my mouth. I have pretty nails!!!!

I started to cry. It came to me like a flood the regression workshop I had May 10th!!! I have not talked to my mother in several months and I was in such a turmoil because of it. But several days after the workshop I had so much peace in my heart. Patricia this is a big breakthrough for me. Thank you so much from my heart.

Hearing Pat's enthusiasm, I couldn't help but smile. Her experience in the regression and learning she could never make her mother happy allowed her to let go. It mirrored, in many ways, her lifetime with her mother now. Pat's soul was getting another opportunity to heal and grow in her current life.

It had been nearly six months since I'd seen Pat when she e-mailed me, telling me what she had recently experienced:

Hi Patricia, I have to share this with you. Two days ago: Early in the morning about 6:10 am. It was still dark outside. I went to my car for work and I had to put some trash in the dumpster. After throwing trash away I turned around and looked up at the sky and the tops of the palm trees I could see a sliver moon. I looked down and I was a little girl age about eight years old, wearing a white dress, knee length with a piece of rope tied to my waist for a belt. I had dark hair a little shorter than my shoulders and a white fabric wrapped around my head like a towel. I was barefoot carrying a wooden pail of water. As I looked up at the sky seeing the tops of the palm trees gently move.

It felt like Jerusalem. It felt warm as the wind brushed against my cheeks. Then it left me. Patricia, one of my past lives was a little girl at the water well in Jerusalem. In my sessions with you we did not dig deep into this past life.

Sometimes after a regression, more awareness can come to you through dreams, while in meditation, or through coincidences. In Pat's case, it was in the form of a vision. She knew the little girl was herself in a past life because she recognized herself from her regression. But more interesting is that she *felt* the warm air brush against her cheeks.

Although there was a slight breeze in the air, it was cool outside. There was something about looking at the tops of the palm trees with the sliver of the moon in the dark sky that triggered that memory.

~

The next experience that Pat had is a good example of an overreaction to an event or situation. Have you ever had a time when something bothered you far more than it should—when your reaction was far out of proportion to what was happening? It may have not have made sense because nothing had happened to you in this life to warrant that reaction. Pat's e-mail continued:

The second aha moment was this morning. I work at the front desk of a private school and the school had a Civil War Reenactment today. We had several people come on campus dressed in blue and gray coats. The women had on the proper dress with hoops and wearing a shawl as well. Everyone who comes on campus has to get a badge from me. I looked up and there stood a man dressed in a blue coat and hat with a full beard and a lady standing next to him in a long hoop dress. Her hair was dark brown and braided back with old fashion ear rings. I about fell off my chair!

All the emotions started to flood in of my past life as a soldier and missing my wife. Being on the battle field all started flooding in. My eyes started to fill with tears and I had to look away. All I wanted to do is hold this lady. Knowing I could not...and that I missed my wife. Her eyes and face were so comforting but yet sad to me. I had to share this with you.

It had been several years since I'd seen Pat. She stopped by my office and expressed how well she was doing. Although she wore her nails short now, they looked healthy, and her relationship with her mother had improved as well. As she retold her story of being Carly, she began to cry. It was still emotional as she described what had happened the day in the barn. She said the wind she spoke of, as her mother hung the sheets on the line outside, was the cause of the barn door slamming shut so hard it knocked down the lantern, which started the fire. She no longer clears her throat like she once did.

ALEXANDRA

Native American Woman, and Belle, African American Woman

Alexandra* discovered me through a coworker and told me she carried my number for a while before calling me. She is a nurse and a Yoga teacher. She told me her mother was very psychic and they had gone to Cassadaga (a spiritual community in Florida) together a few years earlier. Happily married, she had been with her husband since 1993. She was alone when he was on the road as a musician, and Alexandra wanted to discover why she felt so uncomfortable when she was alone, as well as to understand the feeling of being alone even when she was with others.

Once she was in hypnosis, I told her, "There's a feeling inside you don't like. It has everything to do with why you are here today. In a moment I'm going to count from one to three, and I'd like you to let that feeling become very real within you at the count of three. One, two, three. Now notice a long hallway with many colored doors, and find the door that you feel drawn to that holds all the answers you seek today."

"It's a peach door."

"In a moment, I'm going to have you open the door and step into a beautiful mist. Are you ready to do this?"

Alexandra shook her head up and down.

"Now open the door and step into a beautiful mist. In a moment, I'm going to count from three to one. At the count of one, the mist will disappear, and you'll find yourself in a scene, situation, or event that has everything to do with why you are here today. Three, two, one. Notice your feet and what, if anything, you're wearing on them."

"I don't think I'm wearing shoes."

"Are you standing or sitting?"

"Standing."

"Notice or feel what you are standing on."

"It feels like linoleum."

"Notice your hands. Are they big or little?"

"Kid."

"Your hands will tell you how old you are. How old are you?"

"Five...six."

"What color is your skin?"

"White."

"Notice your surroundings. Are you inside or out?"

"Inside."

"Daytime or nighttime?"

"It's dark. Nighttime. Dark out. I'm in a room...bedroom...square... smaller...not a room I know," she said and then paused. "One window."

"Look outside."

"I can't tell. Scared, but I don't know why."

"I'm going to give you a flashlight so you can see better," I said.

"Wood floor. I have shorts on. I see my legs...my feet. I'm a girl. I see lamps, but I can't turn them on. I can't turn the knobs. Walls are white... plain. Like an empty room. There are three lamps on the floor. I don't see anything else. Like we moved out or...like I was left alone."

"You can rewind the scene like a videotape. Find your answers. Three, two, one."

"I'm inside. Still alone again...light...afternoon. I'm alone. A little kid. I don't know where anyone is."

"Go even further back. Three, two, one."

"I'm with parents. Inside. Daytime."

"Who's with you?"

"I don't see anything." She paused for a moment and then said, "I'm in a dining room."

"Describe it to me."

"Table and chairs...wood. Dark wood. Almost looks like childhood. Shorts. No shoes."

"Let the scene unfold."

"I'm outside. In yard. I'm still little in the backyard. Talking...on lawn chairs. She's not my mom I don't think. I don't know who she is. I like talking to her. I don't know who she is. She's asking me if I'm in school, what my favorite color is, and what I like to eat."

"Notice everything you need to notice."

"I'm looking at the fence...wood."

"How long do you spend with the woman?"

"I don't know why I'm there. Where's my mom?"

"Ask the woman where your mom is," I instructed.

"She said she'll be back soon. She's at work or the store."

"Move the tape forward and find your answers."

"It makes me sad. I want to cry."

"It's OK to cry. You'll feel a lot better if you get those tears out." I paused, allowing her the time she needed to cry. Once her crying subsided, I asked her, "Is this a new feeling or an old feeling?"

"New."

I didn't sense it was new, and I said, "Go back to when this feeling first began."

"It's dark. No shoes on. I'm bigger, like an adult." She had regressed to a different lifetime.

"Let the scene unfold," I urged.

"My feet are brownish. I have a long white skirt...light. Cut-out things on it...eyelets. I don't have shoes on...bigger feet. I think I'm...big hands... an Indian person or a...I have long straight brown black hair...or Spanish. I think I'm Indian...female...standing in dirt. My stomach hurts."

"Because…?"

"I feel sad again. My head hurts. I think I was crying. Maybe I'm older now…sixties. Dry hands…dry feet. I can't see my face, but I feel it. It's dry, too. It's like a Wild West scene."

"Mountains?" I asked.

"No. It's all flat. Now I'm in the middle of a road. All dirt. Horses. Daytime. Morning. Ten o'clock. I don't understand. No one is around. Maybe it's earlier."

"Move time ahead to when there are people."

"Now it's all crowded. I'm still standing there. I can't tell if I'm Mexican… Indian…I'm alone. I don't know why I'm there. I'm not going to a store. I don't need anything."

"What's your name?"

"I don't know."

"Move time ahead to your next meal."

She smiled. "I'm eating out of a big thing…a gourd…a round thing. Looks…" Her voice trailed off. "Couscous…quinoa?"

"Are you with anyone?"

"On the floor, sitting with people I don't know. There are tables, but I'm on the floor. Ten to twelve people."

"Go now to the morning of the last day of your life."

"It's daytime. Waking up. I'm in some kind of a hut. Sunny. Hot."

"Are you aware in any way this is your last day?" I questioned.

"No. I'm older. Old and thin. Not dry, though. Soft but old. Really thin."

"How do you feel?"

"I like the sun on my face. There are other huts…dirt floor."

"What is the hut made of?"

"Like a teepee, but not. Not wood, dirt color. Flat."

"Looking back on your life, how would you describe it?"

"Good."

"Are you leaving anyone behind?" She didn't answer. "Go to moments before you pass."

"My stomach hurts. It's dark. Neck hurts. Back aches."

"When is the last time you ate?"

"Many hours. I'm inside. Lying down."

I sensed she had died. "Times passes. What is it you wanted to learn on a soul level?"

"I don't know how to say it."

"A wise and loving Being comes to you now. This Being has loved you through all of time, knows everything about you, and loves you unconditionally. This Being can take any form whatsoever. It could be light, an angel, an animal, or something else. Feel the love as this wise and loving Being comes to you, reminding you that you are never alone. Any negativity from those lifetimes is released to the light for healing." I emerged Alexandria from hypnosis.

"Oh, my goodness. That was good!" she exclaimed.

In both time periods, Alexandra had felt alone, and I was curious to see how her story and healing would unfold. Alexandra returned two months later. "My husband was out of town, and instead of playing the old fear tapes, I remembered my younger self and cried and let it go. It dissipated." I was thrilled to hear how well she was doing.

"I'm curious about what my connection is with gospel music. I feel like I was a black woman before."

I asked Alexandra to feel the feeling of being connected to gospel music and her belief of being a black woman. I then regressed her to when that feeling first began, going once again to the hallway and the door that held all the answers she was seeking.

"Blue door. I can't open the door. I don't want to."

Whatever lay behind the blue door, she seemed afraid of, so I put the scene further away from her. There was a reason she was at that door, and I knew it held all the answers she sought. "Notice a large movie screen, and you are sitting safely in the back row of the theater" I began. "In a moment I will count to three and the movie will begin. One, two, three. The movie begins. Are you inside or outside?"

"Outside."

"Is it dark or light?"

"Dark."

"Alone or with others?"

"Alone…it's like a swamp." She paused. "It's hot! I'm in the water…like up to the middle of my calves."

"Notice your hands."

"Big."

"What color is your skin?"

"Dark."

"Soft or calloused?"

"Calloused."

"Your hands will tell you how old you are. How old are you?"

"Sixties…maybe."

"Move time forward five minutes or more, and when you are ready, tell me what is happening."

There was a long pause before she began. "I'm hiding. I don't know why. I'm scared. I think I'm alone." I noticed the inflection in her voice had changed.

"Move time forward half an hour or more," I suggested.

"I'm being chased. Running away from someone. I have a dress on. It's in my way. I have to lift it up. I don't know who it is…a man is yelling."

"What is he saying?"

"Come here! Come here!" she said before adding, "I don't know what he wants." She paused again, as though seeing the scene in her mind. "I think I'm far away. I'm running away from his voice."

"Have you run away before?" I asked.

"Probably," she said. Her voice sounded flat—or perhaps defeated.

I wanted to get more information. Who was this man? "Go to a significant event before this night," I instructed.

"I'm inside."

"Notice your hands. How old are you now?"

"I don't feel much younger. I'm an adult. Sitting at…a dining room table. By myself again."

"Notice the room and describe it to me."

"Old table. Like wood, not treated. Broken down, dreary and dark…gray."

"What else is in the room?"

"Not much...I must be poor...I don't know if it's my house."

"Where do you sleep?"

"There's other rooms. I can't see...I have slippers on. Old-lady slippers. They're old. Like I have the same dress on."

"What year is it?" I snapped my fingers.

"Thirties, maybe."

"What time is it?"

"Sun just set."

"Walk out through the front door and notice what you see."

"There's a field. Things growing tall. Maybe wheat...corn...something tall. Huh. Huh. I think I'm black!" she said, sounding surprised. "I have braids tied up. They look stupid. Like loops around my head."

"Go now to dinnertime. Do you eat with anyone else?"

"Huh! I want to say no, but that's sad. There's four chairs."

"Notice what you're eating."

"Corn! Hmm. Hmm. And some other thing...white...cream of wheat, but not."

"How do you spend your days?"

"I'm outside. I see a cow! Huh! Just one...a big, big open field. One little house. Like a farm. A dirt area in front of house. A long dirt road. Trees...green."

"What is the name of the town or farm?"

"I don't see a name...Mississippi...Alabama..." she said as her voice trailed off.

"Go back again to an even earlier time of great significance."

"Humph! I'm in a bassinette. In a white thing. Like you carry. Baby..."

"Notice who's carrying you."

"I see her...loving me."

"What is your name?"

"Belle."

"Move time ahead now, Belle. Where are you now and how old are you?"

"Five or six years old. I have the same dumb braids! They're like horse-shoes pinned up. I think I'm in a church. A little tiny church. There's people there with my mom. I don't know who she is (referring to someone in her current life), but she's my mom. I'm sitting. She's standing. I'm wearing a dress. An old, beige, boring dress. I think she's singing in a choir. I feel like I'm alone. There are people there, but I'm not with them. I'm watching."

"Move time ahead to the next significant event, Belle."

"I can't. She wants me to stay sitting there."

"Your mom?" I asked, wondering who was telling her to do so.

"I don't think so."

"Because...?"

"I don't know. I feel like I'm in heaven. I love it there. Like my second home."

As wonderful as heaven sounded, I wanted to know what had happened to her. "Belle, go to half an hour before you pass," I instructed her.

"That man!" she exclaimed. "I don't know him. I'm scared. In my house... alone with him. I must know him." She paused. "I ran out to the water. Like a marsh. I'm trying to hide. He wants to hurt me. I'm scared. He's crazy. He's angry. He's tall...broad...black...black eyes. Black hair, buzz cut. I don't like him. He feels like my husband." She paused. "Yeah. He's my husband. He's craaaazy!"

"Go fifteen minutes before you pass, Belle."

"I'm still there in that water."

"Go through the death scene until you find yourself floating above your body."

"I think he strangled me."

I emerged her.

"Oh, my God! OK, if I made that up, that was weird. That was cool. My mom was Michael. A friend of mine who passed. My husband was my dad in this life. Dad left when I was five. He was violent with my mom. They divorced, and then he got sober but drank again when his next wife died. He died alone. Rotting."

~

Alexandra's next appointment was nearly two months later. Once she was settled in the comfortable blue chair, we talked about her last session and her experience. "Do you have neck issues in this life?" I asked Alexandra, remembering how she was strangled.

"Yes, the left side of my neck from a car wreck." I wondered if standing in the marsh had to do with her knees cracking. "I don't feel aloneness anymore," she continued. "Only once, and I think that was hormonal. I just held the younger me. As fast as it came, it left. I still feel like I was making it up, but I keep coming."

Nearly four years had passed since Alexandra's first appointment. I asked her how her neck was feeling. She responded, "The pain subsided for a long time. It's just been in the past six months it's returned, but now it's in a different spot! I guess I need to come see you soon! There are no more feelings of aloneness, though, which was the initial reason for coming. It doesn't affect me anymore. I think knowing I was both a black woman and man just validates all my deep feelings and thoughts about gospel music, soul food, and how deeply affected I seem to get about racism. It all makes sense now! And to know that my best friend, Michael, was my mom in a past life just touches my heart."

The soul knows exactly where to go to heal itself.

BILL

Fred Colton, West Virginia and Louis, French Sailor

Bill came to me to work on his past connection with his ex-wife, whom he'd been married to, divorced from, and then remarried. He said, "I thought I could fix her." They divorced again.

He had been dating women who were smart and beautiful but said he had no feeling about them, and he didn't understand why. "I felt I knew her the moment I met her," he said, referring to his ex-wife. This is typical of a soul recognition.

During the past year, he said, he had felt "Stuck in the mud. I can't seem to move forward." Bill had attended an experiential group past life regression with Brian Weiss, MD, so he was familiar with the process and went into hypnosis beautifully.

"I'd like you to go back in time and focus on the feeling you had when you first saw Jennifer and make that feeling very real within you as I count from one to three. One, two, three. Now notice a hallway with many colored doors. One of those doors has everything to do with why you're here today. Feel yourself being curious about, interested in, or drawn to one of those doors, and let me know when you are standing in front of it."

"Purple door."

"Notice if you are wearing shoes."

"Boots…black. Leaning on…like leaves."

"Notice your clothing and how it feels next to your skin, soft or scratchy, heavy or light."

"Scratchy...heavy...tan...jacket."

"Notice your hands now. Are they big hands or little hands?"

"Big hands. Hard. Old. Sixties."

"Now reach up and feel your face and hair."

"Scruffy. Stubble."

"Daytime or nighttime?"

"Nighttime."

"Let the scene you find yourself in expand and unfold," I said.

"I'm standing near horses. Talking to a younger man."

"What is your relationship to him?"

"Father."

"Look deep into his eyes. Deeper than you've ever looked before."

"Green eyes."

There didn't seem to be any recognition, so I continued. "Move time ahead to dinner."

"There's a pan on the stove. Inside. Familiar. It's small. There's another person. Brown hair. Rolled. Woman. Green eyes...looking at me." He began to cry. "It must be her."

"She says your name at the snap of my fingers." *Snap.*

"Fred. Fred Colten."

"What year is it, Fred?"

"Eighteen..." His voice trailed off.

"What is the name of your town or village?"

"Johnson, West Virginia."

"Go now to the next important event in your life, Fred. Three, two, one." *Snap.*

"I'm outside. Daytime. On horses...riding near a lake...with someone."

"Who are you with?"

"Long dress on...green eyes."

"Notice your hands. How old are you now?"

"They're smoother. I have gloves. It's dark. Her green eyes looking...feel warm."

"Who is she?"

"My wife...Ginger...green eyes...riding home. Soft and warm, peaceful."

"What happens next?"

"We're holding hands...storm, clouds...her eyes are so close."

He didn't get any further information, so I moved him forward. "Go to the next significant event, Fred."

"It's cold. Fire. Outside. Boots on against the fire."

"Are you alone or with others?"

"One other...son."

"What are you doing there?"

"Horses...stars glowing...campfire."

"How old is your son?"

"Twenty. Twenty-something. Strong." Suddenly his body jumped in the chair, and he gasped. "Something bit me," he said, sounding startled. "On my arm," he said for clarity. I could see his eyes moving beneath his eyelids as though he were looking for what had bitten him. "It's not good," he said before pausing.

"Because?"

"Poisonous. Big rattlesnake. Big head. On left. Son shoots it, cuts it... my arm." He paused before continuing, "See blue sky...brown grass. Laying down. Son gone. One horse left. It's peaceful...green eyes...soft...wife's soft." His voice trailed off.

"Go through the death scene and float above it looking down."

"I'm old. Son not there." I wondered if the son had gone to get help and hadn't arrived back in time.

"Looking back on your life, how would you describe it?"

"Hard work, calm, good."

This seemed to be too peaceful of a life, and I wanted to find a stronger connection with his ex-wife. "Notice Earth gently spinning below you in the far distance. When I count from three to one you'll be back on Earth in a scene, situation, or event that has everything to do with why you are here today. Three, two, one."

"Hmmm. Rolled-down boot tops…big boots…formal. Floating coat. Male…soft beard…strong face…rough brown hair…weathered hands…I'm thirty-five. Outside, daytime…on a ship. The ships are tall. I'm on a ship. I'm not a captain, but I'm part of the ship. Other men are working for me."

"What is your name?"

"Louis."

"What year is it, Louis?"

"Sixteen…"

"Let the scene unfold and expand, and when you are ready, tell me what is happening."

"Sailing from the East…the Old Country. Lots of ships…the islands… a trade ship…loading, big boxes, lots of ropes. Spain. I don't live here." He paused before continuing. "Long eyelashes. A woman I see in my mind. She's at home. Not with me. Her dress has a silver cross in the front…I can see her eyes."

"Move time forward to the next significant event, Louis."

"I'm in a carriage. Loud. The streets are loud. I've been away a long time." There was a long pause as the scene unfolded in his mind before he spoke again. "I'm looking in the window. Candles lit. Beautiful chandelier. It's my home. It's in France. I don't know where she is, though. She's not there. Her silver cross is on the chair. The room is empty. It's dark."

"How do you feel?"

"Anxious."

"Because?"

"She always wore the silver cross. Long eyelashes…hazel color…not happy…in pain. She looks like she's in pain…in bed."

"What's wrong with her?"

"I don't know. She looks like she's suffering. She's scared. I'm not there. She's young. Twenty-nine. Long eyelashes. She's not well. I'm not there. I'm away." He sighed deeply. "Always on the ship."

"Go to the next significant event, Louis."

"Dusty...house seems old now. I'm old. White beard."

"Where's your wife?"

"Not here."

"Because?"

"I think she died," he said softly, before tears poured down his cheeks, wetting the collar of the shirt he wore. "She died a long time ago. I wasn't there."

"What did she die from?"

"Loneliness...sick...everybody had it. No one would come. Lots of people died. I have to go again, but I won't come back."

"Because?"

"It's empty. The silver cross is on the table."

"Go to the morning of your last day, Louis."

"It's beautiful. I'm on an island. Palm trees."

"What is the name of the island?"

"Tortola...beautiful bay. I can see it out the window."

"Tell me about your life."

"I was lonely but driven. Always on the ship. I'm old...beautiful bay... peaceful, easy."

Louis had passed. "In this place you find yourself, notice your wife walking up to you now, Louis."

"I'm sorry," he said through tears. "I'm sorry I wasn't there."

"Let those tears out, and you'll feel a lot better," I said, encouraging him to release his sadness.

"She said it's OK. Beautiful lights...white light streaming."

I had a wise and loving Being come to him, and he had a very emotionally powerful conversation with this Being. I was looking forward to hearing more about the woman who wore the silver cross and the powerful insight he received from his Being. I emerged Bill from hypnosis. I looked forward to hearing his thoughts about the regression and finding answers to the connection he felt with his past wife. He felt he had failed her by not being present, which was why he had such difficulty leaving her in his current life.

However, Bill's first response surprised me. "Whew!" He looked at me with a shocked expression. "I have always had a *deathly* fear of snakes." He then pulled up the sleeve on his left arm and pointed to two hardened drops of blood the size of the top of a pin about half an inch from each other and underneath, what looked like a small, white scar. They looked like snakebite marks.

"How long have you had this?" I asked.

"All my life."

"Let's see if those disappear."

"I can scrape them off, but they always come back." He paused, taking in the experience. "Some images were crystal clear. Sometimes there was a purple haze, and I couldn't see the face...just her eyes. My son then is my daughter in this life. I could hear people talking when I was in Spain, but I knew I lived in France."

"Have you ever been to Tortola?"

"No. And I've always been afraid of death," he said, looking off to the side as though remembering what he'd seen. "Hands were coming through the clouds for me. It was the 1500s or 1600s. And I knew it was the Spice Islands."

"Do you cry much?" I asked, as it was a very emotional session. His shirt collar was drenched with his tears.

"No. I was told not to cry, and I taught my children the same. If a bone isn't sticking out, don't cry."

"Well, you cried through most of the session. How do you feel?"

"I was devoid of feeling for so long...then I saw her eyes and started crying."

Later that day I received an e-mail from Bill:

Patricia, Again, thank you for an amazing experience today, it has left me bewildered, exhilarated, and thirsty for more. So I looked up the plague in Europe and found a few things...oddly enough, the plague was most likely spread by rats common on "merchant ships" and came into France in the Port of Marseille. I must have lived in Marseille. Intense and powerful. And I can't thank you enough for this life changing experience…it has left me wanting more understanding.

Bill went on the Internet and sent me links to the information he found that explained what he experienced. The death of his wife and many others was a result of the bubonic plague, known as the Black Death. It was one of the most devastating pandemics in human history and was thought to have been carried by infected fleas on rats that were regular passengers on merchant trips.

The plague is reported to have arrived in Marseille by a boat from Italy in January of 1348, but the last of the significant outbreaks of bubonic plague arrived in Marseille in 1720, and in a two-year period, an estimated 40 to 50 percent of the population of Marseille died.

Bill ended his e-mail by saying:

It's been a long time since I've felt this good—free almost, like some level of weight has been lifted off of my chest and my heart. I can't wait to continue to explore this path further. There is so much left to learn! I'm fine with whatever you want to use for your book. Anything that will open the door to more people understanding how healing and life changing this can be. Thank you, Patricia, you truly opened a new chapter for me…and looking forward to more!

More than a year passed before I spoke to Bill again. He told me he had shared his regression experience with many. "The wonder and amazement in their faces says it all! One person I shared this with, a twenty-six-year-old woman who clearly has an old soul, remarked, 'Then you don't fear death anymore, since you've already experienced it.' Very insightful for one so young. My life was so forever changed for the better after our session. That weight was gone from my heart, and my soul just opened up."

Three years passed before I saw Bill again. I asked him to stop by the office so I could take a picture of his scar. The red blood scabs I saw after his regression were gone. He said they come and go less frequently now, but the scar that he remembers having all his life remains.

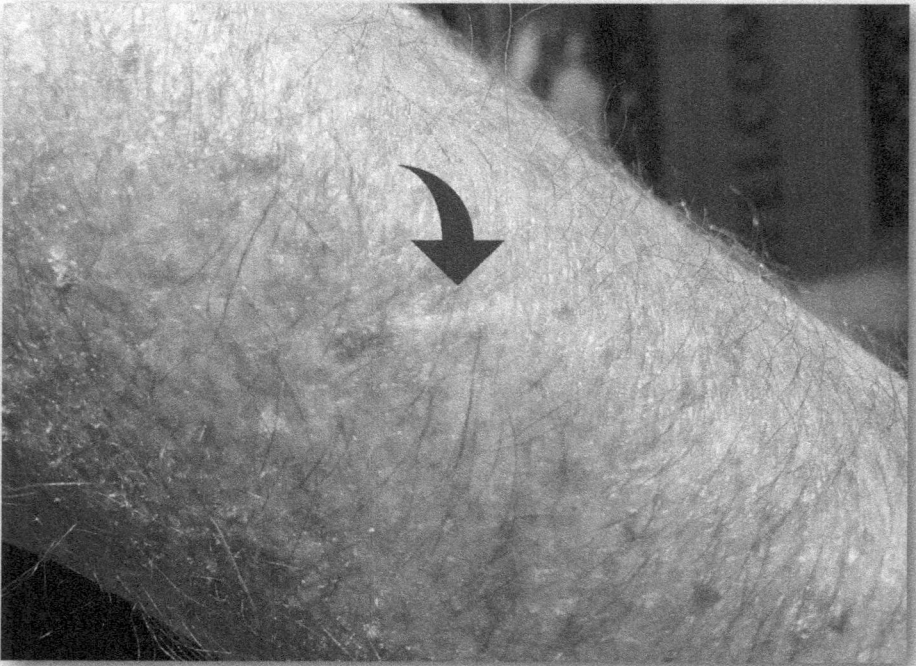

Bill's scar

Bill likes to hike but said he is no longer fearful of snakes. He told me how he used to be vigilant in looking for them as he walked.

As we chatted about his session, he said he somehow knew he wasn't the captain of the ship, but he did oversee the men on the ship. He told me he took a sailing lesson for the first time when he was twenty-two years old, and it all came instinctively for him, so much so that his instructor asked him, "You've done this before, haven't you?" Bill was excited to tell me he had planned a trip to Tortola. He wanted to find the beach he was on in his last years as Louis. His deathly fear of snakes is gone. His fear of dying is gone. And there is no longer a heart tug with his former wife. "Everything is crystal clear now."

DIANE

Mary Todd Lincoln

When I am with people who are skeptical of reincarnation and past life regression, I am often asked if I've met people who claim they were Cleopatra or Elvis Presley. The questions are usually accompanied by a hearty chuckle and an eye roll. I have not met either of them. Yet. But famous people reincarnate, too, so why should it be so startling?

Diane* and I met when I facilitated a group past life regression workshop. A lawyer by trade and very analytical by nature, she was open minded in her spiritual beliefs and was interested in exploring her past lives in private sessions. Over a period of seven months, Diane explored three different lifetimes and had a spiritual experience.

In her first regression, she was a brown-skinned woman who lived in the Netherlands in the 1700s as a disadvantaged or orphaned child but grew up to have her own family. In her second regression, she wanted to explore her fear of poverty, explaining that if her budget wasn't balanced, she felt out of sorts: "It overrides my life." She then told me that the most terrifying part of having cancer was her fear she wouldn't be able to work and thus make money. During her regression, she found herself living on the streets in England as an eight-year-old girl with a little boy, perhaps her brother. They were both hanged, and she felt confused about why she was being hanged. She learned that poverty equaled death.

Her confusion about the hanging left her feeling unbalanced. Interestingly, she has neck problems in this life. In her third regression, she returned to a lifetime she had experienced in a group regression, in which she was a young woman whose husband was a merchant captain. It was a "normal" life, she said, and one she'd like to replicate, as she was happy in that life. During her fourth session, I guided her to a place where she spoke to her deceased parents. Later, she told me that during her first session, she would see scenes in flashes but was mostly outside it, watching. With each regression she reported she was seeing more.

Nine months passed before the topic of Abraham Lincoln came up from Diane. Perhaps it took that long for her to feel safe enough with me or the regression process to confide that she had a "feeling" surrounding President Lincoln. It was a feeling she had shared with very few people.

Diane began by saying she had been fascinated with Lincoln since she was a little girl. While visiting family in Missouri when Diane was five years of age, her mother had made a point of traveling to Springfield, Illinois, to see the Lincoln home. Diane said, "On that visit, the house was undergoing renovation, and one couldn't really get a feel for the house. I didn't appreciate what I was seeing on that first visit, but I did later. I actually remember that visit very well, despite the fact that I didn't understand its significance then."

She became interested in presidents in school, especially in junior high school. She read several books about all the presidents, but Lincoln stood out for her. She read everything about him during that phase of history studies, and once out of law school, she said, she went through another Lincoln phase. She described being drawn to read more and more about him.

I found myself fascinated as I listened to her story unfold. Diane described how she had a sense she was somehow around Lincoln but couldn't figure out who she was, because he felt so *familiar*. "I never thought I was him, but I thought I knew him. I couldn't figure out who I might have been during that period," she said.

Diane continued by saying she recalled a time after a mild argument with her minister, regarding something about a church committee she was responsible for; they settled the disagreement, mostly by him agreeing to handle something her way in the future. Afterward, he smiled at her and said, "Other than that, Mrs. Lincoln, how was the play?"

"He had no idea that I had been immersed in the question of who I was around Lincoln. I don't think he was even thinking of my reincarnation philosophy, since I didn't keep it secret, when he said it. I had never heard that expression before that day, although I have heard it many times since. But coinciding as it did with my passionate question *at that exact time* about who I had been, I had to—hypothetically, at least—take that question of his as the answer to the question I been asking myself."

His response resonated deeply within her, and it became a hypothesis that she wanted to test. It made her more interested in reading about Mrs. Lincoln's life. She said she wanted to "see if it fit—and it did." She said, "It helped explain my strong, strong attachment to Lincoln and many other things about my current life."

Nearly thirty years had passed since she began to have the feeling of somehow knowing Lincoln. Diane was ready to discover if she could finally find her answers and put that feeling to rest somehow. Was she Mary Todd Lincoln? I was certainly curious as well, although uncertain of the outcome.

Once Diane was in hypnosis, I had her to go to a hallway with many doors and find the door with the date 1860 on it. I knew from our work together that it often took a while for her to get information, so I waited patiently for her to answer each question.

"Open the door and find yourself in a scene or situation in or around the time of 1860. Are in inside or outside?"

"Inside. It's the afternoon."

"Notice your feet."

"Black shoes…long skirt…sleeves on dress…"

"Notice your hands," I instructed.

"Small hands. Little. Wedding ring."

"Your hands will tell you how old you are. How old are you?"

"Forty-two…forty-one. I'm with others."

"I'm going to snap my fingers, and you'll know what year it is." *Snap.* What year is it?"

"1860."

"Let the scene you find yourself in unfold, and when you are ready, let me know what is happening."

"Getting ready for a party. People are helping me get ready."

"How do you feel?"

"Excited and a little stressed. Everything needs to be perfect."

"Someone calls out your name," I said.

"Mary…Molly?" she said. "I'm afraid of getting a headache."

"Do you get them often?" I questioned.

"Yes. I take drugs that wipe me out. People are starting to come to the party."

"Is there a special reason for the party?"

"We need to entertain…so people will vote for my husband."

"Notice the people at the party. Is there anyone you feel especially close to?"

"Yes, my sister Elizabeth. My sister Francis is there too…with their husbands."

"Is your husband there?"

"No. He'll be coming…he's with the boys."

"What is your sisters' role there?"

"They come to help me so I'm ready."

"Is there anything you are especially proud of?"

"We serve the finest food. There are a lot of people in the house. I'm excited. I like to entertain."

"Listen to what your guests say to you."

"We've done a nice job decorating he house. Some talk about Mr. Lincoln's political chances. They're excited…most of them. He's in the corner talking to the guys. I think he's going to be president! I've always thought that," she said, sounding confident.

"How will that affect your life?" I asked.

"Elizabeth won't think I married beneath me. We'll show the world we can move in those circles just like everybody else…people are starting to go home."

"What are the names of some of the people there?"

"Norman Judd." (I later discovered he was a US Representative from Illinois in 1860 and said to be Abraham's close friend.) "My sisters. It's over. It's time to go to bed. My head is killing me. Now I can take the medicine."

"What medicine do you take?" I asked.

"Different ones you buy from the druggist."

"Do you talk to Mr. Lincoln?"

"Not tonight. He's still down talking to people."

"Where do you live?"

"Springfield, Illinois."

"Move time ahead to the next significant event."

"I'm in the same house, waiting for Mr. Lincoln to come home. When he comes home, he tells me he's been nominated."

"What is your reaction?"

"Extreme excitement!"

"How do you feel about him?"

"I love him," she said and smiled.

"Go now to the next significant event."

"We're on the train to Washington, but they're going to put Mr. Lincoln on a separate train. He tells them I'd be hysterical if I couldn't find him." There was a long pause before she continued. "He's opposed to slavery. The South is proposing to secede. They say horrible things about him…there's a lot of security people. Several of my family members…"

"What is the purpose of the security?"

"He's to be inaugurated."

"He's been elected?"

There was a long pause before she said, "Yes…that's as far as I want to go in this session." I sensed she knew how the story would end, and she didn't want to relive it.

Diane opened her eyes, looked at me, and said, "You just hypnotized Mary Lincoln."

I thought it was an interesting comment for someone who later told me she felt she'd made the whole thing up.

Two months passed before her next session. As Diane sat down, she said, "I found the last session useful, but I still feel resistance to experience it fully. I had a little bit more emotion. I want to experience the past life phenomenon to convince me one way or another whether it's true."

Once Diane was hypnotized, I told her, "Go to a time that gives you the knowledge you desire."

"It's light. I'm inside…alone…in a dumpy hotel room. Female. I stay in the hotel room a lot."

"What do you do in the hotel room?"

"Lots of time…read letters…from various people I correspond with…"

"How long have you been in the hotel room?" I asked.

"I live there."

"What year is it?" I asked, as I wondered where she was.

"1860…not in good health. Not really working for me anymore to live alone. I can't really take care of myself. I decide to go back." I realized we were back to her life as Mary Lincoln.

"Go back to where?" I asked, unsure of where she found herself. I learned later she had been in Europe.

"Illinois…people there…my sister. She says I can stay with her."

"How do you get back?"

"On a ship…I'm in my sister's house. It's dark. I keep the blinds drawn all the time. Light hurts."

"Notice how you feel emotionally being with your sister."

"I really don't have a choice."

"Are you close with her?"

"Sometimes."

"Is she able to give you comfort?"

"She doesn't comfort. It's just a place to stay. Her grandson is nice to me. Louis. Teenager. I mostly stay in the room. My name is Mary."

"Go to the last day of your life, Mary."

"I'm ready for it to be my last day…there's nothing left."

"How old are you?"

"Sixty-four."

"Is anyone with you?"

"No."

"What are your last thoughts?"

"My husband and sons."

"Move through the death scene, and much time passes where you have all the knowledge and all the wisdom. What was your purpose in becoming Mary?"

"We went there to be together, and he (Lincoln) had to be there to do what he did, and I had to be there to help make it happen. It was a joint project." She was referring to a joint soul mission.

"What did you learn?"

"Lots of things. Fame isn't all it's cracked up to be. Isolation is painful. Pride is a waste of energy. Love is all that matters. Sadness gets old." She rattled off the list.

"Do you feel you learned it?"

"Learned."

"What have you brought forward as Diane?"

"Try to take care of myself economically. Be with people more."

"Because?"

"That's what caused the worst problems before. I'm trying to do things differently. I'm glad I'm here and not there. I still have a few things to learn. I brought forward the sadness and feelings of helplessness."

I emerged her from hypnosis. Her first remark to me was, "I feel like I made the whole experience up."

"You certainly seemed to have a lot of details, and you spoke in the first person," I offered. "Why do you feel that way?"

She answered me by saying she had already known the information she told me during the regression because she had read every book written about Mary Lincoln.

When I asked how many books that would be she replied, "*Many*," before letting out a deep sigh. I asked her why she felt so compelled to read every book she could find on Mary Lincoln. Weren't one or two enough?

Diane responded by saying, "I keep thinking that the rest of the clues I'm looking for will be in the next book or that I'll encounter something that I am sure that I truly remember. I *have* to read them to find out what they say."

From my perspective, when someone needs to read everything possible on a person or a time period, this is a sign of a previous life.

Diane summarized what she'd learned through all her reading. "Mrs. Lincoln got into debt after the death of her husband. She tried to sell the dresses she wore as the president's wife, as women couldn't make money during that time. Mrs. Lincoln was from Kentucky, and her brothers were Confederate soldiers. One of her confidants was a black woman. She wasn't accepted by the North or the South. As a child, Mrs. Lincoln would say she'd marry the person most likely to become president and told her sons to look up to their father, as he'd be president one day. She died in her sister's house, probably of diabetes. If it weren't for Mary Lincoln, there wouldn't be a presidential pension. She set the precedent for retired presidents and their wives."

I did some research and discovered that Mary's father, unlike most men of that era, felt women should be well educated. Diane had become a lawyer in her current life...specializing in pensions. A remnant of her lifetime as Mary?

Diane said she didn't remember ever being so deep in hypnosis that she wasn't sure she wasn't imagining it all. "I think I'm too much of a control freak to really let loose for hypnosis. I've read about the therapeutic effect that many people get from their regression sessions, and I don't think I've really gotten to that point—it's all still more in my head than my emotions." Diane's analytical mind was having a difficult time absorbing her regressions.

In an e-mail to me, Diane wrote, "Some of the "parallels" (and direct contrasts) in her life and mine are interesting. A few examples follow:

* Mary was terrified of being in poverty, and lobbied her friends and acquaintances heavily for a pension. She eventually got one, and later it was increased when a pension was also given to Julia Grant after Ulysses Grant died. Eventually, all presidential widows, and now presidents themselves, get pensions. Mary's work on trying to get her

own pension laid much groundwork for the later granting of pensions to others. This is interesting because in this life, I am a pension lawyer (among other things).

* Mary only wore black from the time Lincoln died. Except when required for business attire, I virtually never wear black. I like bright, pretty colors.

* Mary had severe migraines. I gather she would take things like paregoric, which would put her to sleep to get rid of them. I also have had migraines my whole life (from age 12), but fortunately, there are better treatments now.

* Mary never again sat in a theater after Lincoln was killed. I went to movies and theaters as a kid and when my son was at home, but in later years, as my stress levels were increasing, I stopped enjoying being trapped in a theater to watch something. I find it kind of weird that I really don't like to go to them anymore.

* When Mary was left a widow, she wasn't allowed to do anything to enhance her economic security. She tried selling some of her fancy dresses and everybody got upset over that. In my life, I had made sure I could earn my own living, possibly as a reaction to needing income but not being permitted to earn it."

Diane said that her Mary Lincoln hypothesis is a deep part of her psyche, yet she herself is skeptical about it. I contacted her for permission to use her story, and she said, "Even now (ten years later), I am skeptical about reincarnation in general, even though I have believed in it consistently since I was 16." Diane had discovered the concept of reincarnation in a Methodist Sunday school unit on comparative religions and read *The Search for Bridey Murphy*. "I've never really known if it is true. (That she was Mary Lincoln.) The logical scientist in me wants hard and fast evidence and I've never felt I had that, because I've read so much of Mary's history. There is no way I could encounter anything in a regression that I could take credit for to prove that the memories are real. However, the *feeling* that I was Mary Lincoln has stayed with me my whole life, and I keep finding events and characteristics in this life that fit really well in terms of what Mary Lincoln might well do in a later life to try to correct the many things she got wrong in that one."

What may not be related but is interesting, if not thought provoking, is that my lineage goes back to Dr. Samuel Mudd, the doctor who repaired the leg of John Wilkes Booth, who assassinated President Lincoln. Was there some type of ancestral healing that happened I was unaware of? When I discussed this with Diane, she said, "Interesting idea. I have read a little bit about John Wilkes Booth in recent years, but I mostly avoid him. I also don't like books focused primarily on the Civil War battles. I have read a couple of small books about Dr. Mudd—one when I was in junior high school, motivated in part by the fact that my fifth-grade teacher was named Mrs. Mudd, and I knew even in grade school that her husband was a descendent of Dr. Mudd as well."

My head cocked to the side like a dog hearing the word *treat*.

SUNNY

Marisha, Saudi Arabian Girl

S unny* came to me for smoking cessation. After finishing my usual work
to help her to stop smoking, as I drew a breath to emerge her from hypnosis, she suddenly said, "I'm in the clouds. There's a door."

"Hmmm," I whispered to myself. I use doors to go to other lifetimes, but
she didn't know that, and in fact, nothing in our conversation while I was
getting her history led me to know she was open to past life regression. "Will
going through the door help you to quit smoking?" I asked.

"I don't know. I just feel drawn to it," she replied.

Drawn to it. Those are the same words I use in a regression. Another
coincidence, I wondered? I glanced at my watch to see how much time I had
before my next client. I was very curious myself about what she might discover
behind the door. "Open the door and walk in. Tell me what you see."

"Ahhh, green." She breathed out the words as she exhaled. "Birds are singing. I'm home." Tears began rolling down her cheeks as a blissful look came
over her face.

"Become aware of your feet and notice what, if anything, you are wearing
on them, "I instructed.

"Sandals."

"Are your feet big or small?"

"Small."

"How old are you?" I asked.

"Twelve," she replied. "I'm at a well. There are women there. I was taken, but I've come to tell my mother I'm fine. She sees me." She described being taken by men on horseback through a desert, and my mind went to movie scenes that made me think of Saudi Arabia.

Sunny had spontaneously regressed to a different time period. Questions raced through my mind. How did she find her way back home after being taken? As though she had heard my question, she answered.

"My name is Marisha," she told me. "Oh," she interjected, sounding surprised. "My mother is Rhonda. (Her sister in this life, I later learned.) She has ancient fear and worry." A tear slipped down her cheek. "Oh, my friend is here...Eli," she related, seemingly elated. "He says that as a result of the work we did, my sister will heal."

I had no idea how her sister would heal or for that matter what needed healing until I emerged her from hypnosis. She simply stated that her sister suffered from anxieties, but I still didn't understand the connection until she came to see me again a few months later.

Sunny returned to me to help motivate her to exercise. She was excited that she no longer smoked, but she had more important information to tell me. Sunny sat in a chair across from me and began telling me she had spoken to her sister shortly after our session. Her sister told her that the day before had been the anniversary of the death of her baby, Carmen, stillborn at seven and a half months, a loss she'd mourned for fourteen years. Sunny explained her sister had panic attacks almost daily during those fourteen years, due to the loss of baby Carmen.

Her sister was surprised because, for the first time in fourteen years, she hadn't cried her eyes out on the anniversary of the baby's loss. She told Sunny she had gone to Carmen's grave, as she had all those years, but she hadn't felt sad. Perplexed by her lack of pain, she spoke to baby Carmen in her mind and, for the first time, she knew her baby was OK.

Excitedly, she also told Sunny that all her anxieties were gone. Even more amazing to Sunny was that her sister was open to hearing about her past life regression experience, information that would have made her uncomfortable in the past. I remembered Eli's words to Sunny that a healing would happen for her sister. It all made sense now.

What I learned was that past life regression can heal not only the individual experiencing it, but others who are involved. Sunny's sister was initially unaware of the work Sunny had done when she shared that her anxieties were gone and haven't come back and that she knew her baby was OK on the other side. When a loved one passes, we all want to know that he or she is OK. Sunny's spontaneous regression had healed her sister and their relationship, all because she came to me to quit smoking.

I find it interesting to see who shows up at my door and why they've come to me. Often, the reason they think they've come can be a catalyst for an even greater healing. Sunny thought she'd come to me to quit smoking, but her soul had sought an opportunity to heal. Something much greater than ourselves was at work.

GINNY

Fear of Heights

Ginny was referred to me by my husband, Tim, a licensed mental health counselor. He had been instrumental in her healing process, so when she told him of her fear of heights, he asked her if she was open to considering hypnosis. She had been hypnotized successfully years earlier for smoking cessation and was interested in seeing me. She later told me she felt safe with me immediately because of her connection with Tim. We would later learn our connection went much deeper.

Ginny walked through my office door as I was opening a box containing the first copies of my book *Angel Babies*. We began casually chatting right away. Not all my clients are metaphysical, so I keep the conversation clinical when appropriate. When she asked what my book was about, I hesitated, as I wasn't sure what her reaction might be when she heard the book's premise of communication from early-loss babies. I took a deep breath, told her about the book's contents, and waited for a response while wondering if I'd lost a client.

As always, there are no coincidences. Ginny replied that her best friend's daughter, Susanna, to whom she was very close, had experienced three miscarriages. I sold my first copy of *Angel Babies* to her. Little did we know that day how far our journey together would take us.

Ginny was retired and a youthful sixty-two. Her beautiful red hair was cut in a stylish bob that framed her face. She was a very upbeat person who I

knew had done a lot of emotional therapeutic work healing old wounds origi-
nating in her childhood that had affected her throughout her life. "The thing
I'm most proud of about myself is that I took the time and the money to seek
recovery and that I was worth it. It wasn't the easy way out. It was the only
way out," she said confidently. I liked her spunk.

Ginny had been severely physically abused as a child at the hands of her
mother. She was hospitalized three times while in kindergarten, and she lost
her hearing in one ear as a result of the abuse. She said the physical abuse only
ended when she was old enough and big enough to fight back, but the emotional abuse never ended.

I asked Ginny what the catalyst was for her appointment to see me. She
told me that, while driving on the Blue Ridge Parkway a month earlier, she
had experienced enormous fear while looking down the side of the mountain.
I asked her what the fear felt like, and she explained, "I began hyperventilat-
ing, and I felt like my chest was closing in. I felt fear!" When I asked how
long she had the fear of heights, her response was, "I have had this feeling
forever." So I was a bit surprised when she mentioned she had parachuted with
no problem.

"Do you remember the first time you ever felt this feeling?" I asked.

"The first time I remember was when I was three years old. I was terrified
to get on a plane." I was surprised once again by her answer, as most people
don't recall events that happened when they were three years old. "At five or
six, I felt it on rides in an amusement park," she added.

I asked Ginny about her religious or spiritual beliefs, and she told me that
what governed her life was spirituality. "I believe in a higher power, a universal
source."

I stepped out on a limb and asked her if she believed in reincarnation, and
she responded, "It's possible."

She went into hypnosis effortlessly, and I began. "There's a feeling inside
you that you don't like. It's the feeling that has everything to do with why you
are here today. In a moment I'm going to count from one to three, and I'd
like that feeling to become more real within you. One, feel it coming up; two,
stronger; three, very real now. In a moment I'm going to count backward from

three to one. At the count of one, you'll be at a scene, situation, or event that has everything to do with when this feeling first began. Three, two, one. Be there now. Daytime or nighttime?"

"Nighttime."

"Inside or outside?"

"Inside."

"Notice your hands. Your hands will tell you how old you are. How old are you?"

"Three."

"Are you alone or with others?"

"With others...Mom, Dad, brother, sister...grandparents."

"Notice your shoes. Describe them to me."

"They are Mary Janes."

"Notice what you are wearing."

"I'm wearing a dress with cows on it."

"Become aware of your surroundings now, and when you are ready, tell me what is happening."

"*Noisy* plane. It scares me."

"Like a videotape, move time ahead a little," I coaxed her.

"I don't want to go with my mother. I'm walking...still at the airport. I'm afraid of her strength and power."

"Because...?"

"She hurts me a lot. She scares me. I don't trust her. I don't trust her to keep me safe. It's being in a box (the plane) with *her*."

"Let the scene fade now and be back in my office. This time, I'd like you to go back to that scene as your grown-up self, as though you are a third party. Be there at the count of one. Three, two, one. Notice the younger you."

"She's terrified," Ginny said in a hushed tone.

"Pick her up, and take her out of the situation. Tell her who you are, that you are her, all grown up." I paused, giving her a chance to talk to her younger self. "Do you love that little girl?"

"Yes."

"Tell her you love her. Tell her how beautiful and precious she is. Hold that little girl in your arms, and feel her little arms wrapped around your neck. Tell her you will always be there for her now. Do you have her back?"

"Yes."

"Tell her she'll never be alone again. Life may have its speed bumps, and even a few potholes, but you'll be right there with her through it all."

"It makes me sad, seeing how damaged she was as a little girl."

"Let the scene fade and find yourself in a room with two chairs facing each other. Go ahead and sit down in one of the chairs. In a moment, your mom is going to walk through the door. She can't say anything to you. She can't touch you. She is there to listen to you. You can move the other chair as far away from you as you want before she sits in her chair. Let me know by nodding your head when your mom is present." Ginny motioned her head up and down, indicating that her mother was present. "Now tell her how her actions affected you."

After Ginny told her mom how her abuse had affected her throughout her life, I then directed her to watch her mom growing younger until she was just a little girl about five or so. "Look into your mom's eyes. What do you see?"

"She's more afraid than I was," she said, sounding surprised. "My mom's here for both of us." There was a long pause. "She loved us (referring to herself and her siblings)...she didn't have control to keep us safe (from her)."

"Is there anything else you'd like to tell your mom?"

"No," she said.

"And now you have an opportunity to truly heal if you are ready. Would you like to know how?" Ginny nodded her head. "In one word, forgiveness. Not because *she* deserves it, but because *you* do, Ginny. I'm not saying what she did to you is OK, because it's not, but this is a gift from you to you to heal and to cut the cords that have been attached to you for more than five decades. You've carried this long enough. And you don't have to carry it for another minute, let alone a month, year, or decades more. Are you ready to forgive your mother so that you can heal that little girl within you who *deserves* to be free?"

Without a moment's hesitation, Ginny replied, "Yes."

"Tell her 'I forgive you, and I set you free.'"

"I forgive you, Mom, and I set you free. And to my grandmother, thank you for being there."

"How is the younger you doing now?" I asked her.

"She's swinging her legs on a chair," she said with a broad smile.

"Let's go back to that scene again on the plane," I gently instructed.

"I'm not afraid anymore!" Ginny exclaimed. "I'm sitting in the plane next to my dad."

"Now tell the younger you that the engines are about to start, so she knows that the plane engines will be loud, but it's OK," I instructed.

"She's not screaming!" she said, surprised.

"Now explain about taking off and what that feels like, so she knows what to expect."

"We're up in the air. She's fine. She's sleeping. The sun is bright and pretty."

"Now let that scene fade. I'd like you to go now to the next time you had that feeling. At the count of one, be there. Three, two, one. Be there now. Daytime or nighttime?"

"Daytime. I'm up in an abandoned garage," she said before pausing. "My brother dared me. We were told not to play up there. He called me a chicken. I got to the top of the stairs, and I won't go further."

"Notice your hands. How old are you?"

"Five or six. He told me about a ghost that lived there…a butcher. I'm so scared I can't go down…I finally run down. I don't want to be with a ghost!" she exclaimed. "Oh, my gosh, I forgot about this!"

As mentioned earlier in the book, in hypnosis a part of you is always watching what is going on. You aren't asleep or unconscious. You are still able to think while in hypnosis, but I don't want clients to analyze while they're hypnotized, as analyzing is in the conscious mind. That's the part of you we want to step aside as we talk to the deeper part of you. The subconscious mind remembers everything.

"Let that scene fade now and be back in my office for a moment," I continued. "I'd like you to go back to the scene in the garage again as your grown-up self, as a third party. Be there at the count of one. Three, two, one. What do you want to tell that younger you?" I asked.

"There is nothing up there but an old apartment. Going up the steps, the stairs are safe. She's laughing now." (Referring to her younger self.)

"Take her to the steps," I suggested.

"My brother is gone. We're laughing." (Referring to herself and her younger self.)

"Let that scene fade. Go now to another time when you had this feeling."

"I'm ten years old…up on a roof…another garage. I thought I was going to get in trouble. I'm hiding."

"Let that scene fade, and now take your adult self back to that scene as a third party."

"I tell her it's just as easy to go down. If you get that feeling again, I'll help you." She paused. "She's not sure of that."

"Reassure her that you are there for her."

"Her body relaxed again," Ginny murmured.

"Go to the next time you had that feeling, Ginny."

"I'm flying back from college."

"Have the younger you remind the college girl it's OK."

Ginny hid her face in her hands. "You aren't afraid anymore," she said to her younger self. "She's OK!" she blurted out.

"Go ahead to the next time you had this feeling," I continued.

"I'm outside. It's daytime. My mother is visiting and complaining about the television reception. I go out on the roof to fix the antenna. It doesn't seem scary anymore."

"Notice the harder you try to find the fear, the calmer you become." I paused a moment. "How do you feel?"

"There's just a little fear…the trees…when I get near the edge. But I look fine!"

"Now find yourself at the time in the Blue Ridge Mountains."

"I'm on my trip. I don't like being on the outside lane. I drive slow and go on the inside lane—which isn't safe. This feels different than my fear of flying."

"Let that scene fade now and be back in my office, comfortably relaxed in the chair." I emerged Ginny from hypnosis, knowing we had more to do.

Ginny opened her eyes and looked at me. "When I was on a rung of the ladder, stepping out, I had little fear. And all those other events I had no fear…but anything on the edge."

"Human beings are born with just two basic fears as a form of self-preservation: the fear of loud noises and the fear of falling," I told Ginny, yet I knew we had more to do. We set up an appointment for two weeks later.

~

As I explained earlier, during a regression, clients notice more information than what they share with me. For example, they may find themselves in a beautiful ballroom but will focus on answering the question I ask of them even though they notice much more. For this reason I suggest that clients write down the regression session with as much detail as possible when they leave my office. Although they will remember the session, smaller details may be forgotten but are of interest when they reread their notes years later.

Ginny wrote about her sessions in a private journal she copied for me to read. She has allowed me to share her journal notes with you so that you can see how she felt about her regression experiences from her own perspective.

GINNY'S JOURNAL NOTES

I started seeing Patti to get over my fear of driving on the Skyline highway in Virginia and the Blue Ridge Parkway in North Carolina. I was petrified. I can ride on high mountain roads but I was very uncomfortable driving those roads. It seems like I have always had a fear of heights and of flying.

Patti took me back to myself as I was at the age when things happened to me and let my adult-self protect my younger self. I was three years old at the Chicago airport waiting to board a plane for Miami Beach for a vacation and I was petrified to get on that plane. I realized that my fear was not of flying but of being in a big dark box with my mother. On the plane they gave me a little cardboard box of two Chiclets gum. I could recall what I was wearing, how I felt, what the weather was like and if it was day or night. I could see the real fear and then protect and love that little girl as my adult-self. It felt like it took away all my fear of flying.

Patti had me go to myself at age five and then have my mother there also at age five to see what she looked like. She looked more scared than I have ever been. I felt so much compassion for her. I wanted to tell her, "It wasn't your fault." It rid me of all my hate for Mom.

Patti directed me back to my fear of heights. When we got to the edge of something like a roof or mountainous road, I said it felt different than my fear of flying. We stopped the session there.

I loved the whole experience. It felt like I went to a completely different level of therapy. It felt very healing, soothing, warm and restful. Fascinating!

GINNY

John, Builder and Carver of Walls in Babylon and Rachael Haley, Young Girl in TB Clinic

Two weeks later, Ginny returned to my office for her next appointment. As she sat down in the large, overstuffed blue leather chair in my office, she excitedly said, "This is fascinating!" As she reflected on her last session, she told me her heart had opened up to her mother, and she felt such compassion for her. She talked about a trip she had taken to Italy a year and half earlier and said she had no problem with heights while there. She also said Italy felt familiar somehow. She let her intuition lead her on where to go and how to get there, and it was always 100 percent accurate. This can happen when there is a soul memory of a place we have lived before.

I guided Ginny into hypnosis, and we began. "There's a feeling inside you that has everything to do with why you are here today. It's the feeling you had when you were on the edge of the highway in the Blue Ridge Mountains. Three, two, one. Notice your feet and what, if anything, you are wearing on them."

"I'm barefoot...tanned."

"Notice what you are standing on."

"It feels like dirt, gravel, and rock."

"Become aware if clothing covers your legs. Is it rough or soft, heavy or light?"

"It feels old and worn. It's loose. It covers my arms." I sensed she had regressed to a past life.

"Notice your hands. Are they big hands or little hands? Soft or calloused? Are you wearing any rings or ornaments?"

"Big...calloused...male. No rings."

I looked for any sense of surprise in her face, but there was none. "Your hands will tell you how old you are. How old are you?"

"I'm thirty."

"Daytime or nighttime?" I continued.

"Daytime...sunny."

"Are you alone or with others?"

"Alone."

"Notice your surroundings."

"Flat...Hilly around me. Crude wooden structures," she said.

"Let the scene unfold, and when you are ready, tell me what is happening."

"I'm taking a break. I'm building something. Old time...no cars. Too big to see.

Scaffolding. I'm outside. I'm the only one around right now...Hmmm. I'm just looking around, enjoying the view."

I wondered if something was about to happen as she was on the scaffold. "Is there anything else important you need to be aware of in this scene you find yourself in?"

"No."

"Go now to the next significant event at the count of one. Three, two, one."

"Someone is bringing me food...someone from the village. I'm very happy. My life is good...A woman...my wife. There are children with her."

"I'm going to snap my fingers, and you'll know her name." *Snap.*

"Mary."

"Look deep into her eyes, deeper than you've ever looked before. Do you recognize her or any of the children from your life as Ginny?"

"Oh! The little girl is Suzanna!" (Her best friend's daughter, for whom she bought *Angel Babies*.)

"I'm going to snap my fingers, and you'll know your name." *Snap.*
"John."
"What happens next, John?"
"I'm eating…watching the kids playing in the grass."
"I'm going to snap my fingers, and you'll know the year." *Snap.*
"632 BC." (When a client knows a year, it is because he or she is using his or her current knowledge, which he or she can always access. This is also why she used the word *kids* when she referred to the children.)
"What is the name of your town or village?"
"Near Babylon…it's a long walk…a couple of days. We are all in big baths with other people…with other children, animals…there's birds." She paused, as though taking the scene in. "It's the end of the day…we're relaxing…already had dinner…sounds like music or bells…everyone's gone home. We're all going to bed. It's an ordinary day. Kids are little. We're just…happy."
"Move time ahead, John, to the next significant event. Three, two, one."
"I'm walking…void…grayish."
I wasn't clear on what was happening or where she was. "Go back to when you were going to bed, and then slowly move time forward. What happens?"
"I think Mary died…the kids are all grown up…fifty-six years old. I feel very lost. She's gone. She got sick. She was in a lot of pain. Like she was rotting."
"How long has she been gone?"
"A while…eight years…we were building supports for roads."
"Go to the last day of your life, John."
"There's another bath…a cleansed baptism. I'm not sad. I'm aware. It's a ritual. A stone pool. My family's around. The ritual makes them happy. There are children playing."
"How old are you now?"
"Sixties…sixty-two, sixty-three?"
"Go to moments before you pass."
"My life was full of love, happiness, sunshine…I loved everything," she said and then paused. "I think it's my heart."

"What are your last thoughts?"

"I'm at peace. I feel proud of the life I had. I was a good person...I'm next to a courtyard."

"Go through the death scene, and much time passes. What were you to learn as John?"

"It feels like I deserved that life."

I felt as though we still had not gotten to the core issue of the fear of heights. I asked Ginny to focus on the feeling of fear she had when she was driving on the Blue Ridge Parkway. "Have that feeling become real within you as I count from one to three. One. Feel it coming up. Two. Stronger now. Three. Now at the count of one, you'll be back moments before you ever had that feeling. You can go back as far as you need to go. Three, two, one. Be there now."

"I can't see...a place...feeling...fear...Don't have legs. It's gas lit or candle lit."

"Find your answers," I gently coaxed her. "Let the scene unfold."

"It's so vague. Like I fell out the window and broke my legs. I'm in a Victorian house...garrets...rug is so vivid...silk red, Persian, but not..." Her voice trailed off as she noticed more as the scene unfolded in her mind. "I'm a ten- to twelve-year-old girl...by myself, but someone's coming, and I'm looking out the window. It's dark...overcast outside...waiting for someone to come...in a horse-drawn buggy. They aren't coming fast enough. I'm afraid of someone in the house...an older woman...she's very strict. I think she's a guardian." She paused before continuing, "She watches me. I'm alone in the house...hiding from her. I think it's my mother and father." (Referring to who she was waiting for to come in the buggy.)

"How do you feel about the guardian?" I asked.

"We don't like each other...my life is stuck...waiting for them to come." Ginny paused for a few moments. "I'm at a TB (tuberculosis) clinic. My family didn't come in time...I don't think I fell out the window," she said, as though still not sure. "She has nurse's clothes on." (Referring to the woman.)

"I'm going to snap my fingers, and you'll know the year." *Snap.*

"1844."

"What is the name of the town or village you live in?"

"Sir (phonetic spelling)...United States or England...Ohio? They called me Rachael...Haley. I died on the floor...I collapsed." She paused. "She cried!" Ginny exclaimed, referring to the nurse, as though it surprised her. "Hmmm." She sounded genuinely shocked the nurse cared about her. "She cried," Ginny softly repeated.

"Do you recognize her?"

"No."

"Go through the death scene, and much time passes. What were you to learn?"

"Wow! I died so young. The lesson is it's just a body...my legs...didn't work...paralyzed."

After I emerged her, Ginny described the place she was in as a sanitarium. During that time period, people who had tuberculosis were often placed in sanitariums. She did not seem surprised by her past life experiences.

~

GINNY'S JOURNAL NOTES

I had my second session. I never did get to my fear of being on the edge of mountains. Instead I had two past life regressions. In my first regression, I was John. I was married to Mary and we had three children. We lived a few days walk away from Babylon. I was building something and worked on scaffolding (like building and carving a wall). I worked on this job my whole life and I was very proud of it.

In my second regression, I was Rachael Haley, age 10 or 11, somewhere in Ohio in the early 1800s. I'm in a beautiful luxurious building but it is a sanitarium. I'm there because I have some kind of palsy in my legs and can't walk. I didn't like my nurse because of what she had to do to me but I loved her. I could hear her coming to me because I could hear her petticoats rustling. I thought she was coming to tell me my parents weren't coming so I tried to walk and fell on this beautiful pink and rose red silk thread rug. My neck broke in the fall and as I admired the colors in the rug, I died. My nurse was very sad that I died.

I was unsuccessful in finding a town beginning with Sir in Ohio, but when I tried the spelling of Cir in England, I found a town called Cirencester, Gloucestershire, England. Tuberculosis, commonly referred to as TB, is a potentially fatal contagious disease that mainly affects the lungs. In the 1800s in Europe, one in every seven deaths was caused by TB, also known as consumption at that time. The only means of controlling the disease was to isolate patients in private TB sanitariums or hospitals. The usual progression was for the disease to spread from the lungs to locations outside the lungs, including the bones. It can attack the spine and the ends of the long bones, where the vertebrae may collapse and cause paralysis in the legs. Children are especially prone to spinal tuberculosis. Perhaps this is why she couldn't move her legs and fell.

GINNY

Joseph, a Fisherman in Spain;
The Council;
Elsie Gruenwald, Polish Girl in Birkenau-Auschwitz

One month passed before Ginny's next appointment. I was curious to hear what might have unfolded during our time apart. Ginny told me that since our sessions, she had been getting more information in the dream state. "I would awake remembering even more of the past life, as if I went back to that life in my dreams, but there is still some fear."

"How do you know the fear is still there?" I asked.

"I saw the Grand Canyon on television and felt it." Ginny then told me she was raised Catholic and told me about a scorecard. "Catholics believe you were born in sin, and most people die in sin." (People who have just been to confession and have been forgiven for their sins, people who profess their faith at the time of death, or saintly people, etc., do go directly to heaven.) "There were two types of sin: venial and mortal. If you die in mortal sin, you go straight to hell. Otherwise you die in venial sin (less offensive sins against God) and you go to purgatory. Purgatory is limbo and is like hell, but you know it won't be for eternity. That's where you do time for your venial sins. There are ways to shorten your time in purgatory while you are still alive. Saying the rosary, doing novenas, making the sign of the cross, making and keeping sacrificial promises during Lent and Advent. There are lots more I can't remember, but each one of these had a number value that represented time lessened in purgatory. I don't know if they teach this anymore, but that scorecard is *gone* since we've been doing this work."

I was very happy to hear Ginny's scorecard was gone, and since she was open to where we might go, I suggested we allow her inner guidance to take us to a time that offered the most healing or insight and that was in her highest good. Ginny went effortlessly into hypnosis.

"I'm walking on cobblestones. Humph!"

"Daytime or nighttime?"

"Daytime. I'm at a wharf...we're loading up a ship. I'm helping them load up. I've come from the hills...bringing food for the workers. I'm a young boy. I don't think I have shoes. I'm helping my dad and uncles. We're not going on the boat. We brought food. We're on a wooden cart. Everybody's excited."

"Tell me about the ship," I instructed.

"Spanish? Portugal? Near the southern tip...going East, but a new way this time. Melons, breads, oranges, wines, hard things...like jerky."

"Do you know anyone on the boat?"

"No. We've prepared for months. I've never seen so much busyness. Happy...everyone energetic. They're going exploring."

"I'm going to snap my fingers, and you'll know the year." *Snap.*

"1460."

"What is your name?"

"Joseph."

"OK, Joseph. I'd like you to go to the next significant event at the count of one. Three, two, one."

"I'm in my twenties...twenty-three. I stayed and became a fisherman. The ship comes back. It's back for a while...women happy with silks, fireworks, color. I like the activity...by myself."

"Are you married?"

"No. A family took me in...taught me how to fish...a friend. Warren!" she said excitedly. "He died twenty-five years ago!" She had recognized a friend from her current lifetime. "Looks just like him, too."

"Now go to the morning of the last day of your life, Joseph."

"I'm twenty-seven. I was at the wharf. There was a celebration, and I wanted to bring fish in, so I left early. There was a storm. A big wave came and enveloped me."

"What were your last thoughts?"

"I'm going to miss seeing everyone. I'm not upset."

"Float above and look down."

"Fish all around."

"Float higher now, and much time passes. In this place you find yourself, Warren comes to you," I instructed. (In this state you can speak to those on the Other Side, often called the in-between state. Tibetans call it Bardo, while others call it Heaven or something else.)

"He was a good friend," she said, with a warm recognition in her voice. "He's saying we've been together for a long, long time."

After a few minutes with her old friend, I wanted to see if she could discover why she had chosen her current lifetime. "Go now to the planning stage. The time when you were preparing for your lifetime as Ginny."

"Looks like a council. There's a lot...sitting in three rows...a semicircle... very loving. I'm on the floor...with those who are going with me."

"One oversees you?" I ask.

"Um. Hmmm. Um," she muttered, hesitating before continuing. "A part of me that I don't love, and that is why I'm here. They're going to strip it all away so I can bear it."

"How do you feel?"

"I feel good...safe. I know they're with me. Decision...family. One is a relation of my dad's."

"What will you learn from this family?"

"Deep, small, little part...has to do *without* love to see it."

"You can ask."

"It's like we all know. I don't have to ask. They put people in places so you can do the journey...float down to Mother. The council never completely lets go." She paused, as though getting more information. "Very unhappy person (as Ginny)...it's the lesson. My mother is there. I feel such love from her. I've never felt that in this life. She loves me so much, she volunteers to be the mother."

"Is the deep, small part of you there?"

"I think it has to do with…blame."

"Who do you blame?"

She paused a few moments before saying, "Huh! I blame God for something."

"Go to the time, the event where you blamed God. Three, two, one. Be there now."

"I can feel it and more being there…a war…tanks and metal things. I'm a young girl, twenty-one, Poland…it's the Gestapo. They took my boyfriend. They took everybody. My family went to…(inaudible). They separated us. They knew we'd be gassed. We got off the train…so miserable on the train…ugh! It smells so bad! Ugh. It's human feces. Ugh. I *hate* that smell!" she said as she made a face that exemplified her smelling something awful.

"It didn't make any sense," she said before she paused. "Tons of people… packed in a gas chamber. I'm twenty. Twenty-one. Elsie Gruenwald…G-R-U-E-N-W-A-L-D." She spelled out her last name, letter by letter. "All the women and children…go right to the gas chambers. We knew what was going to happen by the women's faces at the fences…Belsen-Bergen? I can't see. The lights are on the people."

"What are your last thoughts, Elsie?"

"Horrified. Watching children die. The children and elderly died first. I watched them die. How could anybody do this? How could *you* do this, God?"

"What are your last thoughts before you pass?"

"It would have been easier if I had never loved…or been loved."

"Time passes, and you have all the understanding now."

"So sad…I think I'm still learning."

"Did you know how your life would end?"

"I think I did…it's just a body."

"A wise being appears to you."

"I know who it is…she died before I was born…my grandmother's sister."

"Listen as she helps you understand."

"Evil exists. She pats me on the back. Doing a good job." She paused. "I came back fast. Within two years. They wanted me to unlearn the thought that it would have been easier to not love or be loved."

I emerged her from hypnosis.

～

Ginny continued, "My mother…I felt such enormous, deep love from my mother during the planning stage. I have *never* felt love like that from her when she was alive," she said, sounding amazed and absorbing her profound feeling of feeling loved by her mother for the first time. "She volunteered to be a loveless mother for me to learn." Ginny paused, trying to absorb the information she had received. "She *volunteered*," Ginny said, sounding astounded by that realization. "I thought it would be easier to have a life where I wasn't loved, and I didn't love anyone including me…so that it wouldn't hurt so much."

I shared with Ginny the findings of Rabbi Yonassan Gershom, whom I mentioned earlier. In his book *Beyond the Ashes*, he presents compelling evidence, based on the stories of people he counseled, that people who had died in the Holocaust have reincarnated and live today. He noticed that often their last thoughts had quite an impact on their current lives.

～

GINNY'S JOURNAL NOTES

I was Polish. 1944. My boyfriend had been taken by the Gestapo yesterday and when I came home today, my whole family was gone. My grief gave me away to the Gestapo who picked me up tonight and put me on a train for Birkenau or Bergen-Belsen where I was immediately sent to the gas chambers. To this day, I can't stand the smell of human feces because of that train ride with no toilets. In the gas chamber, we were all nude. The babies and older women died first. I blamed God for allowing something so horrible to exist. My last thought before I died was, 'It would be better if nobody loved me and I didn't love anybody including me because then it wouldn't hurt this bad.' After I died, I went before my council where it was agreed to send me back to unlearn that idea. My mother volunteered to be a loveless mother in this life. She loved me enough to volunteer to do that for me. Apparently, there's a lot of evidence that a lot of us came right back and most are very Aryan looking. (According to Webster's Dictionary, the word Aryan has no validity as a racial term, although it has been so used, notoriously by the Nazis to mean a Caucasian on non-Jewish descent.)

It's hard to think that things like that are for the greater good of the human race. I know it's the universe's vision and not my human vision. It gave me great closure and acceptance of my mom.

~

Ginny had told me the train arrived in the middle of the night, saying, "I remember seeing a wrought-iron sign overhead. All I could make out was a *B* and a few other letters." I googled Bergen-Belsen and learned that it did not have gas chambers, but Birkenau did. Birkenau was also known as Auschwitz. When a train carrying Jewish prisoners arrived at Auschwitz-Birkenau concentration camp, "selections" would be conducted. Birkenau camp was a parallel system to the main camp in Auschwitz and surpassed all previous records for mass killing. Those deemed unfit for labor, including the ill, the elderly, pregnant women, and children, were sent to the gas chambers. Often, 70 to 75 percent of each transport was sent to immediate death. These people received no serial numbers and were not registered, so they were not entered into the records; thus, the number of victims can only be estimated. Of those given serial numbers and prisoner status, approximately half were Jews and half were Poles and other nationalities.

I discovered an organization called the International School for Holocaust Studies and looked at the list of names on their website, www.yadvashem.org, but did not find Elsie Gruenwald. Many of the names on the list were known as being missing by family members who survived the Holocaust. This was not the case for Elsie. Her parents passed and perhaps her boyfriend as well. She was ushered off the train to the gas chambers so quickly, perhaps she was among the many not listed.

GINNY

Julia, Mentally Challenged Twin

Two months passed before I saw Ginny again. We talked about her last session and how she felt after learning she had been in the Holocaust. "My last thoughts were that I blamed God. I'd be better off not loving anybody and nobody loving me. Then it wouldn't hurt. I went right from the Holocaust to the council. There were three rows. They were there to help me get through it. I saw my mother volunteering to be the unloving mother." Her next lifetime would be her current one as Ginny, whose mother was verbally, emotionally, and physically abusive.

She continued, "The hard part is the best part. I felt like I had to go through the Holocaust to learn love—to cure the problems of the human race. There are no victims. We all volunteer. It changed how I look at everything."

Ginny's mother's Higher Self appeared to her during the council. A person's Higher Self is that part of a person that is always on the Other Side. This is why, when we return to the Other Side, we are always greeted by loved ones who have passed before us but who may have reincarnated as well.

I decided to regress Ginny to discover whatever was in her highest good. She walked through a glossy, smooth, turquoise door and found herself on a boat, drifting. "I'm grown up...cool summer day...a gentle wind."

"How old are you?"

"Twenty-five."

"Notice your hands. What color is your skin?"

"White."

"Male or female?"

"Female. I have a big hat on...blue ribbons. I can see land. I'm on a river... banks on both sides...grass, trees on side. No stones. A man is powering the boat with a paddle. Humph. Humph."

I realized she was seeing something that was surprising her, as she often reacted with a *humph*. "Let the scene unfold, and when you're ready, tell me what is happening."

"We're going to a picnic, but we're not in a hurry to get there. He's some-body I feel so at ease with...close to."

"Someone calls out your name. What is your name?"

"Julia. I think he's my twin...Edward. We're just enjoying it. It's beauti-ful out. Summer, lush and green. We've got food in a basket. We're not in a hurry. We're going to meet a group of people. We're waiting for a ship to come back."

"From where?"

"I think," she paused, "a long voyage...China. We don't know when they'll be back. It's just so beautiful out. We're waiting for our dad. Grass... blankets...other people from our town. It's a ritual we do."

"What is the name of the town, village, or country you live in?"

"Arlington? Argyle? England."

"Are you alone or with others?"

"There's some girls around my brother. He's teasing them. He wanted to be on the ship, but he wasn't old enough when it left."

"Go to the next important event, Julia."

"My dad's come back. He brought all these wonderful things. Little toys, figurines, fabric and tools, clothes, and foods. My mom's so glad to see them...my dad and other men from the village. I remember loving hearing the stories of the people they met. We live in a house on a hill...a lot of grass... met him in town...carts...dancing...Mom's running out...brother...met him at the ship."

"Do you recognize your dad from your life as Ginny?"

"No. His name is Walt Rooten." She said the name clearly. "Big, sparkly blue eyes…dancing like he is…" Her voice trailed off. "He knows I love those stories."

"What happens next, Julia?"

"A lot of love, everybody's happy and safe," she said, before she paused and added, "I think I'm not…fully mentally developed…very childlike…a grown-up, but I get tucked in to bed. I have long, dark curls, my dad's sparkly blue eyes. My brother…he's fine. It's me. They like me this way."

"Because?"

"I'm always happy. I don't have any worries. No responsibilities. Humph."

"Go to the next significant event, Julia," I instructed.

"My brother is getting married. It's his wedding. He's worried about leaving me. I'm an adult, but…doing the maypole with ribbons with the young girls."

"Your parents?"

"They love me. I'm happy all the time. It doesn't feel retarded. It feels happy. I feel like I'm the blessed one. I'm still in my twenties. His wife…it'll be fine. I've known her. She loves him. She loves me."

"Where will he live?"

"Not far. I'm taking care of the kids. I'm fine."

"Go to the next important event, Julia."

"I'm at that picnic place again…waiting for the ship…my brother."

"How old are you now?"

"Thirty-two. There's another baby…up to four now. I get a sense I live everywhere…doesn't matter. Now his son wants to go on the ship. I'm fifty now."

"Looking back on your life, how would you describe it?"

"It's been great. I walk…have a bicycle. Take things from house to house. Letters, baked goods…my father is still alive. I love the stories and ask to hear them over and over again."

"Your mom?" I asked.

"She's a mom, and she takes care of me."

"Go to the morning of the last day of your life, Julia."

"Parents still alive. I think they know…but I'm not sick. She's sad and crying. Dad tucked me in. I go in my sleep."

"How did you die?"

"My lungs stopped. I never felt sick. I'm early fifties."

"Much time passes, and you have a full understanding of that lifetime. What was it you wanted to learn in your lifetime as Julia?"

"I wanted to be with somebody, so I got a twin."

"Did you choose to be mentally challenged?"

"I *know* I did."

"Because?"

"I wanted to feel free to just love. I didn't want any chores. Almost not be human. Very happy. I wasn't burdened with anything except to love people."

I was touched by the simplicity of her words. She came into this life for the sole purpose of loving people. I emerged Ginny from hypnosis.

~

GINNY'S JOURNAL NOTES

Julia, Argyle, England 1789. I was retarded. I had a twin brother named Edward. The men in our town, including my father, went off sailing. They fished and then took their catch to far off places to trade them for goods—olives, tangerines, fabric, shoes, tools, silks, ribbons and lace. My mother was very shy. She was a seamstress and made beautiful clothes for royalty. She made pretty things for me with her leftovers because I was her princess. Edward married and eventually had six children. His wife loved me and was good to me which is one of the reasons Edward fell in love with her. When Edward went to sea, I sometimes stayed with my sister-in-law, Claudie, and helped her take care of their children. Every time my father came home, he told me tales of his wondrous adventures of faraway places of camels and Arabs and deserts and Arabian horse races and snake charmers. She…the shop woman who was the bakery widow…let me lick spoons and make deliveries. She never had children and I filled her lonely places. When I got tired

at her home, I would lie down on a small bed under the window and spend the
night there. I lived to be fifty years old.

My lungs gave out. My last night, my mother was crying. She knew I was go-
ing to die even though I wasn't sick. My father tucked me in and I fell asleep to one
of his stories. I died in my sleep that night.

The purpose of this was to experience complete and unconditional love both
for me and from me even from the point of my conception with a twin. Love with
no expectations. Just love for its own sake.

I was moved by the power of her last words.

~

I discovered that a ribbon dance, dancing around a maypole, is regarded as
the most traditional of May Day's traditional characteristics in England and
Scotland. Dancers hold a colored ribbon and gather in a circle. As the dance
begins, the ribbons are intertwined around the pole.

Argyle is a region on the western coast of Scotland, but I discovered there
is a village in England called Arlington in East Sussex. The parish is on the
River Cuckmere, which means *fast-flowing*. It flows into the English Channel.

GINNY

Twelve-Year-Old Girl in Cambodia

"For some reason I feel very apprehensive about coming today," Ginny stated, as she sat in the big blue leather recliner.

I placed the familiar quilt over her legs. "Why is that?" I asked her.

"I was watching a television program on Croatia, and there was a panoramic view from a cliff and I thought *there it is*. The feeling of fear. It doesn't happen with a water view or, surprisingly, even when I've been skydiving." To me, skydiving would be the ultimate fear of heights, and yet it didn't affect her.

Once she was hypnotized, I asked Ginny to go back to when she was watching the commercial on Croatia and focus on the feeling she had as she watched it. "As I count from one to three, just allow that feeling to come up strong within you, Ginny. Just for a moment. One, feel the fear; two, allow it to become stronger; three, very strong now. I'm going to count from three to one, and at the count of one, you'll be back at a scene, situation, or event that has everything to do with when this feeling first began. Three, two, one. Be there now. Notice your feet and what you are standing on."

"I very softly feel it...not intensely...I can't get to the feeling."

I changed direction. "Be in the car driving in North Carolina. Remember it. Imagine it. Now allow the feeling to come up as I count from three to one," I continued. "Three, two, one. Be there now."

"I'm seeing a walking bridge."

"Describe it to me."

"Ropes…wood."

"What does the bridge go over?"

"A huge crevice…so huge. I don't know what's at the bottom," she said softly.

"Where are you in relation to the bridge?"

"I'm in front of it."

"Are you alone?"

"I will be."

I wasn't sure what she meant by that but continued. "What color is your skin?"

"Light."

"Notice what you are wearing."

"Like a toga."

"Have you gone over the bridge before?"

"No. It's…" There was a long pause before she continued, "Whew."

"What is on the other side?"

"I don't know…it's a sacrifice!" she exclaimed.

"Who or what is being sacrificed?" I asked.

"My first thought is to a god…whew…well, for a punishment…whew…not anything *I* did…sacrifice to appease a punishment…something didn't happen that was supposed to…with nature…I don't know…it's very green…I think I'm in Cambodia. Only one is being sent across the bridge…it's what we do."

"Notice your hands," I suggested.

"Rings…paintings, inks, like rays from the sun."

"What is behind you?"

"Whew…there's, um…whew…it's the end of a ceremony I think…I'm fourteen. Maybe younger. I'm at the end of a long path…it's almost…" Her sentence trailed off.

"How do you feel?"

"I don't want to do it…I thought I'd cross the bridge, but…I thought you'd go across and stay…sacrifice for a volcano…I walk halfway…" she said, her voice fading.

"Are your parents there?"

"No...the chief...priests...leaders."

"How many are there?"

"Several...dancing...they have sticks with points to make me go on the bridge...I thought I was going to the other side of the bridge. I turn around. I thought I could outrun them to the other side. They're cutting the ropes!" she exclaimed, sounding shocked. "I was prepped for this. (Referring to being a sacrifice.) I know how to pray...knew it was for the good...tumbling into nothingness."

"What are your last thoughts?"

"How nice it smells, mossy and green...it feels like I never hit the bottom."

"Float above and discover what you were to learn in that lifetime."

"It took that fear...to trust in God...the fear is gone..."

"How do you know?"

"On the way down, I trusted God. No fear."

"Now look at the scene, the path. What do you feel? Any fear?"

"No, but I remember it."

"As I count from five to one, know the fear and become aware of what the fear was. Five, four, three, two, one."

"The fear was I didn't have a choice."

"Replace that thought with something else. What will it be?"

"To believe in God."

"Are you willing to place this new thought within you?"

"Yes. It's not about the heights. It's thinking I didn't have a choice."

"Imagine the fear leaves you and goes into the light."

"I feel lighter."

We then did an exercise in which I had her imagine the different scenes of heights, and she cut the cords to those scenes and watched the cords shrivel up and disappear and watched the scenes fade. "Now I'd like you to go back to a scene where in the past, you had the fear. Where are you?"

"Arizona."

"Try to find the fear, and notice the harder you try to find it, it's just not there."

"Yeah, it's fine."

"No, go back to another scene, where in the past, you were afraid."

"Roller coasters…feeling is the same as falling."

"Try to find the fear, and notice the harder you try, it's just not there. Any fear?"

"Hmm. No."

"Now go to a new place."

"Blue Ridge Mountains…still don't like it."

I emerged her, realizing we still hadn't gotten to the root cause of her fear of heights and wondered what I was missing. I asked Ginny to tell me more about her regression experience. "I felt it was between 6000 and 8000 BC. I was pulled away from my family. The priests took me in and raised me for this purpose, to be a sacrifice. I lived with the priests. They thought I was special but not loved. I was being trained religiously about the gods. I can almost smell the dust from this memory. I've had this fear for a long time. I never saw my parents again."

~

GINNY'S JOURNAL NOTES

I was walking along a narrow dirt path leading to a manmade foot bridge made out of rope and green wood-like bamboo. It crossed a deep chasm that didn't seem to have a bottom. I was a young woman, 12–14 years old, light skinned, and dressed in a white toga. I had been raised my whole life to strongly believe in the gods and that my purpose was for this sacrifice. Behind me were men like priests or elders dressed in ceremonial garb carrying bamboo poles that had been whittled to a fine point at one end. I thought I was being led to this bridge to cross it by myself and never come back and live my life on the other peak as a sacrifice to the nature gods. When I got to the bridge, I didn't want to go so they poked and prodded me with their pointed poles and made me go. When I got about halfway out, the bridge started shaking.

They were cutting the ropes. I tried to turn to run to the other side but I didn't have enough time and I fell into the chasm below. Somewhere on my descent, I regained my faith and I wasn't afraid anymore, I don't remember hitting bottom or my dying because it didn't feel like death. It was lush green with ferns and moss, and it smelled wonderfully earthy and enveloped me. My fear wasn't the height but that I didn't have a choice. While still in hypnosis Patti directed me to high places like the Grand Canyon rims and it felt okay to be in these high places. She had asked me if I was wearing any jewelry in that life. I wasn't, but my body, especially my arms, had been painted with sunbursts or sun rays or maybe lightning bolts.

GINNY

Pi, Eskimo Boy in Fjords, Norway

Ginny was content to let her fear of heights be put to the side. She found her past life experiences fascinating and wanted to explore more, so I let Ginny's inner knowing take her to where she needed to go and directed her to a hallway with many colored doors. "One of the doors you'll feel drawn to or curious about."

"It's a yellow door," she responded.

"Go through the door and find yourself in a scene, situation, or event that has everything to do with why you are here today," I began.

"I'm a...hmmm...I'm...ah...bundled up. We're on reindeers."

"Who's with you?" I asked.

"A whole lot of us. We're hunting. It's so pretty here. Like twilight. Norway, Finland, the Fjords...it's beautiful. We've come from an inland village to go whaling. We have harpoons. I'm...hmmm...I've never done this before. I'm young. I've never seen the water before and um...hmmm. I'm about five or six...playing with the reindeer. The water...oranges and purples everywhere."

I assumed she was seeing the Northern Lights. "How many people are there with you?"

"There's a herd of reindeer. All the men are going out on boats. They're going in a circle. There's some kind of chants that will attract the whale. We're on snow...the ice. I can see their breath. We're sitting on skins of...huddled together. Mothers and children…it's like they're sewing homes out of hides. And there's…like, um…maybe young reindeer, dogs, like guard dogs to keep us away from the water. The children…the women are all busy. They're chanting for the safety of the men at sea. It's very methodical…like they're saying it to the wind. They've got a whale. It's on the beach, and they're cutting it up. Getting the fat…hurrying…it's freezing…like they're packing it up to save it for winter…to last the winter. Everyone has jobs. They are sewing together skins to hold the fat…meat. They use everything. The boats are made out of the bones." She paused before adding, "Oh…they feed the reindeer with meat too. And the bones…they're big! The make, um, sleds to haul back."

"What are you wearing?"

"We're bundled up…skins on us. Like mountain goat skins."

"Go to where you live now."

"We're in a cave. Nice and warm from the fires. We live huddled together to stay warm. There's pens…corrals of the whale bones…for smaller animals…for food. There are paintings on the wall. The fire makes them dance. It's very dark all winter."

"Where do you sleep?"

"We all sleep together to stay warm."

"Become aware of your mother and father."

"I have older brothers…I'm a boy. My name is Pi."

"Go now to the next significant event."

"It's getting light outside. We're all going to go out. It's slow paced. The light outside is coming. We are gathering food, oil, and animals during the light time. It's nice to come out. I'm about six or seven. Everything is mating."

"Are there any animals you have to be concerned about?"

"I'm…too…yeah, there's dogs…or wolves. They smell us. The reindeer protect us. We're getting ready to hunt for whales again. I don't see um… future…"

"Go to morning of the last day of your life."

"I'm still young. It's light out. I don't see any danger. It's, um…hmm…It feels like I'm not very strong. I'm on the shore watching. I never get to go. I'm like a sickly kid. I'm being rocked by my mother. It was expected."

"Do you hurt?"

"No. Like some kids are weak. It's a special ritual for children. We're taken somewhere and buried to protect us. The men go to sea when they die. Special kids' grave site so animals don't eat us. Like under rocks and ice and stuff...very warm, very loving. There's a lot of children. Some just don't make it. Accepting...never feels cold to me."

"Let time pass now, Pi. What were you to learn in that lifetime?"

"I'm going up to the sun. It's warm like the fur. I couldn't participate, but I could observe. It was enough. The cave drawings...anyone who wanted to. There's joy in observing. Simple joy."

"Find yourself at an ancient library now," I said, "where someone greets you."

"It's a man. Old."

"He takes you inside now where there are endless rows and rows of books. Now notice a table with a book on it and sit down at the table. This book is all about you. In a moment I'm going to have you open the book. There may be words written on the pages or pictures that come to life," I told her. "Now open the book."

"It's me! It's a good story. He's happy I can see that," she said, referring to her guide. "I trust him. It's a great feeling. There are pictures of my life, and if I've done my lessons. I can see the pictures more...he's happy and I'm happy. It's a very loving interchange."

I emerged Ginny from hypnosis.

"Wow!" she exclaimed. "I could have stayed in the library forever. He was so happy. There was blue and purple smoke, like a wisp of smoke from a cigarette."

~

GINNY'S JOURNAL NOTES

Pi (my name) in reindeer village in far north like maybe Iceland. We lived the harsh winter months in a big cave warmed by the fires we built. It was important for us to harpoon one whale at the end of the summer to sustain us though the winter. Our colony's survival was based on catching one whale at the end of the summer. We used everything of that whale. Bones for the hull of the men's boats, bones to haul everything behind the reindeer, fat (blubber) for fire, organs for our small penned animals for their food until we ate them (hares, moles, etc.) skins for clothes. The women chanted like the whales to attract them to our shores. There were paintings on the cave walls that moved and danced to the flickering fires. I wasn't physically strong and only lived to be seven. Weak children were common so woman tried to get pregnant every spring to get enough healthy babies. Weak children were honored by being buried in a special graveyard just for us. Everyone else was returned to the sea to give back to the whales. Reindeer herded around us to protect us from wolves.

I died in my mother's arms wrapped up like a papoose.

Patti then directed me to an ancient library. She said someone will take you in. I was a young lad about fifteen and he was a man of about forty with the kindest aura and a most loving face and he was so happy for me. Patti told me to sit at a table with a book on the table and to open the book. She asked if I could read any words. The book was about me and it was a book of pictures and if I had done my lessons, then pictures moved and came to life. This pleased me and the man tremendously. He was so proud of me. There were books on the walls on shelves that went as far as I could see. I loved being in that library. I could have stayed there forever.

When I came out of this session, I asked Patti where I was. She said, 'I thought you may be ready to see the Akashic Records.' I think they're like computer records of all of your lives.

~

The Akashic records are a book or books that contain the entire history of your soul; every thought, every emotion, every action and experience that you experienced in all your lifetimes is recorded.

Wild reindeer are still found in Norway, Finland, Greenland, Alaska, and Canada.

The northern lights are unique with each appearance. The lights may appear as rolling smoke, as flickering curtains, or as luminous bands of green light, often along with other colors.

GINNY

Colonel Claude Louis Hector, Duke of Villars

When I first met Ginny, she wasn't even sure she believed in reincarnation, and she hadn't read anything on the topic, but nearly a year had passed, and Ginny had truly gone on a soul exploration. In our early months working together, I had asked Ginny not to read anything about reincarnation or past lives, as I didn't want her experiences influenced in any way. Enough time had passed, and I thought she might find validation in reading about others' experiences. I had suggested she read Dr. Brian Weiss's book *Many Lives, Many Masters*. It was the first book I had read on reincarnation, and it was so profound to me that I felt as though I had discovered an ancient secret holding more truth than any religious upbringing I had been exposed to. I was excited to hear what she thought of the book.

"It was affirming but not startling information," she offered with a ho-hum tone. "After all, I've experienced it myself."

I was surprised it wasn't as impactful to her as it had been for me, but she made a good point. In the year we had worked together, Ginny's first regression seemed to eliminate her fear of small heights, such as being on a ladder or on the roof of her home, but we still had not discovered the root of her fear on the Blue Ridge Parkway. Instead, what she had discovered was herself and her soul's journey. She had learned who she was, allowing her to understand how it affected her in her current life. She told me repeatedly how fascinating she thought the journey was, and she did not seem to care about her nagging fear of heights, but I felt it was time. I asked her to walk me through the fear again.

"I feel fine if I'm a passenger in the car. It only happens when I'm driving—when *I'm* in control. I don't like being in control," she said. Ginny's words *only when I'm in control* echoed boldly in my mind. The fear wasn't necessarily of heights but of being in control. I suspected this is what I'd missed earlier.

In hypnosis, I guided her to an ancient healing temple. "When you are ready, describe it to me," I instructed.

"It's made out of stone...there are several steps going up...there are domes and different sections...waterfalls all around. The waterfalls are all around... all different...they all sound different. Very serene...cleansing."

"Find a place to sit down," I instructed.

"I'm in the center of it, and there is a courtyard with mosaic floor...a mosaic circle. The sun is very warm and bright."

"I'm going to hand you your *I Don't Like Being in Control* book. When you are ready, describe it to me."

"The covers are wooden...carving on them...bound together with a leather string. The carvings are of these waterfalls..." Ginny muttered as her voice trailed off.

"Open the book now, and it will open to the page of the first time you had this feeling."

"I've been in this temple before...now it's like a ruin...can't..." Long moments passed before she continued, "I'm a general. I got off a horse, and I'm looking at maps. It's cold here...thick coat. I'm with a lot of others...it's an army. They are in dark uniforms. I'm a general, so I have gold tassels on my uniform...gold buttons...dark navy. I have a hat. I'm holding all these maps under my arm with thick gloves on. There's a mountain ridge...between France and Spain. I get the feeling that I'm their last shot. It's a pretty hopeless situation, and, um...I'm on the French side, but we're in Spanish country. And, um, the men are tired, thousands...battle fatigued."

"Who are you attacking?"

"The Spanish, but they have a lot of help from the Moors, and we didn't know about that! I'm talking to my men...planning...splitting up? We're in

the mountains with open valleys. The plan is to make a big *C* and attack...
with Berbers." There was a long pause before she continued. "Colonel Clau...
Clausant...Quissant?" She struggled saying the name, because she either
couldn't pronounce it or couldn't hear it. "Sixteen or seventeen hundreds...
end of sixteen hundreds? We didn't know about these Arabian fighters. They
are dirty fighters. We were slaughtered...almost all of them. They knew our
plan and were ready for us...we lost thousands and retreated in shame."

"How many are left?"

"Five thousand...of thirty thousand." In my mind's eye, I tried visualiz-
ing that many people fighting. "It was the end of my career. I retreated to an
island off the Mediterranean as a recluse."

"Go to moments before you pass."

"I feel like a failure...to my country. I was a good general until then. I was
patriotic, and I feel like I let everyone down."

"What is the name of the war?"

"I don't know."

"What were you fighting over?"

"Land. Conquer..." her voice trailed off.

"Is there anyone you loved?"

"No. Only my country."

"What do you remember when you think back to that time?"

"I'm on horseback...a black and white horse, beautiful...at a distance...
over a valley...I'm high on a ridge...on a ledge, on my horse, it's black, looking down...it was a new kind of war...barbarians...they knew our plan of the
C formation and used it against us. There was a spy. I witnessed the worst
bloodbath. They killed thirty thousand of our men brutally with machetes
that were no match to our piddly swords."

"Go to the last day of your life," I instructed.

"It's like I willed my heart to stop...it's daytime...sitting on a lounge
chair."

"What were you to learn?"

"I don't want to be in control. Like control has a high price to it. I felt...
responsible."

I could hear the guilt in her voice as she spoke her last words and suspected it had bled over into her current life. I wanted to be certain there was healing and decided to take it one step further. "In this place that you find yourself, notice that all of your men come to you. What do you want to say to them?"

"I'm so sorry!" she cried out. "Hmmm...they didn't see it that way at all. They knew they were fighting for their country. They are *cheering* me for such a valiant attempt. They didn't see *me* as the cause of their death. They would gladly and proudly soldier under me again, they are telling me."

I wanted to be sure she was clear about their feelings. "Are they at all angry at you?"

"No!" she said, surprised by their reaction. "Huh."

"So twenty-five thousand men don't blame you?" I asked.

"No, they don't. I want to thank God," she said as a tear spilled down her cheek. "It's so powerful...oh, my gosh...it's beyond my comprehension."

"Be on the horse, on the cliff above them, looking down," I instructed.

"Unbelievable!"

"Your book has a new title now," I told her.

"I can't remember the old one. I don't know...I can't remember the old title."

I had goose bumps as she spoke. "Find yourself back in the library, and go to one of the waterfalls, and sit under it, and feel the water wash away any negativity you brought forward from the lifetime you just experienced." I watched as her face softened, and then I emerged her.

"Oh, my God! I *hate* war! I hate war movies! It wasn't guns. It was swords and shields. The Pyrenees mountains, maybe? It was a boundary war. We were protecting what was ours more than overtake someone else's."

Wanting Ginny to understand her experience more, I said, "I want you to be aware that you were on a high ledge, on the edge, in control, and responsible (the words she had used when describing her fear of heights) for thirty thousand men as the general. Sitting on your black horse, looking down on the valley from a great height, watching your men being killed and powerless to help them. It was the feeling you had, while you were in control on a high ledge looking down that caused your fear, not the height itself."

She looked at me and shook her head up and down, agreeing with me.

~

By the time I saw Ginny again, she had researched her lifetime as a general and said she found that there was a war during the time of Louis XIV. "It was called the War of Spanish Succession between French, Spanish, English, and Austrians, where thirty-three thousand men were massacred. Claude Louis was the most revered general in his army. The dates I saw were correct! Europeans feel it was the First World War. The French lost; they lost Canada. England won the war. Even the map formation split like the *C*. Generals were picked from royalty back then. But Claude earned his ranking. It was in the Austrian mountains, not Pyrenees. I found a picture, and I looked like Villars—who had a black horse."

GINNY'S JOURNAL NOTES

I made a comment that I don't like to be in control because then whatever happens isn't my fault. She then suggested I go to a healing temple and I saw one immediately. There were red domes in each corner of a courtyard and a large round mosaic in the middle of the courtyard floor. I sat in the lotus position in the middle of it basking in sunlight. She then had me holding a book on control. The front and back were carved wood. The book was bound with leather strings. I can't remember the title. There were carvings of two of the four waterfalls around the temple. Without opening the book, I knew the story was about me as a general for the French army. I was in my late fifties and I had been an exceptional officer and general. The army was my life's work. My love was my country, France. We were at war with Spain who was trying to take over the Pyrenees Mountains. We were losing the war and I was called in to run the war. It was a last-ditch effort and I had a history of greatness at my job. I was on a black and white horse. It was cold and I wore a long dark blue coat with gold tasseled epaulets and gold buttons. My strategy was to split our fronts in two with a "C" formation coming in to the valley from two mountains passes. We didn't know that the Spaniards had brought on board the Moors or the Berbers—savage barbarian warriors. This greatly outnumbered our army of 30,000. Plus, they had a spy who knew our plans. I positioned myself high on a ledge on my horse where I witnessed the worst bloodbath. They killed 25,000 of our men brutally with machetes that were no match to our piddly swords. I hung my head in shame feeling I was responsible for all these deaths. I retired to an island in the Mediterranean as a recluse. I willed my heart to stop and I finally died on a lounge chair on the porch. She had me go through the death scene and then visualize the army in front of me again but now alive. They were all cheering for me for such a valiant attempt. They didn't see me as the cause of the loss or their death. They would gladly and proudly soldier under me again. The feeling was overwhelming! 25,000 men cheering for me and forgiving me.

Patti then had me go back to the healing temple and go to one of the waterfalls. I sat on a rounded warm rock and let the water cleanse me. It felt wonderful. After the regression, she pointed out that I was on a high ledge on a horse and looking down on the valley. It wasn't the height, it was the scene in front of me (and knowing I was in charge). That is a big part of my fear of heights—it's not the heights, it's the view.

I now remember the title of the book—If I'm not in charge, then I'm not to blame.

This was a very healing session.

~

Ginny had struggled when saying her name when asked, but she knew it began with a *Clau* sound. We discovered *Clau* was Marshal Claude Louis Villars (1653–1734), who was considered one of the most brilliant commanders in French military history. He was commander in the War of the Spanish Succession (1701–1714), fought over the possible unification of the kingdoms of Spain and France.

The Berbers, who assisted the Spaniards, were from North Africa and as tribesmen had a long history of having fierce fighting skills. They were strong enough to have control of parts of Northwest Africa and Spain. So there was a strong likelihood they could have been involved in the war as well. The date range was accurate, and the war was about acquiring land just as Ginny had said, but what really caught my attention was reading the number of men who were in that war—thirty-three thousand.

GINNY

Louis Marchand, Harpsichordist

Ginny attended an experiential group past life regression workshop I facilitated, in which I guided participants to several lifetimes. Afterward, when I asked if anyone would like to share their experience, Ginny's hand shot up.

"My name was Marchand. It was the 1600s. My wife's name was Mimi. We had no children. I was a musical prodigy. I was so good so young, my parents practically made me their life's work, and I loved them very much for that. When I married, my wife was also very devoted to me and my talent. We lived in a three-building dwelling: my parents in one building, my wife and I in another building, and the third building was my music studio where I composed music all the time on a harpsichord. A white dove frequently perched on the windowsill when I was composing like a muse. My father died, and my grief of that inspired me to write my beloved music. This lifetime is the source or some of the source of my love for music today. It might also be the source of my desire to build a three-building home in this life."

At her next appointment, I asked Ginny to tell me more about her experience. She told me she had never heard of a musician named Marchand, and yet she knew a lot about music, so she was a bit surprised. Also, she doesn't like the harpsichord. She said she found Louis Marchand quite easily on the Internet. He was a French Baroque organist, harpsichordist, and composer.

He was a child prodigy and established himself as one of the best-known French virtuosi of his time. Despite his success, few of his works survive to this day, but *Grand dialogue in C and Fond d'orgue in E minor* are considered classic works of the French organ school. Known for his arrogant personality and violent temperament, his life was filled with publicized scandals discussed both during his lifetime and after his death.

I could hear the arrogance in her voice as she referred to herself as Marchand and said, "I knew I was good at what I did. If they have a problem with it, so be it."

GINNY

Gretchen, Holland

Ginny and I had been working together for two years when we decided our journey together of soul exploration would soon come to an end. She had discovered twenty of her lifetimes (not all are included in this book) and how they had affected her life today. We had a strong bond, and since we travel in soul groups, I was curious to know if we'd spent a lifetime together. She wanted to know as well, so we decided our last time together would be to explore this possibility but as always leaving it to her highest good.

Ginny began describing the scene she was in immediately. "Hmmm. Umm. I'm in Holland. It's spring, and there are tulips everywhere. I'm a young girl about eleven.

There's another girl with me...I don't know if it's you...blond braids... we're walking on a stone path. We're excited. We're going to a festival. I think we're going to be in a pageant, and there are windmills."

"Notice what you are wearing."

"I think it's our costumes. Dutch clothes with white aprons," she said, before pausing for a moment. "Yeah, we've got those hats that come to a point on each side. We've got wooden shoes on. A game. A little ditty (meaning a song)...rocking on the stones that you and I are playing. There's something very fun going on because we're laughing a lot. Must be a Dutch game...like a teeter-totter in our shoes. There's a rhythm that goes with it. We have baskets.

When we fall, our skirts fly up, and our petticoats show. We put tulips in our basket. Um...I'm trying to figure out the feeling. Oh! We're identical twins! I thought it was the costumes. We're in a pageant. I felt a closeness beyond friends. It's like you're...we're one. I think, ah, umm..." Her voice trailed off.

"Is there a name of the pageant or—" I asked, before she interrupted and answered me.

"Something about the wooden ships. Hmmm. There's a spring festival for the return of the wooden ships. We're going to be one of the stars, because we sing," she said. Her words brought immediate goose bumps on me.

"What is your name?"

"Gretchen and Grendel Van Hoks."

"What is the name of the town or village?"

"We live in one little town...that's on the sea. There's a *Z* and an *H*...like a hook or...Zeider. Brother is Gunter. There's long flags that come to point at the end. Buildings and bridges. It's...I'm trying to see when this is. It's hard because we're dressed in costumes. There's white handkerchiefs. They wear lace handkerchiefs on their heads. The men kind of look like Pilgrims with the buckle belts. It's mostly women because it's for the men to come back from the ships. They go to exotic places. They bring back teas, spices, flour, bulbs, seeds. The seeds are, hmmm, big. It's cocoa. The things I thought were seeds. It's rice. They come from...there's all kinds of songs about this. Round-the-world song. Something about...there's like a children's song about our alphabet, cities, countries that start with those letters."

We had worked together long enough that it was as though she knew what question I was going to ask and answered it before I voiced it.

"The men are coming back. I'm trying to figure out what year it is. 1825? There's a whole...it's called a troupe. Everything is symbolic. There's jugglers, oranges...because the men need oranges when they come back. We line the docks with tulip petals to show them the way home. There's a big windmill that's very brightly colored. It's going to be the center of the bonfire...to help them find their way back. And there's, hmmm, they're special made breads baked one time a year for this. The bread is braided and full of...hmmm... there's some kind of surprise in them."

"Is it something you eat?" I asked.

"No, like a coin or a ring that's put inside. It's the...I'm only eleven, but these breads are for the young maidens. Something like their betrothed will come back. Might be a key. Something metal," she said, describing the item put inside the bread. "It's something that's been secret, and she matches it up when they come back. Something like that."

I was curious and asked her, "How do you know when the men will return?"

"It's very predictable. They must land somewhere...around May first. They are gone for months."

"Move time ahead now to the next significant event," I directed.

There was a long pause before she began. "Hmmm."

"What is happening?" I asked.

"Um...I can't quite make it out. Another festival has come. Seven or eight years later. You were the one with the coin that year," she said, referring to the matching coins. "But something has changed. It's a bittersweet thing. I think what happened is your boyfriend went off on the wooden ships, but mine didn't. A war...yours is good. Yours is coming back. The ship is OK, but I don't know if it's war or...whatever it is, I'm not happy."

"Something with your boyfriend?" I asked, trying to understand.

"Uh-huh. But I'm very worried about him. He didn't want to go, but he went. It's weird, because when I look out and picture him, I just see a dark cloud. Not in the sky. In front of me." She paused, as she let the scene unfold in her mind's eye. "It's not my boyfriend. It's my brother. Our parents didn't want him to go, but he was set on doing it. It feels strange because we've never had anything like this in our life before. It feels like he went to a war that wasn't ours."

"Do you get a sense of whose war it is?"

She paused for few long moments before saying, "No. I can't. Somewhere in Europe. Because he doesn't take a ship to it. He thinks it's about our land. We have a farm."

"Is he older?" I asked.

"He's a little older. My mother thought he was too young."

"Do we still live in the same town?"

"Uh-huh. There's a cloud over this. There's not the singing like before. The men come in the ships…four or five ships. They need that much for what they bring back."

"Move time ahead to the next significant event."

"Hmmm. I can't picture much. I have a sense of being left behind. I think they went to America. My brother was running away…because whatever happened, he left for his freedom. I think it was you and your husband. You had children, and you were worried about them and went, too. I stayed behind… my parents. But they didn't live, they died. I'm staying on the farm. I feel very sad because I feel left behind. It was like freedom fighters. We had known your husband since we were little kids. I don't have anybody because of this freedom fighters thing. The men were leaving."

"What is the name of your town or region?"

"Hook of something. I want to say Z."

"Move time ahead again."

"I have moved into the city. I couldn't do the farm. I sold it. I'm forty or fifty now. I work with some other ladies, and we make laces. I'm seeing…this is strange…I'm very reserved. I'm sending packages to all of you in America. Letters. I didn't want to go." She paused again before adding, "I make breads."

Curious, I asked, "What did you farm?"

"Tulips, and it was the low country…rice, too. Something with the canals changed the farming. I'm giving little girls lessons on old customs. There aren't wood ships anymore. It's symbolic. They don't do that anymore. I'm really a shy, quiet person. I live upstairs. I make lace. I'm in a bay window. That's where I sit. It's a little town off the beaten path, and we don't progress much."

"Are you happy?"

"Um…yeah. I teach the old dances. My family is gone. I have a close-knit group of friends."

"Go to the morning of the last day of your life. How old are you now?"

"I'm younger than I look. I'm only sixty. I have long, gray hair. I'm dying but not in pain. I have a couple of friends around me. I'm holding a heart. It's from…it's been sent to me from a grandniece. A red heart with lace around it. Gold thread with name sewn on. Lisa. Not a Dutch name. I'm rubbing the letters with my thumbs."

"Go through the death scene. Much time passes. What is it you were to learn?" I asked.

"Boy, this took a long time...that I didn't want to be left behind again. If I could do it over, I would have gone. I chose to stay behind." She paused before adding, "That was the life that made me follow you in this life."

Her last words gave me goose bumps from head to toe. I emerged her from hypnosis.

~

GINNY'S JOURNAL NOTES

I immediately went to Holland. Patti and I were identical twins, eleven years old in period costumes because we were going to sing in a pageant that welcomed back the wooden ships. We were Greta (Ginny had said Gretchen in the regression. Perhaps this was her nickname, or she had meant to say Greta) *and Grindel. We were raised on a farm that grew tulips and rice and we were walking along a stone path that led into town. Greta and I were doing a little dance on the stones in our wooden shoes that mimicked the movement of wooden ships. That dance went with a folklore children's song that went with the pageant. The ships which had been gone to India and spice islands were returning. It was a fleet of about five ships. Aside from carrying the crew's supplies, they had been to India and the Caribbean and brought back teas, rice, cocoa beans and spices. Braided bread loaves were part of the festivities in one of the loaves was a coin. The coin represented marriage and prosperity. My sister got the coin.*

Her boyfriend came home in the wooden ships. They got married and had two children. Our brother joined a group of men who were clandestine freedom fighters against Belgium. They were looking for him to arrest him. To escape that, he immigrated to America. My sister and her family went with him (Hans) because they feared for their children. I stayed behind to take care of our parents and within five years, they were both dead. I sold the farm and moved into Zeeland town. I never married and spent my life there making lace with a tatter. I sold the farm because it wasn't necessary anymore and I was too lonely. The wooden ships stopped coming.

I had a nice circle of friends and I never married. My sister had more children. None of them ever returned to Holland and I never went there. I felt left behind. I had stacks of letters from them. I died a quiet peaceful death with a friend stroking my temple. I was holding a felt heart with lace border. The name Lisa was sewn on the heart in gold threads. While researching this time period on the Internet, I discovered that Belgium was then invading south into Zeeland. Zeeland was part of Holland in the Southern region and it no longer exists. It's a part of Belgium now. Also, because of the uprising, the ports in Holland were closed and the shipping business as they knew it ended.

I remember mentioning that the farmlands were ruined and I thought it had something to do with the canals. Apparently, Zeeland was very low land and a terrible flood destroyed the farms.

~

Through my own research, I also found that several provinces were flooded in 1825 through serious dike breaks and that Zeeland is the westernmost province in the southwest part of the Netherlands. Large parts of Zeeland are actually below sea level.

GINNY

Spiritual Experiences with the Virgin Mary and Ginny's Father

The childhood abuse Ginny experienced at her mother's hand was extreme. Beatings with belt buckles, a broken nose, loss of hearing in one ear, and other events caused three trips to the emergency room for her before she was six years old. Ginny was now at peace with her mother, but she wanted more understanding about her father and his role in the events that had happened, so I decided to take her to a place in the in-between state where she could speak with him. I asked her to pose the question *Why did you let this happen?* in her mind.

Once she was hypnotized, I began, "As I count from one to ten, find yourself going higher and higher to where your loved ones are waiting for you."

"I see hands…a man's hands…it's like a catcher's signal to a pitcher… two fingers down. Hmmm. They are my dad's hands! He had a growth in the palm of his hand. I don't get a body…just his hands…he's catching. He's signaling where to go. I keep…ah…telling him I don't know what he means. I don't know baseball. One or two fingers down. He points his finger to right or left. I don't know this game…almost like sign language.

"Hmmm. What I'm getting is that he was trying to tell me how to get out of my mother's way without talking. My brother knows baseball. I could tell my brother…this is weird…something I totally forgot about…my sisters had one, too…a (window) shade that would be up or down to signal me. Up, come in;

down, go to friends. He was always trying to protect me from her. He's telling me to remember the time we did this…the time we went shopping for the coat." Ginny paused for a few moments, taking in all the information she was getting.

"Is there anything you want to ask your dad or say to him?" I asked.

"At the time I didn't understand it, and now I do. It's so…like he was one (of the people)…at the councils…" she said, her voice trailing off. (She was referring to the planning stage for her current life.) "He came with me."

"Because?" I asked.

"He was like a shield. We all knew it wasn't going to be easy…so there were protections for me. This is kind of weird because…um…for all the times I've been alone, I'm OK. I like it. (She was referring to her current life.) What I'm feeling is that wasn't right. We are *never* alone."

"How does it feel knowing this?" I questioned.

"Feels good. It actually feels *right*. Balanced. The other lifetimes when I was alone were just part of a lesson…not the whole purpose. A lesson regarding whatever I needed. It's like I'm hearing I needed to be alone and be comfortable with it. Once I accepted that…then…I now know I'm never alone."

"Get a sense of what that means," I said.

"It's all in this life right now. It's like I can see…my dad is saying, 'When I got you a coat, it was to get you out of the house.' Here's the thing…I had a very unrealistic opinion about my dad. He was on a pedestal," she said, before a deep sigh and a very long pause. "This is hard to do…I knock him off the pedestal because I thought he was emotionally inappropriate, and that's where I kept him for a long time. He confided in me instead of my mother," she explained.

"Baseball signals again. I'm finding out now he was trying to divert my thinking. It's like he and Mary (her aunt) made a pact…ways to protect me from her. He's showing me all the places and ways he's done it. It's really very sweet. He's getting me out of harm's way to protect me from her. Hmmm. Hmmm. There's so much going on…I see my aunt sitting next to him. She said, 'See? I told you she'd get it!' Like my cheering section. Hmmm. Wow! He had all kinds of people…he didn't want me to feel that way about my mother…he put layers of protection…he was trying to help me mentally, too, not just physically. Hmmm. They have another sister…I'd get farmed out to in the summer. My dad and my aunt Mary and my aunt Bun (short for Bunny, she later told me) are in the back, saying, 'Oh, she got it! I told you not to worry about her. That's our Ginny. We knew she'd come through.'"

"Why baseball signals?" she asked her dad. "'I was the scapegoat,' he's telling me. I used to whimper...I never went on family vacations. Ah. Oh. To protect me. It was very sweet. They never said anything bad about each other. Even my mother. Hmmm. Boy, the packages we put together." (She was referring to the lessons in her lifetimes.)

I asked, "So you are very connected to them?"

"Yeah," Ginny responded. "You are part of it, too. Not related, just like when you pick the package, you know each other in that way. You were brought in because of our lifetime in Holland. We are all in a composition book. It's like we're skyping. My aunts are in the background and came forward. They saw me and then saw you in the background, and they are very glad it was you who had helped me out so much. Kind of like, 'Oh, OK, it's Patti who's facilitating this. Good.' They knew you. They thought I had so much soul progression that I could handle the Holocaust. I had *volunteered*. This life wasn't a punishment; it was 'Let's undo the last thought I had, and let's fix it.' Wow. They are fading away now. I'm impressed he used baseball. I don't like baseball. It feels like I've put in the last piece of a big puzzle."

"A wise and loving Being comes to you now. This Being has loved you through all of time," I said.

"I don't see a Being. I see thoughts, like a spirit dance."

"What do the thoughts say?"

"Go out and have *fun*! Oh, I see now...the things that look like catcher signals with his fingers...he's...spelling out...the word *love* upside down with his hands down."

Tears rolled down both of our cheeks.

～

During another session, I regressed Ginny to an ancient library (Akashic records). She hadn't been in a situation where she could discover if her fear of heights was truly gone, and she was open, as always, to whatever she would discover.

"This is unbelievable. I rode on the back of an eagle to get to the library. Usually when I approach, there is a rock with three steps. This time, it was on top of the tower. The eagle put one wing out to a big window...his wing was a bridge to the library. Oh. Absolutely no fear. I just walked across the wing. It felt like I could fly if I had to. I'm looking at...I'm looking out the windows... not windows, just openings. Um...hmmm...um...I'm to get a book, but I don't know what I'm looking at...it's just, um...like the eagle has...the eagle just wants me to look in his eyes...telling me mentally...I don't need the books. There's another presence here. Hold on...hmmm...I want to say the mother of God. It's a protection...there's a tie to the eagle with her. They're both...it's confusing. Oh, ah, they ask...this is so bizarre. They don't understand why I have this fear. A huge rod of strength goes down my spine. I can physically feel it."

"How does she appear to you?" I asked.

"Like a Virgin Mary...like...her desert robes. I wish I could tell you how this rod feels."

"Ask her if there is another lifetime you need to look at regarding this fear."

There was a long pause. "Ah...it's...no...I'm trying to describe this. It's kind of like I've got your back. Very loving. You've got what you need. Hmmm. Yeah, it's like I went and got a steel rod in my spine."

"Is it possible to move time forward and see how it feels with this rod in your back?" I questioned.

"It feels like, umm...ah...like she's going to send me off with the eagle, and I don't need to worry about it. The eagle can rise above my fears. Don't worry. If I have the fear, she'll have the eagle pluck it out of me. It's such a metaphor. I've got your back. She's laughing. Not sarcastic. They...ah...look and feel like ribbons and swirls...the roads...it's so visual. 'Remember, you are one with everything,' the Virgin Mary tells me. Like she's mother nature, yet...you can't fall off something you're one with. The eagle is on money. She's showing me that, too. She's letting me know that this trip has more in store for me than I think. (Ginny was planning a trip to Portland, Oregon, and the Northwest.) It's going to be very freeing. Wow. I'm just getting swirls of purple...swirls of purple.

"I'm not alone. I'm surrounded in purple spirit over this trip. She has a big smile on her face. 'Just go,' she tells me. 'I've got your back. You know how to do this. Being divinely guided. You've done this before.' Wow! Hah! She's like a fairy godmother, sprinkling me with dust. Thank you. I just got the smell of roses. 'Go and have fun. Wait until you see the roses!' Oh boy."

As soon as I emerged Ginny, she asked me, "Could you smell the roses? It was incredible! Wow! That was amazing."

It was a beautiful end of our journey together through Ginny's lifetimes.

~

Several months later, while Ginny was still on her trip to the Northwest, she sent me exciting news through an e-mail:

You cured me! I walked across this bridge like it was just a sidewalk. I am almost through driving the Oregon coast and absolutely no problems with heights. Not when driving or when hiking or standing at lookout points. I can now go right out to the edge. That, for me, is a miracle! The fear is just gone! This feels incredibly freeing.

On my first day here, I went to a place in Portland called the Grotto known for its beautiful panoramic view. Number one, it was a clear day and I could see for miles and miles. (Apparently, a clear day in Portland is a rarity.) Number two, the Grotto was built by a monk as a thank you to the Virgin Mary for an answered prayer. (I didn't know this until I got there). Talk about goosebumps! Needless to say, I am having an amazing time. Thanks, and many, many hugs, Ginny.

Ginny and I spoke on the phone when she returned, and she said she went to a place that looked like the gorge she saw when she was the Cambodian sacrifice. She stood on the edge and realized her fear was gone. "It's as though I never had it. I even sat in the front row of the Space Needle in Seattle with no fear! And here's what else is interesting. I saw the Virgin Mary everywhere on my trip. It was fall, and there were no flowers, but I kept smelling *roses*," she said, sounding amazed.

Many people have reported smelling roses when they feel the Virgin Mary nearby. I remembered Ginny telling me that as a child she would pray to the Virgin Mary for help, but help never came. She discovered the Virgin Mary had been with her all along. And is still with her.

Our conversation shifted, and we spoke about her last thoughts before being gassed in the Holocaust and wishing she'd never been loved. "So I got to experience that in this life and discovered it was completely false. Because love is everything. I also got the sense I volunteered to be in the Holocaust because they told me I had the strength to do so. This life is part of it. I worked with Tim in counseling, which got me to look at everything in my life. With you, I went back to find love, and that's where the real healing came."

~

Ginny had come to me to help her cure her fear of heights and went on a soul journey that took her back as far in time as 6000 BC in Cambodia, when she was raised by priests to be a sacrifice. She was John, a builder and carver of walls in Babylon, in 833 BC. She was Marchand, a child prodigy musician, and she was a fisherman. She was Pi, an Eskimo boy in the fjords. She experienced a lifetime being mentally challenged, another as a crippled young girl with tuberculosis in a sanitarium, and in another she was a teenage girl exterminated in the Holocaust. She discovered I was her identical twin!

Ginny's fascination with experiencing her past lives led us down many roads, until we finally found the cause of her fear of heights as French General Claude Louis Hector, Duke of Villars.

Perhaps most importantly, she was able to understand and forgive her mother and at long last found peace concerning her. When she saw her mother as a child looking more scared than she was she said, "It rid her (her five-year-old-self) of my hate for her." During the planning stage for her current lifetime as Ginny, she learned that her mother had volunteered to be an abusive mother. She loved her enough to step into that role so that she could unlearn her last thoughts before perishing in the Holocaust: that it would be easier to have never loved or been loved. This understanding healed her relationship with her mother and thus her karma. To her great surprise, Ginny discovered and felt the enormous love her mother had felt for her for the first time. She now has a clear understanding of her father's role and how he protected her in this life, as did her aunts. She had a powerful and poignant experience with the Virgin Mary. Ginny explored other lifetimes not written about in this book as well, and all have helped her discover who she is as a soul.

~

Ginny sent me a note, and typed at the top of the page was the title *Knowledge from Soul Progression Work*: "This is everything I learned through our work together.

* We are one with everything.
* Love is everything.
* Feelings are the paths to everything.
* There really are no victims.
* Faith and letting go of my hold removed fear.
* I am not afraid of death. It is just a metamorphosis.
* We are never alone.
* Forgiveness removes shame.
* Happiness in this life is finding a passion and living passionately.
* My purpose for this has been to learn all of the above knowledge."

Ginny summarized her soul exploration and what she learned beautifully. Ginny found her way to my office for what she thought was a fear of heights. She healed her fear but gained so much more. There are no coincidences in life. Perhaps I was the one needing to be present for her to balance karma, since I had left her in our lifetime in Holland. I still see Ginny from time to time, and she is still as in awe of our work together as am I.

MARTHA

Captain Peter Watson, British Army, Revolutionary War

I met Martha* in Tampa, Florida, at a past life regression workshop Dr. Brian Weiss facilitated. Born and raised in Colombia, where she had graduated from medical school, she came to the United States for her residency and had been a medical doctor for more than twenty years. Martha had beautiful dark hair and deep brown eyes. I had to listen carefully to the rhythm of her words when she spoke, as English was not her native language. She quickly expressed her belief in God and guardians and was metaphysical. Martha told me she had been hypnotized before and had experienced a past life regression while in Colombia two years earlier. In that regression she was a man named John Phillip O'Brien II, born in 1889. Martha went into detail about that lifetime and later sent me an e-mail recapping our conversation.

I was from a very rich family. I had three siblings. My parents died in 1914 from possibly the Spanish Flu and after that I took over the family business. I was the second oldest child but oldest son. We had a financial company, and I was a broker. I married at age 23; following my parents' recommendations, I married a girl chosen by them. I had two younger brothers and was very close to the third one.

My parents did not accept the girl this one married, and he was banned from the family's fortune. He went to live in Brooklyn, and I helped him financially. I lost the fortune in 1929 (Wall Street Crash). My associate committed suicide (he had asked me to sell our stocks months before the crash, since there were rumors about it, but I refused to do it), I sold my house and went to live in Brooklyn. My brother gave me a job at his grocery store. I remember being in lines to get food coupons. I felt humiliated. I started gambling and drinking. My wife and two...sons (?) left me and went to live somewhere in the Midwest.

By 1939 I was already sick from the drinking and bad lifestyle. I lost one son in 1944 (he died in the Second World War). I felt even more depressed after that. I became demented, and remember coughing a lot. My brother would visit me at the hospital. Then, I never saw him again, because he became sick and could not leave his house. My brother died before me. I died alone in a hospital bed, the room was very spacious and bright, my bed was next to the large window, my bed had a white frame. It was a very beautiful day outside. I died in 1946. I stayed in the spiritual life for 15 years. When I searched for John O'Brien, the name appeared 3 times in some sort of census taken in the State of New York—I don't know exactly the year it was taken, but I believe it was a census from 1930, after the crash. I don't know what criteria I used on the search, but two names had ages close to John's, were married, had two children (one son and one daughter each—I did not find anyone with two sons in the census)—one was a BROKER, the other one a GROCERY STORE MANAGER. The broker's wife was educated, the grocery store manager's wasn't. At the time of this census, the broker was age 40. The Grocery Store Manager was 41...I was born in 1889, so I could be either one.

Martha told me that her first pregnancy ended in a miscarriage at twelve weeks. She had a dream before the miscarriage that the baby wouldn't come. As Martha spoke, I remembered that I had been told by an intuitive that mothers of lost babies would find their way to me. I wondered if this was why I met Martha. She told me it had taken three years for her to get pregnant again after the miscarriage, and when she discovered she was pregnant, she wasn't excited. Her daughter, Meghan*, was six years old. "I don't love her like I should," she said calmly. I was curious what the regression would reveal.

Martha went into hypnosis easily. "There's a feeling inside you that you don't like. It has everything to do with why you are here today. Go back to when that feeling first began at the count of one. Three, two, one. Be there now. Notice your feet and what, if anything, you are wearing on them. Notice how they feel," I began.

"Boots," she responded immediately.

"Are you standing or sitting?" I asked.

"Standing."

"Is it light or dark?" I asked the question rapid fire.

"Light."

"Notice your hands." I paused. "Are they big or small?"

"Big hands."

"Your hands will tell you how old you are. How old are you?"

"Twenty-four."

"Male or female?"

"Male."

"Are you inside or outside?"

"Outside...I see trees...we're in a war. I have a red coat. I'm looking for someone." She paused as though assessing the scene she found herself in and then continued, "There are many around." Martha was whispering the answers. Although I was sitting next to her, I needed to lean forward to hear her better.

"Get a sense of what region or country you live," I instructed.

"Virginia...I have a white wig...it's daytime."

"Do you have a role?"

"I'm Captain Peter...Watson...England."

"Let the scene unfold," I instructed.

"I'm entering a home...it's evening now. There's a woman there...I'm looking for someone...I find a man drunk! A superior...I'm trying to take him back. He doesn't want to come. I tell him to come with me...he's upset. He's a *traitor*!" she said with force. "He's helping the enemy with information. He wants me to join them...the other men are in the back now." She paused before continuing, "He's not a superior; he's a friend. I'm upset. We need to come back...they don't let me out." She paused again, letting the scene unfold in her inner mind. "There's four of them, and they're all drunk...friends for two years. Frank."

"What happens?"

"They take off my coat."

"Do you have a weapon?"

"They took it from me. They tied me against the chair...I'm trying to release myself from the chair. They are laughing."

"Move time ahead half an hour or so."

"I'm running away...the woman who lived in the house helped me escape. My friend is coming after me. He tells me that *I* am the traitor. He did not want to get caught."

I noticed her eyes moving under her eyelids, as though she were watching a movie in her mind. "There's a trial...I'm innocent...but they believe I'm a traitor. They believe *him*!" she exclaimed. "They found me guilty. They believe him because he was a post ahead of me. He convinced everyone I'm the guilty one. He was my superior," she said, sounding defeated as her voice dropped. She paused before adding, "I'm against the wall...my eyes are closed...hands tied behind my back."

"What are your last thoughts?"

"Injustice!"

"Go through the death scene. Much times passes, and you have a full understanding of the purpose of that lifetime. What were you to learn?" I asked.

"Forgiveness."

"Did you learn it?"

"No."

"A wise and loving being comes to you."

"He's dressed in white...long beard."

"I'd like to speak to him directly," I said. "What is the connection of anger and injustice between that lifetime and her current lifetime?"

"I'm angry at the court," she stated.

"Ask your guide for help," I instructed.

"He said accept adversities and learn to forgive."

"The people from the court come to you," I said.

"I don't want to forgive!"

"Help her understand the purpose of this lifetime," I asked her guide.

"They say, 'I'm sorry.'"

"What would you like to tell them?" I asked Martha.

"Why did you do this?"

They responded to her by saying, "You needed to go through this to understand. You have done this before."

I asked Martha, "What would you like to say to them?"

"I'm sorry," she stated solemnly.

"Because?" I asked.

"I did not know that."

"How do you feel?"

"Confused. I did not learn the lesson. I feel injustice. I can't let it go. I suffer." She paused, "I love him...my guide...he loves me. I missed him. I ask him, 'Where have you been? I love you so much. Please help me.' He said, 'Let it go and love yourself.'"

"See a little girl coming to you now," I suggested. "As she gets closer, you recognize her. It's you at four years old or so." I paused, allowing her to see herself. "Do you love that little girl?" I asked.

"Yes...I need to love my daughter like I love her."

"Reach inside yourself and pull out that feeling of anguish and anger."

"It's a red ball from my chest. I feel tenderness giving it to my guide."

"See scenes with your daughter, and a white light envelopes you so that all you feel is love, love, love." I then emerged her from hypnosis.

"This is not about Meghan," she said, referring to the lifetime she had just visited. "This is a sense of injustice. As a little girl, I saw my daughter as myself. I love England and London. When I visited England, I had the feeling I'm home. I had on dark boots, white pants, and a red coat. I took the red ball from my chest and felt such tenderness giving it to my guide. I feel a little at peace."

Although the lifetime Martha had visited didn't seem to relate to her daughter, I trusted the process and the soul's need to heal.

I discovered that redcoats did indeed invade Virginia in 1781 during the American Revolutionary War.

MARTHA

Monk

O ne month passed before Martha's next appointment. When she arrived, she said she felt like a heavy weight had been lifted from her shoulders after our last session, but as we talked about her daughter, she admitted she didn't like being a mother to her. She said she didn't feel connected with her during the pregnancy. She'd had a recurring dream on and off for years that was in another time when she had a baby she forgot to feed. She wants to love her daughter. "I know she feels I don't like her."

Once Martha was hypnotized, I regressed her from her feeling about her daughter. "It's dark. I'm wearing a heavy vest. I don't see anything. It's dark... dark. Heavy. I believe I am a monk. I'm in a dark place...alone...standing...I have a candle in my hand. I'm on the ground...I wear sandals...it's a tunnel and a basement. I'm fat. Thirtyish. The candle is guiding me. It's humid. Been there before. Umm. Hmm. I see metal bars. Like a prison. I'm bringing food to someone. It's confusing. I cannot see. Someone had been sent to this place...left to die. They asked me to check on him. The person is very weak... sick. Male. Older than me. I don't know why the person is in here. The poor man is suffering. He's on the floor...shivering. I bring some water. I feel bad for him. I think he was sick. No one wants him around...they're afraid to get sick. I was healthy. I don't want to be there for too long. I'm afraid to get sick, too. He's thin, pale, very sick, shivering. I feel sorry for him," she said and paused for a few moments. "It's a beautiful palace. There's a lot of light and rich furniture. And a garden."

"Go now to the next important event," I suggested.

"There is a woman who works in the kitchen. She wants to be with me. I'm a monk."

"Are you there with other monks?" I asked.

"I don't live there. I spend time there. Helping, cleaning. Things that only monks do. I broom." I assumed she meant *swept* and thought it a curious choice of words.

"Do you like doing this?"

"No."

"Because?"

"I don't know if I want to be a monk."

"How long have you been a monk?"

"A while. My family wanted me to be a monk...or a priest."

"What happens next?" I ask.

"The girl...she works in the kitchen. She wants to be with me... tempted," she paused. "She wants to trick me. Get money from me. She gets pregnant."

"With your child?" I asked.

"Yes."

"How do you feel about it?"

"Guilty. I was not supposed to have done that. I didn't want to be a priest. She got me drunk. I will not say I did not like."

"How do you feel?"

"Luxury...the pleasure."

"Do you love her?"

"No."

"What happens next?"

"I think the baby...dies? There's something wrong...with the baby...boy."

"Are you still a priest?"

"Yes."

"How does she feel?"

"She asks for money...not to tell anyone." Her voice trailed off.

"Look deep into her eyes. Do you recognize her from your lifetime as Martha?"

"I don't recognize her. Baby…newborn…nobody knows baby born. She's hiding."

"How do you feel?"

"Concerned."

"Because?"

"People might find out. I'd be expelled."

"Move time ahead. What happens next?"

"She dies…sick…fever…pneumonia. I sent the baby to an orphanage. Six months old."

"How do you feel about the baby?"

"Guilty!"

"Do you recognize the baby?" I asked, wondering if this could be her daughter, Meghan.

"No."

"Move time ahead and go to the next significant event. When you are ready, tell me what is happening."

"I live in a…not a church…a place where monks go. It's two years later. I'm happy."

"Because?"

"I chose…to live confined. To resist the temptations of the flesh. I heard the baby died before I went to this place. I felt relieved, but I carried the guilt."

"Go now to the last day of your life."

"I'm sixty. I never told. I feel my life was useless."

"Are you aware in any way that this is your last day?"

"No."

"Are you healthy?"

"Yes. I'm getting grapes…Italy…1361…under the sun, I fall. I may have had a stroke."

"What are your last thoughts?"

"None."

"Are you alone or with others?"

"Others come to help."

"Are you close to anyone?"

"We're friends. Antonio. They call for help."

"Time passes, and you have a full understanding of that lifetime. What were you to learn?"

"Sacrifice...my freedom."

"Did you learn it?"

"Yes."

I sensed that Martha still carried guilt. "In this place that you find yourself, the woman and your baby come to you."

Martha's face softened. "The woman smiles. She forgives me. The baby... sad...felt abandoned. He's healing for himself. I'm sorry, baby. I wasn't responsible. I was a coward. I had a choice to abandon priesthood. I did not choose it. He was not taken good care of at the orphanage. Poor baby. Suffered."

"If you could, would you have done it differently?"

"Yes. I'd have had my family take care of the baby. I'm sorry, baby. The baby is my cousin." She recognized who the baby was in her life as Martha.

"Pull the guilt out of you, and notice what form it takes," I instructed.

"It's a stone...rock...size of my hand."

"Give the rock to the wise and loving being before you. A ball of light breaks it up and changes it to something positive."

"Everybody's happy!" she exclaims.

"Because?"

"We forgive each other. The ball of light is so bright."

I emerged her from hypnosis, and we talked about her experience.

"I didn't like the baby. The baby would ruin my life. I had thoughts I wanted to kill the baby so nobody would hear about him. I knew it was wrong. I gave the baby to the orphanage. It was an ugly secret. She didn't blackmail me more, but she got sick. I was in a palace—the cardinal's house."

Although the baby from her lifetime as a priest wasn't her daughter, Meghan, I knew her soul had taken her to that lifetime for a reason and hoped we had begun to peel the layers off her not wanting to be a mother to Meghan. Perhaps this had less to do with her daughter and more to do with the responsibility of being a parent.

MARTHA

Duke, Battle of Worringen

When Martha returned for her next session, she reported she had more patience with her daughter. "I feel closer to her now. Not as irritated. I feel more like her mother now. I'm *much* better," she said, sounding relieved.

Martha wanted to work on feeling addicted to the computer and said she would feel enraged at the injustice of communism, dictators, and topics of a political nature. I guided her into hypnosis: "Find yourself going to an ancient temple where a guide is there to meet you at the entrance. Your guide takes you inside, where you find yourself before a very long row of books. All of the books are about you. Now find the book that has everything to do with this feeling inside you that you don't like."

"It's a big book," she responded quickly.

"In a moment you will open the book and see words or pictures on the page. Open the book, and tell me what you see."

"There's a picture of a knight. He's dressed in all silver."

"Watch as the scene unfolds."

"I see people riding horses, going toward this city...like a fort...like a medieval city. There's some sort of war. Getting ready to fight somewhere, and I'm on a horse, too." She had automatically stepped into the scene.

"Notice your hands," I began.

"I have gloves on...metallic. I'm male. There are many."

"What is the name of the town or village or region?"

"Dussendorf?" she said with a question in her voice, as though she wasn't pronouncing it correctly or perhaps not certain of her answer. "It's summertime…sunny day…a lot of movement going on. 1288."

"Who's in charge?"

"The general. I am an officer. It's an area with different small kingdoms, where Germany is located today. I'm helping organize everything. Hands are cold. We live there. We are getting ready to depart…to invade another city."

"How do you feel about that?"

"I feel OK…excited about."

"Is it your first time invading another city?"

"No."

"Move time ahead."

"We are resting…spending the night in the forest. We feel secure knowing we'll win."

"What is the purpose?"

"Power…claiming it back. We take over the city. We really win. I'm promoted. They give me a lot of credit for the good work. I don't have a family."

"What is your name?"

"Mark."

"Move time ahead to the next important event of your life, Mark."

"I get importance…and they admire and respect me…like they want me to take over. They convince me something is wrong with the king. They want me to find out what it is. It's a peaceful time. We're working on making the army strong again so we are ready—just in case. They put me in charge of this…and the king."

"What is the king's name?"

"King Lyon. He's nice. I like him."

"Go to the next important event now, Mark."

"The king is dead. He was sick. I miss him. I liked him."

"How old are you now?"

"Early thirties…nobody knows who's in charge. There's something going on. He died unexpectedly. There was no plan. It's a small kingdom.

Thirteenth century. There are other kings in the area related to this one. The king wants to take over this place. I say they not do that. I take over with the army and declare myself in power before a decision is reached. I'm the top of the army…a general. Many years had passed. I'm doing what the king would have wanted. The other king is evil to the population. There were three brothers. My king was one…there were three sons. One of the other sons wants the kingdom. He had no heir. We had expanded. I took over the place. They declare me the new king."

"How do you feel about this?"

"I like it. More than I thought. But it changes me. I become authoritarian."

"Because?"

"I want to do how *I* want to do."

"Go to the morning of the last day of your life."

"I don't trust anybody. Five years have passed. I feel isolated. Not happy. They will betray me. They don't like how I've been. They want to give the kingdom to one of the brothers."

"Are you aware in any way that it is your last day?"

"No."

"Go to ten minutes before you pass."

"I was poisoned. I drank something."

"What are your last thoughts?"

"Despair."

"Go through the death scene and float above your body."

"I'm alone. I see how I'm dressed. A metallic shirt. I have bangs. Hair: down to neck. I have sandals that go across lower leg. I was strong."

"What were you to learn in that lifetime?"

"Humility."

"Did you learn it?"

"No. I became very arrogant, authoritative. Power, control…I want everything done *my* way. What I thought was right wasn't. I feel betrayed. I don't trust anybody. Everybody's the enemy. I was fighting my battles, and I don't know what they are…I never finished what I wanted to do. It was interrupted."

"A guide comes to you now to help you."

"I let it go…in my belly. It's a round, white armor ball…well shaped, very heavy…like I treasure it. It was a dear thing to me. I had taken good care of it. I gave it to him (her guide). I know it was not good now. I was holding it."

"How do you feel now?" I asked.

"Better. I have a sword. I give it to him. I have a shield. My shame…I give to him. He loves me and is taking it away."

I emerged her from hypnosis. Martha couldn't wait to begin her research on the life she had experienced.

~

At Martha's next session, she told me she had researched and found validation of her past life in Germany. She excitedly told me what she had discovered. "The battle, the time, and the three brothers were all confirmed! The Battle of Worringen was fought on June 5, 1288. I had goosebumps to find out that was the right year! (It was summertime, as Martha had said, and the year was correct). It was near the town of Worringen (now Cologne) and an important part of history for nearby Dusseldorf, Germany. I looked up Dussendorf and realized it is Dusseldorf I was trying to say! The battle was, in fact, fought for possession of land and was one of the largest battles of Europe in the Middle Ages. Many of the men wore armor. The Duke of Limburg, he was not a king, died without male heirs. All was just as I had said! It was then inherited by his daughter, who married Reginald I, Count of Guelders. She died a year later, and her husband claimed the title of Duchy of Limburg in 1282 and had his demand recognized by the German King Rudolph of Habsburg. He took over the land. And it was the Counts of *Mark*!" The Counts of the Mark were among the most powerful and influential Westphalian (a region of Germany) lords in the Holy Roman Empire."

Although not all of what came through in Martha's regression was verified through research, there were enough connections that were certainly thought provoking. All clients' sessions are important. Whether they can recall the name of the town where they had lived or the year makes no difference if they feel they have learned something about themselves and have healed or grown as a result of their regression. It is always validating when a client finds proof of who they were in a part of history he or she is unfamiliar with in his or her current life.

MARTHA

Becky Smith, a Slave in Georgia

Martha was always ready to get started on whatever issue she wanted to work on for the session, so after we discussed the exciting findings of her last regression, we began.

"I don't have any energy or motivation," she said. "Can I improve this? It's not depression but a trait since childhood."

Martha went into hypnosis effortlessly. "Is it dark or light?" I began.

"Dark."

"Notice if you have clothing covering your legs and how it feels next to your skin."

"Long skirt...rough...my arms don't have clothes."

"Notice your hands. Are they big or little?"

"Little."

"Your hands will tell you how old you are. How old are you?"

"Twenty...I'm carrying something on my head." She paused. "I'm a slave...going to wash clothes...I have a big bag on my head."

"What color is your skin?"

"Black. My skirt is dark...some red surrounding my head."

"Tell me about the terrain you find yourself in."

"Flat...some trees around...walking to the river...daylight...sunny, hot. There are other people washing clothes when I arrive to the river...other slaves."

"Who are you a slave to?" I asked.

"A family. They are from the same house," she said, referring to the other slaves washing clothes. "It's a big property."

"Whose clothes are being washed?"

"The babies…the children from the house."

"How many children are there?"

"Two. One is a baby. One is four."

"I'm going to snap my fingers, and you'll know their last name." *Snap.*

"Smith."

"How do they treat you?"

"OK," she said sheepishly.

"Where do you sleep at night?"

"With the other slaves," she said, her voice drifting off. "It's a big house with high ceilings." She paused. "I sleep on the floor…dirt around. I see something hanging. Nets? Hammocks? Yes. My family is not with me. I miss them. They lived there. They were taken away when I was eight," she said, lowering her voice.

"What is your name?"

"Becky."

"Becky, go to the next important event at one. Three, two, one. Be there now."

"I got new clothes," she said with a hint of a smile and sounding proud. "I have a pair of shoes. Brown. I have some books in my hands. I'm twenty-one. I have a hat. I'm going to a school after church. It's Sunday. I'm learning how to read."

"Who else attends the church?"

"I go because I am the nanny. I'm smart, and they like me."

"What is the name of the town you live in?"

"I don't know…in Georgia."

"Is there a name of the plantation where you live?"

"I don't know." She paused. "I don't want to know…Stanford?"

"What do you grow on the plantation?"

"Corn and cotton."

"Do you do any of the work in the field with the corn and cotton?"

"No. They want me to learn to read for the kids. That's how I got to go to school."

"I'm going to snap my fingers, and you'll know what year it is." *Snap.*

"1824."

"Do you like learning how to read?" I asked.

"Yes. Learning words, writing...I did not know they had pencils. I'm in the bedroom with the kids. It's very hot. I play with them. Read for them."

"Go now to the next significant event, Becky. Find yourself there now."

"I'm inside. I think the mother is dying. The girl is eight. The boy is four years old. The kids are crying."

"What are her symptoms?"

"She has a fever...Yellow fever. I feel sorry for her and the kids."

"Are they nice to you?"

"Yes."

"How are they to the other slaves?"

"OK. Nice, but not super nice. You have to know your place."

"What happens if you don't?"

"They scream at you. Humiliate you." She paused. "After she dies, he keeps her body. Neighbors are there eating. There is a woman there...she's really mean to me. She makes fun of me. Humiliates me. She thinks I should be *outside* the house, not inside."

"Look into her eyes; do you recognize her?"

"No."

"Go now to the next important event, Becky."

"I'm riding horses with the kids. They are teenagers. It's afternoon. I feel sad because I can't learn now. They don't let me. The kids share with me. Geography, history, languages...northeast Georgia...Lafayette? I see myself as sad, depressed. I don't see a reason for my life. I feel alone. I don't have a family. They were sold to another farm. I stayed to take care of the kids. I do as they tell me. I don't have the freedom to do what I want."

"How old are you now?"

"Twenty-eight. I don't want to get married."

"Because?"

"I don't want to. I have no interest."

"Move time ahead to the next important event."

"The girl is getting married…Anna. She doesn't know him too well. It's an arranged marriage. They don't let me go with her. I have to take care of the boy. Sam."

"Find the study and perhaps an envelope with an address," I suggested.

"Samuel Bridgeport. I remember now. I was sold to this family. Becky Smith—family I came from. Samuel Bridgeford, Lafayette County." I noticed she now said the name *Bridgeford*, not *Bridgeport*. They certainly sounded the same. Was she correcting herself?

"Go now to the next important event."

"The boy is gone. I'm still in the house. I feel very sad. The children are gone. The girl is in another country. It's very boring. I help in the kitchen. The girl is in Europe."

"Move time ahead," I instructed.

"It's the war. A lot of movement around. Many slaves are going to the army. I'm in my fifties now. They want to go. They are equals…it's the Civil War. I don't know much about it. The farms are empty. The boy went and the father, too. He's a colonel. Women left behind. We take care of the house. The girl is still in Europe. She never came back. She has written to me, and I have answered. I know how to write. I see France." (Referring to where she lived.)

"Move time ahead until the war is over."

"I don't see the end of the war."

"Go to the morning of the last day of your life, Becky."

"I think I'm sick. I've been coughing. Not much food around."

"What do you eat?"

"Potato. Looks like I died of the same thing Mother did…Typhoid fever." I noticed she had corrected herself from *yellow fever* to *typhoid fever*.

"What year is it?"

"1863. I don't know. I'm in my fifties."

"Did you ever feel happiness?"

"No, I carried sadness all of my life. I was never free. The joy was learning to read, write, and serving the kids."

"Go through the death scene and float above your body."

"It's night. There are candles around me. Some people crying."

"Did you love anyone?"

"Not really. The kids are away, and I don't see them anymore. The war is still going on."

"What were you to learn in that lifetime?"

"Humility."

"Did you learn it?"

"Yes."

"Your Higher Self comes to you. How will this help you?"

"Find joy in everything. There is joy everywhere."

"Is there anything you'd like to ask your Higher Self?"

"Why do I feel so much lack of energy? I felt the same way as back then... because I was depressed."

"Can you let go of that now?" I asked.

"I was so disappointed not going to school anymore. I was so happy to learn. I was so proud of wearing my shoes and going to school," she answered. "My Higher Self tells me I need to have discipline and to set goals."

"Are you willing to do that?

"Yes."

I emerged her. Martha had found the source of the sadness she carried as Becky. Without being consciously aware, I wondered if the joy she had in learning as Becky was what propelled her desire to learn and become a doctor.

Martha pulled out her smartphone and looked up the dates of the Civil War. "1861 through 1865," she stated, looking at me with wide eyes. "I did not know the dates." For her, it was the confirmation she needed. She didn't live to see the end of the war because she died in 1863. "There is a Lafayette, too," she added, looking a bit stunned by the information.

I began research of my own. I wanted to find Becky Smith. The dates Martha had given me during the regression confirmed she was in her late fifties when she died.

During enslavement, slaves were given the last names of their owners. Martha had said the name of the plantation could have been Stanford, but I wondered if it could also have been Sanford. There is a town in Georgia called Sanford. I found a listing of slave owners in Sanford, and Smith was listed as owning sixty-two slaves according to the Jones County, Georgia Slaves Index 1791-1864. Perhaps this is where Becky had originally lived before they sold her.

I also found a town called Lafayette, located in northwest Georgia, where there is a river. Could it be the river where Becky washed clothes? I contacted the Lafayette County Public Library, and with the assistance of its genealogy librarian, I learned that the building that housed the records of slaves' names had survived the Civil War but was lost to fire due to arson in 1883, taking with it fifty years of county records. The librarian could not find a record of Becky or Rebecca Smith; a Samuel Bridge, Bradford, or Bridgeport; or a Stanford Plantation. "But there may have been one. There were certainly corn and cotton plantations in the area," she said. I felt like I had come so close to finding Becky, but I'd run into a dead end.

Slaves were generally prohibited from learning to read and write, but some were taught by their owners or missionaries for the purpose of teaching the Bible. So although it would have been rare for Becky to have learned how to read and write, and almost unthinkable she would have been allowed to attend school, both were possible. I also learned that the most prevalent fatal diseases of the time were typhoid fever and pneumonia.

MARTHA

Lilly, Countess in Belgium

Martha told me her addiction to the computer had been cured over the time since I'd seen her last. She had organized her office the day after the slave regression. She spoke about her daughter, now six, who told her she missed her while she was at work. "Patricia, I don't feel like I'm her mommy." I could see she was still struggling.

Once she was in hypnosis, I regressed her on the feeling of not being her daughter's mommy.

"It's dark. I'm inside. Standing…in a room…dressed in a long, white skirt and gloves that go to my elbow. It's a very pretty dress, like silk."

"Feel your hair."

"It's an updo."

"Are you alone or with others?"

"Others."

"Let the scene unfold, and when you are ready, tell me what's happening," I said.

"It's like a party."

"Daytime or nighttime?"

"Not night. It's the afternoon. I'm drinking tea."

"How many are there?"

"More than fifty. I feel like my hair is blond. I don't see myself married. I'm at the age of getting married. I feel like I'm looking for something. It's a very pretty room. Only well-dressed people are around. I don't feel like I'm nice. Like I'm trying to achieve something. I'm looking for somebody or something. There are people outside in the garden. It's summertime. Marble floor, statues, mirrors. It's very pretty. I feel like it's in France. The south, maybe? I see a lot of sunlight, sunny. Everybody is in a good mood."

"Tell me about the party," I requested.

"Celebrating something. This may be a summer place. Ladies have little umbrellas. Lots of drinks. Everybody's happy. Maybe their arrival in town. (Referring to the reason for the party.) I don't have a mother around. I'm on my own. I'm an adult. I'm pretty...and I know that."

"What is your name?"

"Lilly...I don't know. My shoes are white. Made of silk. Oh, now I can see better," she said, as though she suddenly had full vision of the scene she had stepped into. "The dress is short sleeved."

"What year is it?" I asked.

"Late 1700s...lace below the breast," she said, expanding on what she was wearing. "Little white umbrella. I have a hat. I'm looking for someone...for a man."

"Move time forward until you find him," I suggested.

"I go to his office."

"At the party?" I asked for clarification.

"No. Where he works...a lawyer? I think he's married. I'm his lover. I like him, but he's...not my husband."

"What is his name?"

"French name. I don't know. Antoine? I pretend I'm his client so I can visit him at work. I'm a mistress, and I did not care or feel guilty. It was good. I had money," she said, with an air of authority. "I have a good life...Louis... Louie...I don't have any children. I want to keep my body pretty."

"Move time ahead to the next important event after seeing him."

"I'm riding horses. A hunting trip. People know who I am but pretend they don't. A man comes with me and pretends we're together. My brother—or a friend. They are calling me Countess. They address me as Countess." She remained silent for a few moments before continuing. "I ride the horse well. I'm rich. I think he gave me the title. He was very rich.

A hunting trip…big castle…there are a lot of people there. I'm in my thirties or late twenties. Maybe this is Belgium? It was France at first. Things
are happening in France. A revolution…it's over, but we're afraid. King of
France Louis XVI and his wife…they were killed by the guillotine. We don't
want to go to France anymore," she stated before pausing. "I have a black
horse. Very pretty…Leah…" she said, trying to pronounce a name. "Leah,"
she repeated. She then spelled it out, letter by letter. "L-I-E-G-E. The countryside is here."

I assumed she was spelling the name of the town. "Are you near water?"
I asked.

"No. I think he lives in Brussels. This is countryside property. I am upset.
I like to travel, and we can't travel. We're afraid of what happened. The nobles
were killed or threatened. End of 1700s. When we vacationed, it was *before*
the revolution," she explained. "Rougier. Louis Rougier. He was a noble. His
rank must be high because he gave me a title of countess. He comes from a
noble family. He was born rich. I wasn't born rich."

"Move time ahead to the next important event," I instructed.

"I do a lot of intrigues—manipulation to do what I want. Gossiping, talking—useless, but I was smart. I had studied languages. I know how to keep
a good conversation. I don't want to have a child. They irritate me. I don't
like children. It's pointless…to have children. I think they are annoying little
creatures. I don't care. I'm in my thirties."

Curious, I asked, "What do you do so you don't get pregnant?"

"I never got pregnant. I was lucky. I just enjoyed life. I didn't do anything
useful—just had a good time. I have servants, nice house, I travel. That's my
life…little gatherings…laughing. All the work I didn't do, I do in the next life.
I learned humility as a slave," she said, referring to her life as Becky. "Now I
can see that. I died young."

"Go to the last day of your life."

"I'm barely forty. I was sick…pneumonia, coughing, sweating…"

"Go to moments before you pass."

"Louis is there. He was very sad. He thought I was interesting…intel-
ligent. I was getting worse."

"What were your last thoughts?"

"I was so sick. I was not thinking well."

"Float above the scene."

"I can breathe well. I feel light…happy in my own way. I was useless and hurt many people with my gossips. I would spend my time pitting people against others. Hmmm. Many people got hurt. Shame."

"What were you to learn?"

"I don't know. I'm confused. I don't know why. To find a purpose. I never found it. It's interesting. I could have married well, but I wanted to be with this man. To know he wanted me more than his wife. I was not a hooker. I was a *mistress*," she said with emphasis, as though it was far better. "On Belgium soil. I was loyal to him. He loved me. I did not have her social rank," she said, referring to his wife. "I spent my life hurting her. She was a good person. *I* was the bad one. I'm sorry for the pain I caused. I am so sorry. Please forgive me. You did not deserve it." I could hear the sadness in her voice as Martha spoke.

"Is there a soul recognition of this person?" I asked, curious if it was someone in her current life.

"I don't see who she is. She's very sweet. I don't know if I know her."

I sensed she was seeing her and understanding who she was. "She'd like to say something to you," I said.

Sounding surprised, she relayed the message. "'I forgive you.' I'm trying to recognize her. I'm hugging her. I kiss her hands. I don't know her. I'm so sorry."

"A guide or angel comes to you," I said.

"My friend…he's coming. The same guide…white robe…long beard… hugging me." There was a long pause. "Now I understand my other lives. I didn't do any good to anybody."

"Ask him about your daughter," I suggested, as it was becoming quite clear that she hadn't liked or wanted children in her past lives.

"He says I'm very selfish and still carry that feeling. I have to learn to be a mother. I haven't been a mother in a long, long time. I have to accept motherhood. I've avoided for so, so long. I never had children in other lives as a woman. I have to let this feeling go."

"Ask him to reach inside you and take this feeling."

"Hmmm. It's a rock…it's a grayish, cryptic rock…big…heavy. He disintegrates it, and it turns it into powder, and the wind takes it away. Wisssshhh," she said, making the sound of the powder being blown away.

"How does he fill the space where the rock was located inside you?"

"He gives me a ball of light. A little ball of light to guide me, help me, protect me."

"How does the little ball of light feel?"

"It feels good. I feel light. He tells me to believe in myself. Do not be afraid to love."

I emerged her. Martha looked at me with wide eyes and began speaking, "Now it makes sense. I've been fighting my lack of desire to have children. I despise gossip in this life or to compete. It was a countryside castle. We were in the south of France, near where the Dutch artist van Gogh painted his pictures. We'd go on vacation to the beaches where van Gogh was, but he was not alive at the time. *L-i-e* something (referring to the name of the town). There were towers on the edges of the castle (she described turrets), and it was close to a forest. I was accepted and envied, like I was his second wife. As time went on, Victorian times, it changed. It was a fox hunt I went on when I was riding. He bought the title of countess for me. My name was Lillybeth. His name was Rogier or Rougier…Louis Rougier. He was deeply in love with me and infatuated by my charms. But I simply liked him. I was not in love with him."

~

Martha researched the time period and sent me an e-mail soon after her session:

"Patricia, I did a search on the subject 'mistress,' and it was very interesting. I kept repeating to you, 'I am not a prostitute,' remember? This was emphasized below,

A mistress is not a prostitute.' It is also mentioned, *'In the courts of Europe, particularly Versailles and Whitehall in the 17th and 18th centuries, a mistress often wielded great power and influence.'* I lived in Belgium, a France neighbor, and that is exactly how I felt during my last regression. I had a lot of power and influence in the social circle at that time, and it was an open secret my relationship with that married, aristocratic man. I looked up the city of Liege, and it came up as located in *Belgium*. Even more amazing is the pronunciation of the word Liege by people who lived in that area. Remember I told you that I mentioned the name started with *"L-i-e?"* There are TONS of Castles in Liege. I have no idea which one I used to visit. I do not remember the rank of my lover so I cannot even locate the castle. And I looked for Countesses named "Lilly" and I did not find any...anyway!"

～

I could hardly wait to begin my own research with the information Martha had written.

During the 1700s, a young woman never traveled without supervision, so it was interesting and perhaps necessary she felt a need to explain to me why she was unsupervised at the party. I was unable to find Louis Rogier, but I located a Charles Rogier who was a liberal Belgian statesman and leader of a revolution born in 1800. His father, after fleeing to Belgium, was an officer in the French army, and after he died, the family moved to Liege. Charles Rogier gained recognition as one of the most active among the patriot leaders and became minister of Belgium in the 1840s.

Martha had described a time when summers were spent in the South of France, where van Gogh vacationed. One of the places van Gough lived was in Arles, France, near a beautiful, large beach on the Mediterranean. I wondered if this could be the beach Lilly had visited. When she said van Gogh wasn't alive at that time, it was because he hadn't been born yet and wouldn't be born for another fifty years or more. He was born in 1853. This is a good example of how she could access her knowledge in this lifetime as well.

The revolution she so casually mentioned was none other than the French Revolution, and the king and his wife who were killed by the guillotine were King Louis XVI and Marie Antoinette. Both had been beheaded. Royalty across Europe were horrified at the beheading of the king and queen. More confirmations.

I showed Martha some photos of castles I'd found on the Internet. "No, the towers were lower and wider." I asked her if she'd ever been to Belgium, and she replied she hadn't.

Once again, she wanted to make sure I understood that she was not a prostitute and emphasized she was a mistress and countess. This position held much importance, she said confidently. She was correct, in that titles of nobility were generally hereditary.

Other than Brussels, I was unfamiliar with cities in Belgium, so Martha and I were both surprised to discover Liege is a city located in the Eastern region of Belgium. I was intent on finding the castle she had mentioned, thinking it wouldn't be difficult. What I didn't know was that there are more castles per square mile in Belgium than anywhere else in the world. In fact, there are about three thousand in Belgium! We both began researching the castle, but we were unsuccessful in finding it. None of the photos of castles I'd sent to Martha ever hit the mark. I researched castles off and on for more than a year and was ready to abandon hope when the last castle on a very long list of castles caught my eye. I learned it was constructed in the seventeenth century as a hunting palace. The words *hunting palace* flew off the page at me. There were turrets on the corners, as she had described. I was excited and wondered if this could be the castle where she had hunted.

I began to read more of its history. Castle d'Hassonville, as it is named, was used as a hunting palace and is located in Marche en Famenne, thirty miles from...*Liege.* Had the castle been there all along, and I had dismissed it because it wasn't *in* Liege? I quickly e-mailed the link to Martha and asked her to take a look when her time permitted. Moments later, she responded to my e-mail: "WOW! THAT IS IT! THIS IS THE CASTLE I SAW..."

We had found it! Interestingly, there was an advertisement about the castle, as it is now a château where you can stay overnight. The castle and its initial 1,606 acres had been established as hunting grounds for Louis XIV of France, the Roi Soleil, also known as Louis the Great and the Sun King, who was attracted to the scenery and lush landscapes.

~

Well over a year had passed since her regression as Lilly, but now that we had found the castle, I had other questions about the regression. Martha responded to my answers through e-mail:

Patricia, somehow after that regression, my 'aversion' to being a mother disappeared. I believe that feeling was kept inside me, 'sleeping,' and the spell was finally broken with the memory of that lifetime. It was a blessing. Thank you.

MARTHA

Gustav, New World, and Amsterdam

Martha sat on the familiar blue recliner and said, "I feel so much love toward my daughter. I *never* had this before. She doesn't annoy me anymore. I have more respect and consideration for her." I was happy to hear her regressions were helping her. She then continued, telling me about her anger toward her mother-in-law and wanting to be rid of the feeling. In hypnosis I regressed her on the feeling of anger toward her mother-in-law.

"It's dark. Outside. A house. Close to woods. House in the woods," she began. "I'm a man. The clothes are old. Grayish brownish. Very simple. Old, but clean...and I have a beard. Big...coarse."

"What color is your skin?" I asked.

"White. Long beard...too much. Gray. Midforties. I cut the trees. I walk barefoot. I think I'm resting. I have an axe in my hand. I'm resting, looking. The sun is blinding me...the beginning of the day," she continued.

"Does anyone live in the house with you?" I asked.

"I don't live alone, but I'm alone now. Maybe they're sleeping."

"Move time forward," I instructed.

"I smoke. Like a cigarette type. My hair is a little longer, too."

"Walk into your house and tell me what you notice."

"I have a brother in the house. Younger."

"Anyone else?"

"I can't see, but I know there's somebody else."

"How long have you lived there?"

"All my life. I lost my father…recently. I'm sad because of that."

"Someone calls out your name. What's your name?"

"Doesn't come…can't pronounce." She paused before saying, "Gustav."

"Move time ahead to the next significant event, Gustav."

"I'm taking the logs to sell down the mountain. A horse is pulling an open wagon. My brother is with me. We are not married."

"Because?"

"We never found wives. We live in the mountains. There's a woman in the house," she said softly, before curling up on her side in the chair. "There is a dog that comes with us. I think our mother lives in the house."

"How do you get along with your brother?"

"OK. We get along." She paused before adding, "It's very far away," referring to where she lived.

"What is the name of your town or region?"

"I'm trying to see where is this place. I don't know where. It snows in the winter. Looks like…I have the impression it's in the United States, the East. Smoky. Very isolated. New Hampshire. It was hot, but now it's cold. It's a very boring place. I don't see much purpose in my life. I see me cleaning a gun now. We hunt bears. We use the skin of the bears for winter."

"Look into your brother's eyes. Is there a soul recognition?"

"Looks like he's my daughter."

"Go to the next significant event."

"There are other people hunting. I see a fire in the night. We are drinking. We are all together. Laughing together."

"What are you drinking?"

"Rum? Using metal containers. Now my clothes are heavier. I have boots on. I have my dog with me. It's a big dog. It's always with me."

"What happens next?"

"We are sleeping," she said. After a long pause, she added, "Looks like someone is trying to steal something while we're sleeping. We had already hunted, and it's worth a lot. He's stealing the skins. They're black bears.

(Referring to the skins.) There are Indians there. I sense there are Indians living nearby. I haven't seen any," she said, before pausing. "I'm not English. I don't think I was born here. I've lived here twenty years or so. I'm not English," she repeated.

"Where are you from?" I asked.

"I'm from the country high in Europe. I look Dutch, but I'm not. It was a private ship. Norway…Denmark. I think my parents and my brother came after me to start a new life. He was my baby brother. My father got sick and died. They laugh at us because of our accents. We tried not to go to the Indian territory. They don't kill the bears there."

"Move time ahead to the next significant event."

"We're going back to Europe. We couldn't stand living in those conditions anymore."

"I'm going to snap my fingers, and you'll know what year it is." *Snap.*

"1630. We don't have much money. I'm happy we're leaving. We did not have friends. It looks like I'm Dutch. We're going to Amsterdam. It's a long trip. Weeks…months."

"Go to the next significant event."

"I cut my hair and my beard."

"How old are you now?"

"Close to fifty. Late forties. I work riding carriages to transport food. I stop at a street market. I just mind my business, but my brother is having problems. He's always in pubs, getting into trouble. I try to help him, but my mother is comforting…he's always involved in fights. Oh. It's my mother-in-law," she said, recognizing him on a soul level. "He spends money…gambling. He goes home, and she takes care of him."

"How does that make you feel?"

"Angry. I'm the one who brings food to the house. He brings a woman… another mouth to feed. I'm really angry. I see a baby being born. I complain. Nothing happens. They come and eat when I'm at work."

"Move time forward."

"I move away to another city alone."

"Your mother?" I ask.

"She stays behind…for him. I don't know how she'll support herself. I move to start over. I don't want to be responsible. My mother said my brother would work and change."

"Move time forward to the next important event."

"I think I found someone and got married. She's an older lady. No children. We live together. We are poor, but we get along well. We have food on the table."

"How old are you now?"

"Early fifties. We live in a small house. One room."

"Are you happy?"

"Content, but I carry resentment. I never want to hear about them again. I don't know what happened to them."

"Go to the morning of the last day of your life."

"I have a history of gout. My foot got infected. Gangrene. My wife is caring for me. Midfifties. I went very young to the Americas. The last ten years I spent back in Holland."

"Do you recognize you wife?"

"I think she's a friend of mine."

"Go through the death scene. What were you to learn?"

"Forgiveness. I didn't learn it. I was filled with resentment and regret about choices. I felt guilty leaving my mother."

"Notice now your mother comes to you, Gustav."

"I don't want to look at her."

"What would you like to say to her?"

"Mother, I'm sorry."

"Sorry because?" I asked.

"I'm not sorry!" Martha exclaimed. "I'm angry because of the way you behaved. I felt you were irresponsible."

"Because?"

"You did not care for me."

"Because?" I asked.

"You never listened to me. You never appreciated me."

"Mother, help him understand."

"I feared for him," she said, referring to his brother.

"Because?"

"He could die. I always thought you were stronger, and I knew you'd be OK. I'm sorry. I love you."

"I wish you could understand. I wanted recognition, attention…love." She then added, "I think my name was Gustav."

I emerged Martha. "She was preventing me from helping him. She was doing so many wrong things. I was trying to help him."

I researched and found that the name Gustav is considered both Norwegian and Danish.

MARTHA

Tanai, Native American

When Martha returned for her next session, she reported her symptoms of feeling angry at her mother-in-law had gotten worse instead of disappearing. I knew immediately there was another lifetime she needed to explore.

In her session, Martha discovered she was a colonist who had come to America from a Dutch colony. She explained, "I was a man in that lifetime who was the head of the family. I sold furs to provide for them. Although I had come with a Dutch company, I felt adamant I wasn't Dutch. I had come to organize the colonies. New Hampshire came to mind. After someone came and stole all our furs, I felt defeated and decided to return to the Netherlands. I had brought my mother and brother back with me. I would transport vegetables to the market for an income. My brother didn't adapt well to the move, as he had been raised in America. He was drinking and with women a lot. It was uncomfortable because I was the only one providing. My brother got the girl pregnant, and I just couldn't do it anymore, as now I'd have another mouth to feed. I asked my mother to come with me, but she chose to stay with my brother. I was so disappointed she chose my brother and not me. I ended up marrying and died with gout or gangrene."

She became aware that Gustav's mother is her mother-in-law today. Her daughter today was her brother then. Martha also told me she had researched and found New Netherlands, which is now known as New York, in the early 1600s, but she felt she was in New Hampshire.

I discussed with Martha how we each have a Higher Self and how healing can happen, even with someone who is alive. We can talk to that part of the soul that is on the other side. I quickly recapped Sunny's story for Martha, telling her how after Sunny's regression, her sister's daily panic attacks and deep grief of fourteen years disappeared, and she somehow mysteriously knew her daughter was OK. Sunny then told her sister about her past life when she was her sister's child who had been stolen and died.

Once she was in hypnosis, I took Martha to an ancient temple where a wise and loving being met her at the door. From there, her loving Being took her inside to a library, where she said, "It's very big with high shelves."

I told her that all the books in the aisle where she was standing had to do with her present and past lives. "Find the book titled *Mother-in-Law*."

"It's big and heavy...gray, feels like leather," she quickly responded.

"In a moment I'm going to have you open the book, and it will open to the page that will offer the most healing of your relationship with your mother-in-law."

"There are no pictures, only letters," she began. "The letters form words... horses. I can see a picture of a wild horse. It's brown."

"Step into the picture now," I suggested.

"I'm running in a prayer. It's an Indian dance. I'm in an Indian village. I see children around and women carrying things. There's smoke. It's springtime."

"Notice what you are wearing."

"I have on a long skirt...a long dress..." Her voice trailed off. "I'm young. Not a child or adult...sixteen. I'm helping my mother now. I went to get water. We're close to a river. The sky is blue...it's the beginning of spring. It's a little cold. The men are traveling."

"Where are they traveling?"

"I don't know. I think they went hunting. Only women and children are here."

"How many are there?"

"Many," she said and then paused. "Hmm..."

"What is happening?"

"I see mountains far away. The name that comes to mind…South Dakota."

"Do you have a name for your people?"

"C-ucks," she responded. I wrote it down phonetically. "I have long hair," she continued without prompting.

"What are the men hunting for?" I asked.

"Buffalo. They have to go far away because they're gone."

"What are your living conditions?"

"I have a young brother, mother, and older brother. A small tent, but everything is clean."

"Have you lived there long?"

"No, we are always moving, but we're going to stay here for a while." She paused before adding, "I'm a little concerned."

"Because…?" I waited for her response.

"I don't know…I'm afraid of something." She was quiet for a moment before continuing, "I'm afraid the men are not going to come back. Every time they leave, I'm afraid they won't come back."

"Because?"

"My mother told me a story, so I'm always afraid."

"Look deep into your mother's eyes. Do you recognize her on a soul level?"

She paused. "I think she was my aunt."

"Look now into your brother's eyes, and notice if you recognize him."

"No."

"Move time ahead now half an hour or when the men come back."

"They come back at night. It's dark. They brought food with them. Some of them are hurt."

"Hurt? In what way are they hurt?"

"They were attacked. I don't know. They don't tell me. They don't tell the youth. They ordered me back to my tent. There's a lot of commotion. The sky…there are a lot of stars. It's very pretty. I like to look at the sky and listen to the stories. But tonight is different. I must go back. They are hurt by another tribe."

"Do you have a father?"

"Yes. He's very strong. He's a warrior. My mother is young. My mother is pretty. At least I think she's pretty. She doesn't tell me anything, and I'm afraid to ask. I ask the next day and am told they were attacked by another tribe to steal the horses."

"What is your name?"

"Tan-i." I wrote it phonetically, so I would pronounce it correctly.

"Move time ahead, Tan-i, to the next significant event, and when you are ready, tell me what is happening."

There was a long pause. "I think my brother is sick. I'm caring for him. He's having fever and shivering."

"How old are you?"

"I'm almost eighteen. I'm about to get married…but he gets better. (Referring to her brother.) He doesn't die."

"Do others get his illness?"

"He was the only one who had it. I think he ate something he shouldn't have."

"What happens next?"

"We are moving to another place. Every spring we go to a different place." She pauses before adding, "It's like I'm so naïve. People don't talk to me. I do as I am told. I don't question. I'm very nice. I do not argue. My mother teaches me how to cook…how to care for a husband, how to make the husband happy, how to prepare fire. I'm very silly. Innocent. I like to hear stories and look at the sky. I don't talk too much." She paused before continuing, "My mother is preparing me for getting married. I'm excited, but I don't show it. I do not show my emotions. He's a young boy. I think he is so attractive," she said and smiled broadly.

"Move forward now, Tan-i, to your wedding day."

"I get married at night. They are dancing and clapping their hands."

"Go now to the next significant event."

"I'm pregnant. My husband is very nice to me."

"How old are you now, Tan-i?"

"I'm nineteen. He hopes it will be a boy." She paused and then added, "The place where we live never rains. It's hot. I'm under a tree."

"Look deep into your husband's eyes. Is there a soul recognition?"

"Hmmm. Looks like a friend of mine. Not sure."

"Move time ahead to the next important event."

"Up to now, we only travel time to time. It's very peaceful, actually. I feel more secure when men are around. People are happy. Each cooperate. We respect the elders, love everyone. We respect the animals. Nobody fights with anybody. Everybody is so nice. Everything is very organized. Everybody has one task. Everybody obeys. Boys are behaved." She paused again as though gathering more information. "This is a long time ago...before America was discovered. They haven't seen...the white man. This tribe is very peaceful. They have long hair, leather clothes. We eat fish, meat."

"Move now to the morning of the last day of your life, Tan-i."

"I had been sick—abdominal pain. My belly has been hurting. I'm middle age. My hair is not white. My son is an adult...twenty? Twenty-one?"

"Go through the death scene now."

"My grandfather from that lifetime meets me."

"What did you need to see or learn in your life as Tan-i?"

"How important harmony is."

"Your mother-in-law comes to you now."

"I am showing her happiness and harmony. I have such a nice family. We respected each role...I'm showing her how we lived. She's listening. It was a happy lifetime. Each one respected another. She feels touched. Lead by example."

"See her now as a small child," I instructed.

"She doesn't feel loved. She's jealous of her older sister. She feels insecure with her. I think because she felt that way, she didn't want her daughter to feel that way."

"Understanding and knowing this, can you forgive her?"

"Yes. Hmm. Interesting. She did not know better. She tried to prevent her daughter from feeling what she did. Very interesting." She paused for a few moments. "Little girl, come here," she said.

I have goose bumps.

"I'm sorry you feel that way. It is possible to be happy. It's a matter of being willing. It's never too late to change or learn. I'm sorry. I forgive you.

Grandfather. He's proud of me. A hug and kiss. I missed you so much. He taught me so much...gentle...wise."

I emerged her. Martha and I went to my other office, where I make future appointments. She sat on the sofa, and I sat at my desk with my back to her as I pulled out my calendar. "I'm not familiar with a tribe by the name of C-ucks," I said absentmindedly as I looked for an opening for her next appointment.

"Yes, C-ucks," she said, before spelling it out letter by letter. "S-I-O-U-X."

My eyes widened, and I spun my chair around to look at her. "Sioux? Is that what you were trying to say?" I asked, startled.

"Yes, C-ucks," she repeated. "S-I-O-U-X."

"It is pronounced *Sue*," I said, smiling and shaking my head. "Of course you would pronounce it that way," I said, remembering English was not her native language. S-I is, yes, pronounced like *see*. (*C* in my shorthand.) O-U-X sounded like *ucks*. She told me her name was spelled T-A-N-A-I.

She pulled out her smartphone and googled *Sioux*. A picture appeared. "Yes," she said, "this is how we looked."

I asked her what she knew about native Indians in her South American country. She said she was familiar with Mayans, Aztecs, and others, but they looked different. She knew little of Native Americans. Martha set up her next appointment for the following month. I was already anxious to hear how her session and healing would unfold in her life, but my mind was spinning with the realization that she was referring to being a Sioux Indian.

MARTHA

Forgiveness Work

D ue to schedule conflicts, I did not see Martha for four months. When she returned, we talked about her life as a Sioux Indian, and she said, "I had no clue about South Dakota, but I have always been fascinated with Indians. I had no idea who the tribes were except a few I'd heard about from watching the movie *Last of the Mohicans*. And I had no idea where in the United States the tribes lived. It's interesting, though, that I had bought a video about Indian wars. I was drawn to the photo on the front of it. I didn't watch it until after our regression. While I was in the regression, I thought that the time was before Columbus, as I had not seen a white man, but then I read that horses were brought to America by Europeans. I saw many horses, so the white man must have been there, but I just hadn't seen or even heard about the white man. They did not tell the women and children about them. After the regression I watched *Dances with Wolves* for the first time, and it felt very familiar, but they never said where the movie was filmed."

"I imagine it did look familiar because it was filmed in South Dakota," I told her.

Martha's eyes widened. "I died from acute abdominal pain within days. Appendicitis." She added that she had not gotten better with her mother-in-law after the regression, and she felt she needed to forgive her. "I just want to let go, Patricia. I feel like I hold on to resentment. I want to forgive and let go."

Once she was in hypnosis, I took Martha to a place within her called Martha's Control Room, a place where she could make changes within herself. I had her cut the cords to negative feelings about her mother-in-law and then did forgiveness work until she felt relaxed and peaceful toward her.

MARTHA

John Campbell, England

When Martha came for her next session, she wanted to discuss her Sioux lifetime again, as she had been reading more about the tribe. "The Sioux were the most advanced culture. They were family oriented—not violent like the others. That's exactly how I felt in the regression. They respected the kids and women. I feel healed from the last session. It's always a gradual process for me. I traveled to Miami last weekend, and I was anxious before I saw my mother-in-law, but when I saw her, I had no anger. I only felt sympathy for her. There was no problem at all. I have no anger at my sister-in-law either."

I asked her what she wanted to work on. "This is not the life I planned. I thought I'd be in Colombia. I wanted to specialize in a different area than I'm practicing in now. I feel anxious."

Once she was hypnotized, I instructed her to focus on her feeling of being anxious. "Make it strong within you as I count up from one to three. On, two, three. Focus on this feeling within you, and go back to when this feeling first began. Is it dark or light?"

"Dark. Boots."

"What are you standing on?"

"Stone...loose stones. My pants...the boots are over my pants...long...I have a beard and long hair."

"Let the scene unfold. Are you alone or with others?"

"Alone. I have a dog with me. I don't know, but...I'm looking for something. I'm outside. Late twenties...my hair is dark. Looks like I am looking for a dog. I have many dogs. One, I think, had escaped."

"What kind of dog?"

"Hunting dog. Now it looks like I care for the dogs for somebody else. They aren't mine. They are for hunting."

"How many are there?"

"Maybe a dozen."

"Move time ahead until you find the dog."

"I think I'm responsible for the dogs. I feed them...so they can hunt."

"What do they hunt?"

"Foxes, deer..."

"Where do you live?"

"Somewhere in Europe."

"I'm going to snap my fingers, and you'll know the name of your town." *Snap.*

"York. That's the first name that comes to mind. There's a hunting trip the next day. I was a little nervous that the master would be upset."

"How long have you worked there?"

"Not too long. I just started in the past year. I was in the servants' house with other servants. I'm single. I think I am. I like it, but it's stressful. They have to be in shape."

"Move time ahead to the next significant event," I instructed.

"There's a party. Everybody is having fun."

"Where is it located?"

"It's on the grounds of the property."

"How old are you now?"

"It's only months later."

"I'm going to snap my fingers, and you'll know your name." *Snap.*

"John."

"Last name?" *Snap.*

"Campbell."

"What year is it?" *Snap.*

"1620…I like a girl."

"Is she there?" I asked.

Martha shook her head no. "I have long sleeves…I have a belt and dark pants. My boots go to my knees. It's interesting because I'm…my hair is well treated, I'm clean, not dirty. I'm good-natured, I don't wish harm to anybody. I don't know how to approach her. I'm handsome. Good looking. My eyes… blue. Light skin. Nose…thin. I have a beard, dark hair. My hair has curls to the shoulder. I'm wearing a hat. Sometimes I put something on it to decorate it…drinking beer…it's my free day. It's the end of the hunting season. We're celebrating. End of summer, beginning of fall. She works on the property… daughter of someone who works there. Her name is Claire. I think she may work inside the house. She must be sixteen…name of estate…Gloucester… but I don't know."

"Move time ahead at the party."

"I think her father does not want her to date. I say that's OK, I don't care, not such a big deal. Maybe she'll change her mind."

"Move time ahead to the next significant event, John."

"I really don't care about dating girls. There is an older man that comes to me. That's a secret…nobody knows. That's why I wanted to date her. He protects me…provides for me…like a love relationship…but nobody can find out…I'm *gay*! How interesting! This word did not exist then. People did not talk about it. I do not want anyone to know. He has a high position with the servants. I don't take advantage of him. I was careful with my appearance. My hair was shiny, pretty teeth, my clothes were clean."

"Because…?"

"I have a vanity. I'm not saying I'm a narcissist, but I like to look good. I like to be clean. Clean hair…clean clothes. I think I was kind of delicate, if you know what I mean. The way I talked…walked. People would laugh at me. I don't care. I think they were jealous."

"Move time ahead to the next important event," I suggested.

"I want to move away to a big town. There are people who've invited me."

"To what town?"

"London. I don't know. My brother…cousin invited me to live in London, but for that I have to quit my job."

"What happens next?"

"Eventually, I go to London, and I am amazed at how beautiful the city is. Actually, I was twenty-three or twenty-four. Now I'm twenty-six. I still don't know what I'm going to do…I'm in a little hotel. I go to pubs through the streets. I'm having a good time. I think it's my cousin's…we're friends. He doesn't know I'm gay. He just thinks I'm delicate." She paused before telling me where he was staying. "A little inn…a small one…outside of the city."

"What is your cousin's name?"

"Trevor Stuart," Martha said as she turned on her side in the chair.

"Does he have a job?"

"I don't know. I think he was there before me. I don't know what he's doing. He's nice. We are the same age. I think he works…he likes a good life, fashion, friends in high…good places. But what does he do?" She repeated my question. "Hmmm. I still don't know…oh…no…he's a gigolo. He hangs with rich ladies, and they give him money. He doesn't work…that's why he invited me—to have fun…but he's not gay. He doesn't know I'm gay. I feel ashamed. I don't want anybody to know…so during the night we party—during the day I shop, and I love it!"

"Who gives you money?"

"Trevor. He says, 'Don't worry, cousin. I'll support you.'"

"Move time ahead again to the next significant event."

There was a long pause. "Hmmm. I don't see…I'm having fun with Trevor. Just enjoying going out. I'm concerned with my appearance. I like my boots to be shiny and clean…and when I talk, I make a lot of gestures." She moved her arms dramatically from the chair to demonstrate. "I'm a happy person."

"Is there anyone you are interested in?"

"That's the thing. I don't know what I'm going to do. I'm happy shopping. I see Trevor getting a lot of jewels. I'm sitting in bed with him looking at his jewels. I make people laugh. They like me, but I'm stuck."

"Move time ahead one month to two years. How long do you stay with Trevor?"

She paused before answering. "It's over a year now. It looks like I'm working in a hat store…decorating hats. I'm a hat designer. It's 1624. Plumes, jewels. I don't like flowers. I call it a plume. I notice the street in front…small, good neighborhood, narrow."

"Notice the name on the store."

"It says Tapestry. I'm controlling myself. I always talk like this: 'You look *beautiful!*'" she said, with great emphasis on the word *beautiful*. "This store is for males and females. I decorate hats. They are big. Some have ribbons. I'm a good employee. I'm good at what I do," she said as she waved her arms dramatically.

"Move time ahead again."

"I think Trevor's sick. Poor Trevor. His lungs are weak…too much partying. That's what the doctor said. He's twenty-seven. I take care of Trevor. I give him soups."

"Look into his eyes. Is there a soul recognition? Do you recognize him?"

"I cannot go there. I like him very much. He's my best friend. This time I am providing. He can't hang out with the ladies anymore. I'm very proud of that. I have a servant. Can you *believe* it?" she said, sounding excited. "It's not a palace but a nice neighborhood. He's feeling better but never the same anymore."

"In what way?"

"No energy. I think he feels depressed. I love him so much. I take care of him. I am appreciated. People like what I do. I receive compliments. I have a good energy around me. I have fun at work. I was doing something I wanted to do, and I am good at it," she said before pausing. "And you know what? I don't have a boyfriend, and I don't care. I take care of Trevor. I ride a horse to work every day. I gave Trevor a dog to keep him company."

"Go now to the morning of the last day of your life, John."

"I'm around sixty. I'm old. I have breakfast. I'm in my gown. I did not go to work. Trevor died twenty years before…his lungs. I'm happy because I helped him. Actually helped, and I was not sexual. I was just happy to make people happy…so I had many friends…I never married…had children. There's an older woman—I think she's been my servant. Madeline."

"Go to moments before you pass, and look back on your life."

"I had a happy life. I did what I wanted. I helped many people. I made a small portion. I think eventually I opened my own shop. I was happy. I was a little bald; little glasses; long, white hair—like Benjamin Franklin. I'm having shortness of breath. I was overweight."

"What street do you live on?"

"Mallard Street...close to a square. I live on the second floor. A building with three floors. It was a large apartment. Twelve hundred square feet. So I was not rich."

"Go to the death scene."

"Madeline found me. I was on the floor. She came to serve me tea."

"Float higher. What were you learn in your lifetime as John?"

"To share. I needed to learn how to share material things and happiness. I felt so...I was very generous...I helped people. I did not live in luxury but a comfortable life."

"Your guide comes to you and helps you understand more."

"I was to learn how to deal with adversity. Things aren't always how we want. Need to accept that. Just make one person smile a day."

I emerged Martha from hypnosis.

"I was flamboyant. I felt like talking like he did, with lots of hand gestures. He was feminine and single until he died, but happy and appreciated. I've never had prejudice about people being gay."

~

I couldn't wait to see what I could discover about her life as John Campbell. Until about 1620, the captain was the fashionable hat to wear. It had a tall, conical crown rounded at the top, but by the 1630s, the crown was shorter and the brim wider. It was often worn cocked or pinned up on one side and decorated with ostrich plumes. Also, there is a Mallard Street in London, and it's near a square.

Martha e-mailed me and discovered *Gamble* was more common than *Campbell* in seventeenth-century England. She found several John Gambles born around 1600 and deceased by the 1640s, but no Campbell. "So, it is possible that my gay past life name was not Campbell (not Gamble)," Martha wrote. She could not find a Trevor Stewart or Stuart before the 1800s. "But... there are the following names that could match based on death date and city of London. Edward Steward, Charles Stewarde, Sackvile Trevor."

~

I noticed that Martha would make references to people who had not yet been born. When I asked her about it she said, "In regards to the dates: I have a general knowledge of the world history, but I have never been to Belgium or to the South of France. But I *knew* I was there. (She was referring to lifetime as the Countess Lilly.) The same way I *knew* I was in South Dakota and Georgia, for example." (She was referring to her other regressions as Tanai and Becky.) I knew what was happening around me, the rumors about the revolution in France. I mentioned van Gogh because he lived in the South of France for a while, and somehow I believe I was vacationing in the same area. However, I knew that van Gogh was not born yet at the time of my regression. I know he was a nineteenth-century impressionist, so your current lifetime knowledge helps you with this type of information, I guess!"

"It is fascinating how your mind operates during a regression...depending on your level of education and knowledge, you may identify world facts related to it...remember my lifetime as Becky, the slave? When you asked me to go forward to the end of the war and I said, 'I died before the war ended. How could I know?' I said, 'I died two years before the war ended'. I did not think about, it is just what came to me at the time of your question. Later, I found out the Civil War ended in 1865, which is amazing. I mean, I knew the Civil War took place in the middle of the nineteenth century, but I did not know any of these details. Amazing."

Martha inspired me, as did Ginny, to want to write about her fascinating experiences. The lives were not only engrossing, but time and time again, she was able to find validation of her lifetimes. She was curious to explore and discover who she was to potentially heal who she is now. Martha journeyed into lifetimes that spanned more than eight centuries. She found herself to have been a countess and a priest, a king and a slave, a Native American and a colonist, a gay man and a captain in the British army. Interestingly, the only lifetime in which she recognized her daughter was as Gustav. She went to lifetimes in which she didn't like children or want a child as the countess and the priest, and in doing so, her feelings toward her daughter shifted. Her addiction to politics and the computer abated as she learned of her lifetimes of injustice. She also gained a sense of peace with her mother-in-law. The exploration of her soul helped her understand and heal.

LINDA

Lilly McBride, England

Linda is a medium who told me she had seen several of her past lives while in meditation, but she had never been hypnotized before or worked with anyone to guide her to a past life. She was nervous, and I reassured her she was always in control and could stop the process at any time. I also reminded her I wasn't doing anything to her, but simply guiding her into a beautiful state. I knew it would be interesting to work with her, as mediums receive information through some or all of their senses. This is referred to as "the four clairs": clairaudient (clear hearing), clairvoyance (clear seeing), claircognizant (clear knowing), and clairsentient (clear feeling).

I have all my clients fill out history forms before our first session, and I ask if they have any fears. Linda wrote *drowning* on her form. I found it interesting that she did not write *water*, as many people do, but instead specifically stated *drowning*. I wondered where we would go and if that fear would reveal itself. Linda was certain she would go back to one of the lifetimes she had already seen during her meditations, but we soon learned that would not be the case.

Once Linda was in hypnosis, I asked her to find a hallway with many colored doors. "There's so many!" she replied.

"Find the door that you feel drawn to that will help you heal and grow the most."

"The red door." Without being instructed, she opened the red door and began telling me what was going on in the scene in which she found herself. "Cold. Busy, busy, busy, so many people in the street...the market...standing in archway...my feet are cold. Clothes...dirty...long skirt...torn...old."

"Reach up and feel your hair," I instructed.

"Thick...curly."

"Notice your hands."

"Dirty."

"Your hands will tell you how old you are."

"I'm twenty years old."

"Daytime or nighttime?"

"Daytime."

"Let the scene unfold."

"I don't belong there," she began.

"Because?"

"I don't know anyone...ugh," she sighed.

"Like a videotape, you can rewind the tape," I said, wanting to elicit more information.

"Going backward...prison...not prison. Cells...alone...a long time. Long time. Sixteen years old," she began.

"Do you know why you're there? What you are accused of?"

"Ugh. Fighting. No more! I *spit* in his face."

"Whose face?"

"A man."

"Someone you know?"

"No."

"I'm going to snap my fingers, and you'll know what year it is." *Snap.* "What year is it?"

"1892."

"I'm going to snap my fingers, and you'll know your name." *Snap.*

"Lilly. Lillian."

"What is your last name? I'm going to snap my fingers and give me the first letter of your last name. *Snap.*

"*M.*" Snap. "*C.*" Snap. "Bride."

"Go back now, Lilly, to before the cell."

"White...big house...England...sent to work there from home. North country. Northumberland."

"Notice your hands. How old are you now?"

"Twelve years old," she said, before continuing, "I miss my family. I cry... I work long...hard. Harder than I ever did on the farm," she said, sounding surprised. "Don't like to learn...lessons. I want to go outside. I clean, wash, make the beds...must do it right."

"Is there a name to this place where you are?"

"Fetherton," she replied, before she spelled it out letter by letter. "F-E-T-H-E-R-T-O-N."

"How many live there?"

"Many...big house...ten bedrooms. Three...noooo..." She shook her head. "Mother in black. No father, three sons. All grown up but lazy. Useless. The lady is very strict. I don't want to make her mad."

"Go back now, Lilly, to when you were with your family on the farm."

"I miss them," she mumbled quietly, as tears rolled down her cheeks. "Mother is Mary. Father is Charles James. Two names. I'm the oldest," she stated, sounding proud.

"How many children live at your house?"

"Six...disease comes...not for the people...the land...kills all the food... can't feed everybody."

"What type of food did you farm?"

"Potatoes, wheat, beans."

"Notice your mother, and look deep into her eyes. Is there a soul recognition?"

"No."

"Look into your father's eyes now."

"It's Uncle George." She paused and then continued. "I don't read or write. Mother says I'm lazy. I work with my father. I don't care."

"How far away is town?"

"Three miles to walk. McKill...Hilly McKilly. That's what I call it. England. Soldiers in their red coats. We're told to...I'm told to stay away."

"Go to moments before you leave the farm."

"I'm screaming...crying...coach comes...some man gives my mother money! She says I'll be OK and...come home when I can...when I finish my services. I'm angry. I hate them! I'm not *ever* coming home!"

"Now move time ahead to before the cell. Let the scene unfold, and when you're ready, tell me what's happening."

"There's a big party. Lots of preparation. Everything must be perfect. Spotless. Told to go to my room. I want to see the pretty people. I can hear the people laughing—the music."

"What happens?"

"Two men come to my room. Dressed like dandies. (*Dandy* was a term used in late nineteenth-century Britain to describe a man who placed importance on his physical appearance, refined language, and hobbies.) They want to touch me. My one master touches me all the time. That's OK. He likes me. I say no! I spit in his face...*scratch*...fight...ugh...he hit me...struggling. They take me beat up, bloody, going to the hospital."

"Who takes you?"

"The coachman."

"Is the master aware of what is happening?"

"He says I've gone crazy. Ladies come and take me. I feel safe. It smells like...oh, it doesn't smell good. They wash me. Not my clothes. They put me in a cell. Very small window at top...cold."

"What is the name of this place?"

"Hospital. I hear banging, clanging, screaming...all women. I cover my ears."

"Move time ahead, Lilly, to the next significant event."

She whispered her next words. "I'm smart and...I'm very naughty. I'm going to run away."

"Run away from what?"

"The hospital. Twice a day, we walk around. Four of us are going to run away. It takes a long time. The walls are high...there's glass at the top...can't go over," she said, before pausing to see what was happening. "I'm out. The only way to get over...they'll have to lift me up. I feel bad. There's a lady who is very stupid. I tell her if she lifts me, I'll pull her up. I know I can't. There's a big storm. Lightning. The matron calls us in. Girls are screaming. We'll get hot buns and milk...Betty's *strong!*" she exclaimed. "Whoa! She pushes me over the wall! I run, and I hear her calling my name over and over. I'm sorry! I hear the dogs. The men. I run and run...I'm in that busy street," she said. (Referring to the first scene she was in at the beginning of the regression.) I'm hungry and dirty. It's a port. I can see a boat. A big boat. There's soldiers. I can't be seen. I'm in Dublin! How did I get to Dublin?" she said, clearly surprised.

"How do you know you're in Dublin?" I asked.

"I just *know* I'm in Dublin. I just stand there. It's like I'm not there. People can't see me."

"What happens next?"

"If they can't see me, I can walk down the street like a lady...so I do. I want to get on the boat. I don't know where it's going. People are busy. They don't notice me. It's like harvest time on the farm," she said, her face beaming with a huge smile at the memory of her life on the farm.

"How long did it take you to get there?"

"I saw two full moons. My feet are bloody and sore. I sleep in barns and trees...steal clothes off clotheslines."

"Go to the next significant event, Lilly."

"I'm in a nice bed. I'm twenty-five. My husband is a redcoat, and we just had a baby. A girl."

"Is there a soul recognition as you look into your baby's eyes?"

"My daughter."

"How did you meet your husband?"

"In a pub, serving."

"Did you get on the boat?"

"No...Northern Ireland...tum...two penny...T-W-O penny. I never learned to read or write," she said sheepishly.

"What is your husband's name?"

"James Carlisle...married...a year...not quite. Eleven months," she said, correcting herself. "He's gone a lot. It's a little house, but it's warm. I have food. I feel safe. I walk down the street like a lady," she added, quite proud. "I won't go home. They sold me! Why not one of the other children?" she whimpered.

"Go to the next significant event, Lilly."

"Three more children. Every time he comes home...he's home now. He doesn't wear the uniform anymore," she said.

"Is there a reason he doesn't wear the uniform anymore?"

"There was an uprising...against the king...queen. I'm confused. Who is the monarch now? I'm just thirty-one, but I feel old, and I'm coughing too much."

"What are the names of your children?" I inquired.

"James...Bryon...Mary. Two children didn't make it," she said with no emotion. "My coughing is bad. I hide it, otherwise they'll send me away."

"Is there a name for the coughing?"

"Consumption. (What we now know as tuberculosis.) A woman brews strong tea," she said, before adding with a deep sigh, "He's a kind man."

"Go to the next important event, Lilly."

"I don't want to go! I heard them talking in the parlor. I have to go to the hospital! How could they do that to me? I put on my sleeping bonnet and white night dress and go out the back way. It's cold. Very cold. I'm feeling weak. It should be easy. I am going to the river...the water is so cold." Linda began physically shaking and crying.

Sensing she had walked into the river, I asked, "What are your last thoughts?"

"My children."

"Float above the scene and look down."

"She looks so peaceful. She's laying amongst the reeds," she described.

"How long before they discover her?"

"Quickly. Ten minutes. I hear him calling her. (Referring to Lilly.) I left the gate open. He...James finds me," she whispered. "I never loved him. It was a way for me to be a wife...respected."

"What year is it?"

"19...05. The little one is five."

"Much time passes and you have a full understanding of that lifetime. What did you want to learn on a soul level in your lifetime as Lilly?"

Linda chuckled and said, "Stay away from hospitals!"

"A wise and loving Being comes to you who has loved you through all of time. This Being can take any form whatsoever and loves you unconditionally."

Linda sighed deeply. "This is who I really am. I'm this. Not that person. This is real."

I emerged her.

"Wow! That was different. If you put water in my face, I go *insane*."

An interesting choice of words, I thought, and just another reminder that the soul and subconscious mind remembers everything.

Linda continued, "I had reddish hair or light brown, curly, thick, brown or hazel eyes. Big round doll eyes. Fetherton could be the name of the manor. McKillen the name of the town? James Carlisle was a redcoat, but not an officer. I ran for two months. It's funny because I expected to go to my Chinese or African lifetimes! It was on Market Street in Dublin. I've never been to Dublin! When I was eighteen months old, I was at Daytona Beach and started walking right into the ocean and nearly drowned. My mom was asleep on the beach. I always assumed my not liking water on my face was from that event. When I'm in the shower, I can't put my head under water! I was afraid my husband would send me to the hospital like the one I had been in, and I would rather die than be sent back there. I hate doctors and hospitals."

LINDA

Lilly Revisited

Nearly two months passed before Linda returned for her second session, and she wanted to know more details about Lilly.

Once she was in hypnosis, I began, "Go to your lifetime as Lilly, and notice your feet. Describe the shoes you are wearing."

"Leather...brown leather...on the grass...hanging out wash...twenty-five years old. Cold morning...there's a small river. The mist is rising...frost on the ground. Steam is coming from the clothes. Hands are raw, red. I want to get back inside."

I noticed that the details of the image she was seeing in her mind were clear and specific. "Move time forward."

"It's my home. Inside. We have a fire. Two of my children...little girl, baby in the bassinette."

"What is the name of the little girl?"

"Silly. I get the names confused. Sophia. Sometimes my mind doesn't work right. I get anxious and scared and can't think right."

"Scared about?"

"I don't want people to think I'm crazy."

"Is there a reason?"

"Because I was in the hospital."

"For what reason?" I asked, to see if more would be revealed.

"I don't know. Because I hit the man. David James…I don't know. Sometimes…" she said, before letting out a deep sigh. I noticed she began playing with her fingers.

"Sometimes I don't know where or who I am. Sometimes I want to run away."

"Because?"

"I get scared," she said quietly. "I love the children, but sometimes…I forget things."

"Like?"

"To cook. He gets angry."

"Who gets angry?"

"Husband. Most of the time, he's kind to me. I like him. He's gentle. James…five years in the house…there are other cottages…there are five houses…close together. Behind a river and fields. There's a hill. The manor house…the person who owns our homes."

"What's his name?"

"He's a lord. My husband told me he used to be in charge of him when he was a soldier in the regiment."

"How did you meet your husband?"

"I met him in a pub. Dublin. There was a lot of trouble with the people in Dublin. They were fighting about the rules and regulations. They told me if I went with a redcoat I'd be hated. I see…a horse…a lady on a sign…a white horse. I don't read well."

"What is the name of the street?"

"It's in the main square. Market Street. 1872."

I wanted to get more background information about Lilly when she was young. "Go back to when you were a child."

"Ten years old. We lived on a farm. I was the oldest. We had pigs, a horse, our plow horse…in England…Cotswold. It's beautiful. We all work very hard. There's no time to learn. The priest wants me to learn to read, but there's no time. I take care of pigs and chickens. I feed the horse and rub him down."

"What is the name of the town you live near?"

"Tetherby. Where the church is."

"Look into your mom's eyes and see if there is a soul recognition."

"Could be Rebekah...my daughter."

"Now look deep into your dad's eyes."

"Uncle George," she answered.

"Lilly, go now to the next important event."

"Being taken away. Crying." She rubbed her hands together and added, "I'm very confused. I didn't do anything wrong. I'm mad!"

"Did your mom or dad say anything to you to help you understand?"

"Nothing."

"Move time ahead again, Lilly."

"Big house...*big* house. A woman comes. She looks mean. She takes me to the pantry and asks me what I can do. Tells me I'm there to clean the house."

"How old are you?"

"Thirteen?" She paused. "Sir. Always say *sir*...and don't look at him."

"How long of a drive from your house to this one?"

"Long...dark and cold. All day and night."

"Where does it go?"

"Cheshire. Somerset House...but it doesn't make sense. I hear the cooks laughing. They make a joke of it."

"Where do you sleep?"

"In the attic. By myself."

"Go now to the next important event."

"Sir comes and makes love to me. I'm fourteen. He tells me he loves me. I feel really important. I feel special." She smiled.

"Is Sir married?"

"Mariam. His name is Charles, but I must never use it."

"Does he have children?"

"Yes, but older. Only youngest daughter...Mary...Somerset. I don't like her."

"Because?"

"She treats me rude...she's mean."

"Lilly, go to the next important event."

"I was taken away from the house. I was very bad."

"Because?"

"I hit the man."

"Because?"

"He tried to touch me."

"How old are you now?"

"Fifteen. I was taken away…nighttime."

"How did you travel?"

"By coach. Very scared. Mrs. Abbott in the coach. Housekeeper. She doesn't like me."

"Do you know where you're going to?"

"No."

"Find yourself approaching where you are going."

"Big. Big place…gray…early morning…sun's just coming up…and there's a big fence everywhere. I ask Mrs. Abbott where we are. She says it's a hospital because I'm not well."

"Does she say the name of the hospital?"

"No. It's made of gray stone. I've never seen stone like that. She says it's from the quarry. A lady comes out in a uniform. She's in all white. Mrs. Abbott gives her a letter. She takes me inside. People are crying…screaming. Scared. They take me to wash, and I put on a gray uniform…a dress…go to a room with lots of other beds. The women are crying."

"Move time forward, Lilly, to the next important event."

"I hate it there."

"How long have you been there?"

"A long time. A year or two. I don't know. A long time. Too long. I'm scared. I want to get away. Run away."

"Do you know the reason you're there?"

"It's because I hit the man." She paused before continuing, "Then he writes in his book and he goes away. I always ask him if I can go now and he just smiles." Playing with her fingers and sounding like a young girl, she said, "All the girls like him because he's nice."

"By now you've heard the name of this place you are staying through doctors or nurses."

"They call it the dungeon. Doctor comes...I know his name. I *know* his name," she said. I could see her struggling to remember it. "He's nice...blue eyes...I like his blue eyes. Jamison. Dr. Jamison. He's kind. He always asks how I am, and do I know why I am there."

"What is the name of the place where you are now?"

"Aron something."

"Notice the terrain."

"Trees...countryside."

"Is there water anywhere?"

"No. Arondale. (Spelled phonetically.) We're not allowed to listen when they talk."

"Move time ahead to the day you leave Arondale."

"I ran away. I tricked a girl to help me get out. I'm running...cold and wet. I sleep in barns when I can find them. I'm really hungry. I see a boat."

"A fishing boat?" I ask.

"Uh-huh. I ask the fisherman where he's going. He says, 'I'm going to go fish. What's the matter with you, girl?' I say I ran away, and they're after me, and I'm scared and hungry. He takes me home, and his wife makes me porridge. And they give me shoes." Linda began wringing her hands. "And a nice thing for my shoulders. I'm sorry, a shawl. It's got holes in it, but it's still warm. And then I ask him can he please take me away from this. He asks his wife if it's OK, and she said yes. The next day, I go with him on the boat."

"Where do you go?"

"It takes a while...maybe two days," she said, as though not sure. "Before we get to land, I ask him if we're in Australia. He just laughs and laughs and laughs," she said, smiling. "I heard Australia is a long way away. I guess it's not Australia," she said, sounding confused, embarrassed, and a little disappointed.

"Does he tell you where you are?"

She shook her head up and down, "Ireland," she said, playing with her fingers again.

"Notice everything."

"There are redcoats everywhere. I'm scared. He took off. I wave good-bye. John..." Her voice trailed off.

"Move time forward again, Lilly."

"I'm working in the fields. Pick potatoes. Dig up."

"Have you done this before?"

"Yes, on my home farm."

"Go to the next important event, Lilly."

She smiled and said, "Standing in the archway looking into town. So many people. It feels happy. People are laughing."

"How long have you been in Ireland?"

"A few weeks. I'm a mess. My dress is dirty, raggedy. Mother would not be pleased. I'm hungry...always hungry. I go to the pub and ask for work. They laugh because I look so bad. One of the girls said she'd clean me up. They couldn't pay me, but they'd feed me. Soon I was good, and they liked me. Then I go to work behind the bar. Ja...Ja...James," she stuttered.

"Go to the morning of the last day of your life, Lilly."

"Like any other day. Not Ireland. We're in England. James works for the manor. He's a games keeper. We have a cottage. I keep coughing. I cough blood sometimes. I've heard people who cough sometimes go to the hospital."

"Tell me about your children."

"The ones who lived? Two died."

"How?"

"One after I gave birth, and the other had the fever."

"What is the name of the closest town?"

"We go to the market one time a month. It's my favorite day. Starts with a *C*. Chester. I sit on the hay cart with the children. Takes all day to go and come home."

"Go to the morning of the last day."

"When the man comes, it's nighttime. James is talking to him about me. The man says I have to go to the hospital. All of a sudden, I hate him. I *hate* him! I'm not going. I'm not going back! I put on my bonnet, and I go out the back quietly. I go out the garden gate. I don't know what to do. I see the river...they go, and they don't come back," she said. (Referring to people who go to the hospital.)

"Is there a name of your illness?"

"Consumption."

"What year is it?"

"1892. I'm not good with numbers."

"Find yourself floating above your body."

"James is holding me and asking, 'Why?'"

"Much time passes, and you have all the answers. What did you want to learn as Lilly?"

"Trust."

"A wise and loving Being comes to you."

"Like a big sponge cake. It's beautiful, soft, comfortable. I feel loved and... perfect."

"Ask about your time in the hospital."

"It wasn't your fault. Tests were done to you," she said, repeating what her Being told her.

I emerged Linda from the hypnotic state, and we talked about her session. When I asked her what she had learned about Lilly, she responded, "How confused she was. She was illiterate. She couldn't read or write. Everyone made fun of her. She had no education, but she was intuitive. She had promise. The memory loss, the confusion...I remember she'd forget to do things. She'd walk off and forget she had the kids. She didn't mean to...just...you know. The trauma of being around crazy people. There was constant screaming. She never loved him (her husband)." Linda was quiet for a moment before adding, "How confused she was, and I won't go to doctors!"

~

Soon after Linda's session I received an e-mail from her:

Hi. I found the house where James worked as a Game Keeper. Fetherston Family in Ardagh, County Longford, Ireland. The dates match. The town of Ardagh is only one hour from Dublin on the river Shannon, the major waterway through Ireland's central area.

Oh my gawd! I have located the asylum that Lilly was sent to, I had such a horrible reaction to seeing some of the pics, I have printed out some data with pics etc. the name of the place was Countess of Cheshire, Cheshire County Lunatic asylum built in 1829 demolished 2005. In the time period that Lilly was there, there were 90 residents, men separated from the women, it's the place, it makes me feel sick to my stomach. The asylum Lilly was kept was in England."

I found photos of the asylum on the Internet and asked Linda if it looked familiar. "Yes, I have seen these, the color of the stone is not grey, but the early morning light in winter everything in England is grey! LOL. It is definitely the place, I felt such a sickening feeling when I first saw the pics and the building. Fear gripped me and I really had to fight through it.

~

I began researching further to discover more about Lilly.

* Lilly said she was sent from home to work in the "North country. Northumberland." I discovered that Northumberland is in the northeast portion of England, bordering Scotland.
* I asked her the name of the place she lived, and she said Fetherton. I discovered there is a village in Northumberland named Fetherston, as well as a castle. Fetherston Castle was the original home of the Fetherston family. George Ralph Fetherston was the youngest son of Thomas, and he succeeded as heir in 1865 at the young age of thirteen.
* If Lilly was correct in her original statement that she was sixteen in 1892, and she arrived there when she was thirteen, she would have arrived in 1889. George, if he was Sir, would have been twenty-four years old and only twenty-seven when he sent her to the hospital.
* Lilly lived on a farm in Cotswold, England. She said the closest town, called Tetherby, was three miles away. There is no town called Tetherby, but I located a Tetbury, and as she said, it is located in

the Cotswolds. The Cotswolds is an area of south central England containing the Cotswold Hills, a range of rolling hills. Tetbury is a small town situated on the *top of a hill*. Could this be the town she nicknamed Hilly McKilly as a child?

* Lilly said she was on Market Street in Dublin. I found a map of Dublin in the mid-1800 s. There was and still is a Market Street in Dublin.

* As Linda said in her e-mail, the Cheshire County Lunatic Asylum opened in 1829. Today, it is known as The Countess of Chester Hospital. It is no longer an asylum.

* During Victorian times, women who rebelled risked being declared insane, as did women who behaved in ways the male society did not agree with. For women, having an opinion was dangerous. Men had the last say, and if they simply wanted to silence the voices of these women, they were committed to an asylum. This was usually done by the husband or father. Women had no rights to contest this action. They were further disempowered once locked away, where they would likely spend the rest of their days.

* Lilly said she was in England on the last day of her life and that they would go to the market once a month in a town called Chester. Chester, England exists, but what surprised me most was that it's the same city in which the asylum was located. Perhaps this is why, if she was even aware of the close proximity, she was frightened at the thought of returning to the hospital. It was the same "hospital" she had been in before.

* Lilly drowned herself in a river in back of the home where she lived. The River Dee runs through Chester.

~

Nearly a year had passed since Linda had been regressed, and I invited her to be a guest on a radio show called *Soul Traveler* I cohosted with spiritual coach and medium Pamela Latour, PhD. I asked Linda to tell the listening audience about her session with me. As I listened I was amazed at the consistency, as she told the audience about her life as Lilly.

This is a synopsis of the radio interview:

Linda: *I was a little nervous because I wasn't sure what to expect. I felt very comfortable, though. I felt very, very calm and relaxed. I also felt very secure. I think that is very important because there is a level of trust, and I think you have to have that as well. I remember being in a hallway and being frustrated because there were so many doors, and I was quite curious, but you told me to pick a door. It was amazing. It truly was.*

Patricia: Tell the audience about the first scene you found yourself in once you opened the door.

Linda: *I was at a market in town. People were rushing around doing things. I remember standing in the archway and feeling invisible. Then I had the sensation of being cold and dirty. Raggedy clothes and young. There was a lot of busyness.*

Patricia: What did you learn when you went back to an earlier time before you found yourself in the market?

Linda: *I had been sold into servitude to a wealthy family, and the master of the house had become my lover, which was hush-hush. One night, he expected me to have sex with another man. I fought him, and I was sent to an insane asylum. When I researched it and found it, ugh, the memory was so real. It's one of the wow things.*

Patricia: Tell the listeners more about the hospital.

Linda: *It was all women. We slept on floors. Several people to a room. It was not sanitary. Very dirty. One of the doctors seemed to really care. I think he was probably one of the junior people. He was kind. I remember feeling a sense of compassion. That was something I really treasured because it was something I had not a lot of in my life.*

Patricia: Have you had any further insight as to why you were sold into servitude?

Linda: *Many times, they didn't own the farm. It was property they worked. They constantly had to give to the lords, so I remember we had a problem with the crops. We weren't getting enough…a drought or disease. I can't remember.*

The animals weren't eating well. We weren't eating well. I suppose my parents had no choice but to sell their oldest daughter into servitude. I felt very hurt. Very angry."

Patricia: How long do you think you were at the asylum?

Linda: *I think it was years. Maybe four or five. I'm not sure. There was a yard we used to walk in to get fresh air. There was a brick wall. It had glass shard on top of the brick wall. This one girl, a young woman, tall, she was backward, but very strong. I told her if she lifted me up, I'd reach down and pull her up, knowing full well that was impossible.*

Once over the wall, I ran and ran. I heard her yelling, but I couldn't do anything. I remember dogs, hearing dogs and men and just running and grabbing what food I could. I remember grabbing clothes off wash lines. It was very frightening. And then I remember an old man and an old lady. They gave me a meal, and then she said he'd take me on the boat. I thought we were going to Australia. I've never been to Ireland in this life. That was when I was standing in that archway. (The first scene she first found herself in during the regression.) *Because of what she went through in the asylum, she was a little scattered. She had a problem with memory, confusion, but somehow, she got through that point to getting a job in a pub. There were a lot of soldiers around what she called redcoats. That is where she met James. Lilly had times when she would forget things. Again from the treatment she received, there were times she'd forget what she was doing. She might forget and wander off and forget the children. Those were the only times she'd argue with James. He'd be very angry. I think she tried very hard. She was grateful to have a home and family. They weren't rich, they were quite poor, but they had a home. She treasured that. She wanted very much to be a lady. That was important to her. She had been sick awhile with a bad cough. She knew people who had this illness were sent away. She heard James tell a gentleman she was coughing up blood. They talked about taking her to a hospital, and in her mind, she thought she'd go to the mental hospital. She stepped into very, very cold water and laid there until she died.* (I noticed Linda would go from speaking of Lilly's memory in the first person to the third person.)

Patricia: How is that lifetime reflected in your current one?

Linda: *Frighteningly similar to this lifetime. A lot of betrayal, of being used rather than loved. Fear of water. I love looking at water but not going into it.*

I can't put my head in the water. Even in a shower. If someone splashes me, I panic. Also, I'm fanatical about taking care of my health because I will not go to doctors.

Patricia: After your regression I remember you said, "If I get water on my face, I go *insane!*" What an interesting choice of words.

Linda: *Oh wow.*

Pamela: After you realized where these experiences had come from, how has it changed you?

Linda (laughing): *I'm still not rushing to jump in the water. Whatever I was meant to learn as Lilly, obviously I didn't learn very well, but to see similarities— "Oh, that's why this happened." Instead of seeing things just happened as a big mess, I experienced this to understand it differently now.*

Pamela: What was the message for you?

Linda: *That's a deep one. I'm probably still working on it.*

Pamela: Cells have a memory not only in this life but what your soul has brought into this lifetime. When you enter your body, it becomes part of who you are. We know that in the law of attraction, if we don't generate something new, we know it will run the old program. So the question of what did you learn from this? I'm not so sure you have to learn something. It often regenerates because it's already there. It picks back up again. What you need to learn is to let it dissipate and move through you. It will disappear when you stop resisting it.

Linda: *I've been processing this experience, and we do need to learn, but I like what you've said. All I have to do is observe it and acknowledge it.*

Pamela: When the emotion kicks in say, just say "I lovingly allow it to dissipate." Why did you feel a need to research your lifetime?

Linda: *The documentation of it (the regression) is amazing, and when you can prove that these things occurred, it's so rewarding and worth the experience.*

Pamela: Explain the difference between doing a reading and having a regression.

Linda: *When I'm reading, sometimes I get a mental image and sometimes I get a mental hearing, but when I did the past life, I was in that scene. I wasn't the interpreter like when I work. When I was in the past life, I was Lilly, and I felt the cold, I felt the fear. I felt it, and that was completely different. It was a firsthand experience.*

Patricia: Linda, can you tell the audience about when you were a toddler on Daytona Beach?

Linda: *I walked straight into the ocean. No fear. I just kept going. A man got me out. I can only assume it was reigniting the "oh my god, that's the fear." Why would I do that, though?*

Pamela: Lilly just walked into the water, and that's what you did as a child. It was already there.

Linda: *Maybe she didn't like the human world, and the water would get me home. It worked the last time.*

What I found interesting was that everything she said was practically verbatim from her regression. If she was simply using her imagination, I think it's unlikely she would remember the same story she had made up a year earlier with such detail.

Linda later wrote to me, saying the following:

The regression served to help me see that what I have been told by Spirit and all I have learned from reading etc. is true, that we come here to heal and to experience things that can either advance us spiritually or regress us down a lower path, it is up to us to choose, the insights I got from the regression was to be made aware that this life is just a repeat of the past life and that I have to put forth the effort to heal this time around, no time to waste.

Not all the information Lilly revealed lined up with what I discovered through my research, but one must remember that her mind was not the same after the asylum, and at one point she said, "I'm not good with numbers." More importantly, one can better understand how Linda's lifetime as Lilly has affected her current life, from her fear of water—"I go *insane* if water is on my face"—to her irrational fear of doctors and thus her focus on her health, as well as her relationships with men. Her fear of drowning has not disappeared, as typically happens when one revisits a past life, which leads me to believe there are other lifetimes involving drowning yet to be unveiled.

Weeks before sending my manuscript to the publisher, I traveled to Ireland. With the assistance of a librarian in Dublin, I found the pub Lilly had once worked in when she arrived by boat. The address she gave me was 9 College Street. As I walked to the location of the pub, I was shocked as I realized I had eaten at that very pub a year earlier. Of all the pubs in Dublin, I went to that exact pub.

Where Lilly worked. The road to the right goes to the River Liffey, a block away.

BOBBIE

Jessica, Dodge City

Bobbie wrote to me, stating she'd had a reading with internationally known Chip Coffey, a psychic medium featured on the A&E Network television show *Paranormal State* and as the host of *Psychic Kids: Children of the Paranormal*, as well as the author of *Growing Up Psychic*. She wanted to get background information on how television production was done through his eyes and perhaps get a general reading. During their conversation, she discussed her interest in doing a documentary about the paranormal. Chip suggested she consider an alternate route by making the documentary about past lives.

During Chip's reading of Bobbie, he told her about several of her past lives. In one lifetime, he described her as being a person of the clergy, and in another life, he saw her in a death scene where she was hanged or crucified as a male, but it was an unusual crucifixion. In the third lifetime, she was an abused woman in the American West in the 1800s and possibly a female whose last words were "Never again." Those were the only details Chip gave Bobbie about her lifetimes. He told her that she would do the documentary, but it would go slowly because she wasn't ready yet.

Bobbie said her interest in past lives was fleeting at the time of her conversation with Chip, but for the next six months, they had occupied her thoughts. After a period of constant internal nagging, Bobbie reached out to me. "The thoughts about the lifetimes were relentless," she said. "They weren't visions. I've never been a visionary, but I am good at listening to my gut. My intuition." (A reading from a psychic is not as emotionally charged as a regression, and as a result, therapeutic change does not occur.) She was curious about the validity of the past lives Chip had told her about, and she had a sense the lifetimes were blocks for her. "I'm not sure why I want to do this journey other than I feel it's important for me to know what happened, who and what I was," she wrote in an e-mail.

An information technology (IT) professional by trade and former emergency medical technician (EMT), in addition to having a military career, Bobbie was a budding filmmaker. When we spoke on the phone, she asked if she could film her session to produce a documentary. Bobbie had become interested in seeing if she could go to the lifetimes Chip had revealed. She was curious to discover if it was possible for a psychic medium to tell you of a past life that you could return to in a regression. I felt that any opportunity to show someone seeking a past life regression and its healing benefits would be beneficial. And I, too, was curious what we'd discover.

Bobbie arrived promptly for our appointment. Her dark-blond hair fell to her shoulders. I never would have guessed her age, as she looked much younger than her birth date revealed. Raised Roman Catholic, Bobbie had strong connections to the Church as a child, but those ties had waned over time. She told me she had been exploring metaphysics for a year or two through watching several paranormal shows on television and reading articles. "I was familiar with the belief of reincarnation in Buddhism from what I'd seen on television, so I wasn't a stranger to it; I just wasn't a believer. To be honest, I didn't know what the heck Chip was talking about," she said with emphasis and a hearty laugh.

I, too, was interested to see if she would be able to experience one of the lifetimes Chip had discussed with her. Sometimes when clients are too anticipatory, try too hard, or are preoccupied with other thoughts, it can block the process of allowing themselves to go into a hypnotic state where they can find their answers. Admittedly, this was a concern of mine as I watched her set up cameras, sound equipment, and lights in my office.

Would she let go of the concerns of filming enough to allow herself to go into hypnosis? And if so, would she experience one of the lifetimes Chip had revealed to her? Or would she visit a different lifetime altogether.

Bobbie had been thinking of the lifetimes Chip had revealed for more than six months, and she was anxious as to what she would discover. As was I. All my doubts evaporated when Bobbie allowed herself to go into hypnosis effortlessly, as though she'd been waiting for this moment.

"Let that feeling of 'never again' come up in you as I count from one to three. One. Feel it coming up. Two. More present now. Three. Very real within you. Go back to moments before you ever had this feeling. At the count of one, you'll be there. Three, two, one." *Snap.* "Notice your feet," I began.

"Bare," she said softly.

"Is it dark or light?"

"Light."

"If you have clothing covering your legs, notice how it feels against your skin," I continued.

"Coarse…nothing on arms," she answered.

"Notice your hair."

"Black hair. Victorian. Petite."

"Notice your hands," I directed. "Your hands will tell you how old you are."

"Young…not under twenty-one."

"Let the scene unfold," I instructed, "and when you're ready, tell me what's happening."

"Cold." Bobbie began to visibly shiver, even with a big comforter covering her. "It's dusk…inside…alone. Lying there…I can see my hand. I'm on the floor. Wood dresser," she continued, as she observed the room she saw in her mind's eye.

"How long have you been there?"

"I don't know."

"Move time forward," I instructed.

"It's dark…night…still cold. I've been there for a while. Same place."

Hoping to get a better understanding of what had happened, I continued, "Like a videotape, you can move time forward or backward. Move time backward to the beginning of the day." I paused briefly before asking, "Are you inside or outside?"

"Outside...sunny day...warm...red dress...hat...dirt road...in town... wooden porch...saloon. It's cold again."

"From the weather?" I asked.

"No."

I was puzzled as to why she was cold if it wasn't the weather. I continued, hoping to find my answer. "What happens next?"

"I'm in the saloon." She paused before adding, "I'm known."

"I'm going to snap my fingers, and someone calls out your name." *Snap.* "What is your name?"

"Jessica."

"You said you are known. In what way are you known, Jessica?" I asked.

There was a long pause, and she gave no answer. I knew that either she was not getting an answer or she didn't want to tell me.

"When I snap my fingers, you'll know what year it is." *Snap.* "What year is it?"

"1853."

"What is the name of the town you are in?"

"Dodge. I'm inside a saloon...happy...wearing a shawl. I'm of grace. Upstairs." Bobbie laughed. "I'm outgoing, flirtatious...sassy!" she exclaimed and laughed again. "I'm in a brothel. Cold." Her body began to visibly shake again, as though she was very cold. (When you are in a state of hypnosis, your body temperature can sometimes drop a little, just as it does when you sleep, but her intense shivering told me it was cold in the scene in which she found herself.)

"Move time gently forward now, Jessica."

"Cold again...ugh! Man. Jacket. Tweed. Mustache. He's looking at me."

"Do you recognize him?" I asked.

"No." She paused before continuing, "Nose, mustache." Bobbie listed what she was seeing in her mind's eye.

"Move time forward," I instructed. "Find your answers, Jessica."

"Name. Bad name. I'm angry...really angry," she emphasized. "He's hitting me! I'm so angry! He's hitting me!" she blurted out. She then paused and continued, "He has a knife...cold...he's gone. Bleeding...side. Hurt. Thirsty. There's noise...something above me...a voice?"

"Can you see who it is?" I asked, wondering if he had returned.

"Something standing...lying...weightless..." Her voice trailed off. "I see me...black hair...corset...blood left side."

I knew she had been killed, but I wanted more information on her life. "Look back on your life, Jessica, and tell me about it."

"Little girl...sweet...tree house...old home...Daddy."

"Move time forward to Dodge."

"Young...by myself."

"Because?"

"Loss...family...war."

Hoping for more clarity, I asked, "War with who?"

"Gray officer. Daddy!" Bobbie began to cry. "He's dead!" she gasped and then sobbed. "He's my same father!" Without my asking her if there was a soul recognition, she recognized her father in her lifetime as Bobbie. "Mom. Same mom. Hmmm."

"Much time passes in this in-between state. What were you to learn on a soul level?" I asked.

"Obedience."

"Did you learn it?" Bobbie didn't answer. "What were your last thoughts?"

"I hate myself."

"Because?"

"I'm a victim. *I'm not gonna let this happen again!*" she said with great emphasis and emotion. Her words echoed closely to *never again*—the words Chip Coffey had told her. The sentiment of her words and his were nearly identical. Based on her emotional response, I knew this was a recalled memory. Emotions are always excellent indicators.

If you begin to analyze while in hypnosis, it brings you to your conscious state. Essentially, you bring yourself out of the hypnotic state. I knew Bobbie remained in a deep state of hypnosis, so we continued.

"Did you leave anyone behind?" I asked.

"I don't know...a little boy...maybe." She paused for a few moments and then smiled. "He's three. He's my little boy. Mark," she beamed.

"Do you recognize him from your lifetime as Bobbie?"

"No." She paused. "I *love* him." She said the words warmly. "Happy."

I knew Bobbie didn't have children, and until you do, it's hard to imagine or feel how profound the love for a child is. I witnessed Bobbie experiencing the deep love a parent feels for little Mark. "A wise and loving Being comes to you," I said softly. Bobbie spent a few private minutes with the Being before I emerged her from hypnosis.

"Part of my mind wants to know if it's real," she said quietly, as a tear rolled down her cheek. "I left Mark. I abandoned him," she explained, as she tried to compose herself. The emotion she felt was apparent. I remained silent until she stopped crying. "That was different," she said quietly. Bobbie was clearly deeply affected by her experience. "I remember the wood planks and rubbing my finger on the floor. It was like an anchor to know I was still alive. I remember the people. I remember..." Her voice trailed off, as her mind wandered back to her experience.

"Bobbie, do you have pain on your left side?" I gently asked.

Bobbie's head quickly riveted to look directly at me, clearly surprised. "What did you say?" she asked.

I repeated the question. "Do you have pain in the place where you were stabbed?" I asked, pointing to where she had indicated she'd been stabbed with the knife.

She paused as though absorbing the question I had asked. "Yes! I've seen many doctors about a pain on this side. Nothing diagnosed. It has hurt on and off for years."

"Well, let's see what happens with that," I said casually.

Bobbie was anxious to tell me more about all that she had experienced. "The clothes were heavy. Lace trim. Hat. I was pretty!" she exclaimed, as though quite surprised. "The boy had on a white shirt and suspenders. My dad was possibly a Confederate officer—in the Civil War? He had a mustache and beard. He looked different, but I knew he was my dad in this life. And the fort didn't look like a fort you'd see in old Westerns. It was just buildings. There was no protection."

As Bobbie began to dismantle the filming equipment, I could see she was still digesting what she had experienced. Hearing about a lifetime through a psychic reading is interesting and can explain things pertinent to your life, but reliving it is an entirely different experience. It is often emotional and profound. Also, there is a lot more information being noticed than what is expressed to me during the regression because the mind looks to find an answer to the question being asked, but it is noticing much more. Just as when you are speaking to someone and focusing on what he or she is saying, but you are taking in the scene you are in as well.

BOBBIE

Jessica Revisited

Six weeks passed before our next appointment. As Bobbie sat down in the blue recliner, she told me that as she drove home from her last session, she kept thinking about her regression experience as Jessica, and the name *Bender* came to her in her mind. I wrote the name *Bender* down in my notes and wondered how it would relate to her story, if at all. More information can come after a regression, as it did for Bobbie when she was driving.

Most of us have had the experience of driving somewhere and upon arrival wondering how we got there. Driving is something we don't have to think about how to do, so we allow our minds to wander and think about what we have to do that day at the office, our grocery list, or something else. Our minds are focused on what we are thinking about, which is a light state of hypnosis.

Bobbie was anxious to tell me more about what she had experienced as Jessica and began telling me about the man who killed her in detail. "The assailant who stabbed me was a male. He wore a derby-type hat, mustache, dark-colored suit. As I looked forward in the room, there was a door to the left, a dresser with a lace doily. Whoa. I have cold chills," she said, sounding surprised. "The bed was embroidered in some fashion, dark wood, and the walls were a light color. There was light coming through the window, which was behind me. It was late afternoon…in the spring. I was stabbed on the left side, below the rib cage."

"How is your side feeling since our last session?" I inquired.

Bobbie looked puzzled. "What?"

"Where you were stabbed. How does your side feel?" I asked again.

She looked surprised before saying, "It hasn't bothered me for the last month or so. In fact, only one time on Thanksgiving did I have any issues with it. I used to have discomfort all the time, and the doctors couldn't figure it out," she said, before realizing the regression had helped her. "I did not expect that *at all*! Hmmm."

I wanted to know more. "How long had it been bothering you?"

"Years. In fact, for the past decade," she said, sounding astonished. "Oh, and I'm also sleeping through the night now."

I was not aware she'd had problems sleeping, but I was glad she was getting a good night's sleep. It was time to begin our session, and Bobbie wanted to go back to her lifetime as Jessica to gather more details. I, too, was interested to see what more we could discover. It was one of the few times I intentionally regressed someone to go back to a lifetime they had been to before, and I was curious about what more we could uncover about Jessica. Once hypnotized, Bobbie began giving me information immediately, seemingly knowing what questions I'd ask before I asked them.

"My shoes are black...buttons on the side, cloth at ankles. I'm standing on a wood floor."

"What are you wearing?"

"Heavy cotton...red trim...in my room...it's morning."

"Let the scene unfold, and when you are ready, tell me what is happening."

"The window looks down to the street...it's dirt...there are carriages and people. Across the street...there's an intersection...and smaller buildings. I'm on the second floor."

"Read the names of the stores," I instructed.

"General Store. I can't see a name."

"What type of stores are next to the general store?"

"There are two buildings to right, then an intersection."

"Can you read the name of the street?"

"No. No signs...dirt road...opens to country."

"Are you at the edge of town?" I was creating a scene in my mind as she spoke.

"Could be. Saloon is on the left-hand side...same side as me...can't see it. Just know it's there...*L*...and script...can't see the rest of it. I think I'm in the hotel. I'm young. Pretty. Black hair...long, in a bun...skin is very white. Oh gawd. I can see my face. It's porcelain. Narrow jaw...white cheeks...eyes are the same as I have now. Comfortable...like home...children playing. It's my boy. He's playing with a girl. Just a baby. I'm sad. Mark...is two years old."

"Look deep into his eyes," I told her. "Do you recognize him?"

"No."

"Notice your hands. Your hands will tell you how old you are. How old are you?"

"Early twenties. Twenty-one."

"How long have you lived in this place?"

"We just got here. Alone. No father."

"Where do you come from?"

"Barstow...far. Days on train."

"Go back in time to before you went on the train."

"Mother...angry...She's angry at me."

"How old are you?"

"Eighteen...maybe older."

"She's angry because...?" I asked.

"Baby...pregnant," she said, before beginning to cry. "The baby's dad is *dead*."

"Who is the father of the baby?"

"I don't know."

"Because?"

"A soldier was the father...an officer."

"What state do you live in?"

"I don't know. Utah?"

"Describe the terrain."

"Outside...house on a hill...whitish wood trees...lots of trees. She's working. Washing clothes...her heart is broken."

"Because?"

"Of me...Mom!*Mommy!*" she exclaimed, as she began crying. Once again, Bobbie recognized her as her mother in her current lifetime.

"Notice everything you need to notice."

"Summer."

"Rewind the tape to when you first met the father of the baby."

"He's funny. He makes me laugh," she said, before laughing out loud. "I'm happy. I'm so happy," she said contently as she smiled.

"How did you meet?"

"School...he's sweet. I love him. He's older."

"What's his name?"

"George Smith," she said before pausing. "He's dead!" She began crying. "War! No! No! My baby..."

"Did he know about the baby?"

"No. He was away."

"Doing..."

"I don't know...military...I don't know...Indians. Calvary. Hmmm." A tear rolled down her cheek. "He's transferred to Dodge," she said and then began to sob. "He's sick. Something with the fort. He's sick...it's too late. I got there too late. He was dead sometime before I got there. I'm so sad."

"Did he know about the baby or that you were coming?"

"No. I was worried. No letters."

"Tell me about arriving into town."

"Bender..."

"Who is Bender?" This was the name that had come to her as she was driving home from her last session.

"The Bender family?" She stifles a cry. "A ranch...or something awful... passing by it now. People didn't like that place."

"Because?"

"They don't speak of it. It's outside of Dodge," she said before pausing. "Ain't right. That family ain't right!" Her words hung in the air. *Ain't* was not a word that Bobbie used. She was reliving the scene as Jessica. "Stay away from them. *Hatred*!" she said, sounding appalled. "Safe in Dodge."

"What date is it?" I asked.

"187...6? Late 70s? That place is *bad*."

I noted the year was later than she had said in her first regression. Perhaps she was getting the information more clearly now. "Do you discover the reason it's bad?" I asked.

"They are murderers. No one talks about it...stay out of there."

"Move time ahead to the next significant event after you arrive in Dodge."

"The fort is closed. They closed the fort."

"Were you surprised, or did you know this?"

"Surprised. It's not much of a fort, just buildings in a square or circle...no real protection...graves." She began crying. "George. Humph."

"What's happening?" I asked her, sensing she was seeing more than she was saying.

"Nice man. Owner of the hotel. Foreigner. He has a daughter. She's older. She looks after Mark. Her name is Lisa...big hotel...two stories."

"Notice the name."

"G...gold? It's a G and long...long saloon, right-hand side," she said before pausing. "People hate me."

"Because?"

"What I am."

"What are you?"

She paused. "A prostitute." (This explained why she didn't answer me when I asked her in what way she was known in our previous session.)

"You became a prostitute because...?"

"I had to eat...baby crying," she said, sounding as though she had no other choice. "I'm so *ashamed*," she muttered.

"Go to the morning of the last day of your life, Jessica."

"It's spring. Cool, but not so bad...*stupid* horses. They stink! I *hate* that smell. Ugh," she said, crinkling her nose as though she smelled it. "I'm inside my room...sleepy. Mark and Lisa are playing."

"How old is Mark?"

"Two...maybe three. Blue jeans, pants...cute...jacket." She smiled. "He looks like George."

"How long have you been living in Dodge?"

"A year...maybe two. Not that long. I can't wait to go back home. I miss Momma."

"Move time forward through the day now."

"Working...flirtatious...fun...in the bar...saloon...creepy guy."

"Have you seen him before, or is he someone new?"

"He's the man," she muttered, before her voice trailed off.

"Have you met him before?" I asked.

"No."

"I'm not comfortable...other girls are drawn to him. Something's not right with him."

"How can you tell?"

"He's evil. I feel it."

"What's his name?"

She paused for a long time before saying, "I don't know. I'm not sure."

"Is he new to town?"

"No."

"I'm going to snap my fingers, and you'll know his name." *Snap.*

"Frank Beh...Bender," she said, before pausing and adding, "He's killed before."

"Who did he kill?"

"It's a scandal...the whole family was in on it. They didn't kill the law person. The law got a hold of them. He's killed before...family. His family killed before...Ben..." Her voice trailed off again.

"Who did they kill?" I asked.

"Law...scandal...they didn't...whole family was in on it...he didn't kill the law person. He followed me...it's late afternoon. He's yelling at me...kills me...knife...he runs...no one knows...ooh, my baby...I'm floating high and higher. I died in my hotel room...bleeding out."

"Who finds you?"

"Mary...wife of the hotel person. She's protecting Mark. I'm sorry. Baby, I'm sorry," she whispered through tears.

"Float even higher now, and much time passes. What were you to learn in your lifetime as Jessica?" I questioned.

"Obedience," she answered.

"Did you learn it?"

"No."

I emerged Bobbie from hypnosis. She was quiet for a few moments before she began talking. "It was a whole family involved in that. The fort was nothing like Fort Apache. Just a set of buildings. The hotel owner wasn't from this county. Mary was his wife. I think they took Mark in as their own son."

"Do you have any idea for his reason to kill you?"

"No. There was no reason for it. Why would someone do that?"

"What happened to George?"

"Pestilence…rats were in the fort. The fort looked deserted. There was a graveyard and mounds."

Both of us were curious about what we would find when we began researching her lifetime as Jessica, but what we discovered shocked us both.

～

Jessica thought her father might have been in the Civil War (1861–1865). The dates certainly made it possible. Although she sounded uncertain, she said she was from Barstow and thought the state was Utah. I couldn't find a town called Barstow in Utah, but there is one in California. The settlement of Barstow began in the late 1840s as a Mormon settlement, part of what was called the Mormon Corridor, which began in Utah. It was possible that she lived in or was familiar with both places. Barstow was named after William Barstow Strong, the former president of the Atchison, Topeka, and Santa Fe Railway, which had routes from both Barstow and Salt Lake City, Utah. The railroad came to Dodge City in September of 1872 and, as she said, it would have taken "days on the train" to travel there.

Jessica had described "whitish wood trees" when she said she lived in Utah. Aspens are trees native to Utah and have the white bark she described. Bobbie confirmed that aspens were the trees in her regression when she saw a photo of them.

An army fort called Fort Dodge did exist near Dodge. Located five miles east of Dodge, it consisted of simple buildings without fortified walls and was exactly as Bobbie had described. Established in 1865, it was described as one of the most important forts on the western frontier. Its purpose was to protect the wagon trains along the Santa Fe Trail traveling to New Mexico from attacking Native Americans. It was known as the journey of death, as it was often without water the whole distance. The fort was abandoned in 1882. It confirmed what Bobbie had said; the fort looked nothing like what one would expect a fort to look, as it was just buildings with no enclosed wall.

Courtesy of Legends of America
Fort Dodge

Dodge City was founded in 1872. The first business to open was a whiskey bar built by George Hoover from Canada. This confirmed that the bar owner was in fact from another country—a foreigner, as Bobbie had said. He and his wife Margaret raised a foster son, George Curry, who became a Roosevelt Rough Rider. Could George Curry have been Jessica's son, Mark, whom she had left behind when she died? Could she have gotten the names confused? George was Mark's father's name. Could Margaret's nickname be Mary? It was certainly possible.

In 1873, a Colonel Biddle and his wife Ellen were traveling to Fort Lyon, Colorado, where he was to assume command of the post. By then there were general merchandise stores, a dance hall, and a saloon in Dodge. Brothels were established where women worked for dance halls, earning money for dancing and prostitution. Biddle's wife, Ellen, wrote an interesting note in 1907 about the Dodge House in Dodge City, titled *Reminiscences of a Soldier's Wife*, which describes the environment of Dodge.

"The journey to Fort Lyon was full of interest...Dodge City was the terminus of the road, a terrible little frontier town. On arriving we went to the hotel to remain overnight. It was a wooden building, without paint or wash of any kind, with two front doors, one leading into a saloon, the other into a parlor. Fort Dodge was about five miles distant, and the soldiers on pass came to the town, drank villainous whiskey which these saloons kept, and after a drink or two the men would be crazy drunk, their clothes and everything they had with them stolen, and when the saloon-keepers had gotten all they possessed they were thrown out into the streets."

Courtesy of Ford County Historical Society
Dodge City in 1874

Could the Great Western Hotel be the building Jessica described that began with a *G* and was a long word? Could it be where she had lived and was killed?

Dodge
Courtesy of Gunsmoke

Bobbie contacted Legends of America, asking about local forts and their conditions. They wrote to her saying, "Fort Dodge was the precursor to Dodge City. Sanitation at the time in most places was very bad. Water could have all kinds of things in it. There was no refrigeration so food went bad but they ate it anyway. There were probably lots of critters running abound biting people, fleas, ticks, etc. and the fact everything was just built on the ground and a bunch of folks around just leads to disease. All the plagues in Europe were due to bad sanitation, lack of medical knowledge or drugs, rats feeding on garbage, fleas on the rats spreading and biting people causing illness and people in close proximity spreading the disease. Vicious circle."

Bobbie began to investigate if there was a Bender family in Dodge. Her e-mail to me got my attention immediately, as in the subject line she wrote, "Oh My Gawd!!!!" She wrote, "I found the man who had killed Jessica. His name was Bender and in fact, the entire Bender family was quite infamous. John Bender Sr., Kate Bender, John Bender Jr. and their daughter Kate, all of German decent looking to come west for a fresh start. John Bender was described as a tall, slender handsome man with auburn hair and a *mustache*. He would laugh aimlessly causing people to think of him as a half-wit, though later on, many believed it was to disguise his clever nature."

During the regression, Bobbie had said there was "something not right with him." I, too, researched the infamous Benders and learned they used the front half of their cabin for an inn and grocery store. Travelers could find rest, supplies, and a warm meal. By 1873, rumors began circulating regarding ten missing people, including a prominent physician. Many attended a meeting regarding the problem, and all volunteered to have their premises searched. All but the Benders, who remained silent.

Sometime later, a neighbor noticed the Bender Inn was abandoned. When a search party arrived, at first fearful they, too, had been victims, they found a terrible smell inside the inn. On the floor, they discovered a trap door that had been nailed shut. Once pried open, they found a hole with clotted blood but no bodies. They moved the cabin to look beneath it but found nothing until they unearthed a vegetable garden. They found the bludgeoned doctor with his throat cut from ear to ear. Ten bodies were found on the property, some mutilated. There were many other corpses found in the area, and many mysterious disappearances of travelers. Locals believe the Benders killed more than twenty people. Two bodies that were found included an unidentified male and female. The knife that was used was also found. Bobbie reported she had an eerie feeling when she saw a photograph of the knife.

Bobbie wrote to me in an e-mail:

"Bender was my first tangible validation...a name that came to me after our first session. It's all a mystery to me how some of the pieces fit in so well and others are more slowly coming together. I researched Barstow in Kansas and came up with Mary Louise Barstow who founded a finishing school for young ladies in 1884. My head swirled with this...was she Jessica's mother and she founded the school out of grief? Or is this something none other than my mind trying to fill in the blanks. Still though totally blown away by Bender..."

Through a computer program, Bobbie was able to recreate what she felt her murderer looked like.

Courtesy of Bobbie
John Bender

Later we found an etching of John Bender Jr. that looked remarkably similar to her description. John Bender Jr. was actually a man named John Gebhardt.

Courtesy of Legends of America (Photos from *The Benders of Kansas* by John Towner, Kan-Okla Publishing, Wichita, KS, 1913, reprinted 1995.)

The above sketch is the only known likeness of John Bender Jr.

Bobbie was cold, even shivering, at times during the regression because she was bleeding out as a result of the stabbing. The more blood you loose the colder you feel.

Bobbie's initial interest was to discover if psychic mediums could reveal a person's past life, which the person could then recover through a hypnotic regression. Instead, she was documenting the past life itself and finding validation of that lifetime. Her regression experiences as Jessica seemed to be taking her in a new direction. Bobbie wanted to find evidence of the life she had once lived.

BOBBIE

James Bridger

T hree months passed before I saw Bobbie again. She wanted to know more about the lives psychic medium Chip Coffey had told her about and invited Linda Farr, a local spirit medium, to my office. Bobbie was interested in discovering if she could see the same lifetimes Chip had revealed and had already received a brief phone reading from Linda.

However, it wasn't until I had nearly completed writing this book, and long after our regression work, that I asked Bobbie if I could watch the video of her phone reading with Linda. This is the transcript of that reading:

You are being told to journey. Five different places on the planet. There are two in the United States. One in India. I'm not getting clarity on the other two. One is in Washington, DC. I have a strong pull to the actual city. You will recover a great deal of your energy there. The Smithsonian museum. The other place is in the north and middle of the county. Very open land. Vacant land. Acres and acres. Do not underestimate the gifts you will give to humanity. And that's it. She's gone. It's about assisting others. There will be much ridicule. Be prepared. You'll be attacked for what you are trying to bring forward. Stand fast. Stand true to what you know is true. Know that what you're experiencing is real. Know that the people who are ridiculing you are working from a place of fear and ignorance. They can't see what you see.

Neither Bobbie nor I had personally met Linda until she came to my office. Linda's petite frame and short blond hair reminded me of actress Sandy Duncan, who appeared in the Broadway musical *Peter Pan*. Just as I was imagining her flying through the air, I learned her former job was as a patrol officer for the Dallas Police Department. My image of her abruptly changed to Wonder Woman.

I learned that Linda was born into a family of gifted mediums in London, England. She grew up watching her great-grandmother and grandmother read tea leaves and conduct séances. Watching them speak to spirit was normal for her, and before long, she was doing the same. As an adult she trained to develop her gifts and has been helping clients worldwide hear from their lost loved ones for more than thirty years.

Bobbie and I hadn't discussed her phone reading with Linda, so I was curious what would unfold. I knew Bobbie most certainly had numerous other lifetimes in addition to those told to her by Chip. I wondered silently what the chances were that Linda would hone in on those same lives Chip had unveiled until she began Bobbie's reading.

"You've had well over one hundred lives," Linda began. "I see a lifetime where you were in India as a disabled starving child. Another lifetime in Washington, DC, as a politician. Male. In Greece. Female. Many centuries ago, you had to care for someone. A servant—slave. You lived to be sixteen. Australia...as an aborigine...before white man. Medicine woman. Deeply spiritual. Shaman." Linda rattled off lifetimes like a grocery list. "Montana. Open land. Native American. Very painful death. Very terrifying. Tortured. Indian. This is where your anger comes from. Anyone treated inhumanly."

My eyes shot up from the paper I was vigorously taking notes on to look at Linda. Was this the same crucifixion life Chip Coffey had told Bobbie about? I wondered. Bobbie asked Linda to expand on her lifetime as a Native American.

"It's more of a scene of torture," Linda began. "You were hung upside down. They thought you were doing the work of the devil. It was in a large flat area...plains, mountain range, near Canadian border? Blackfoot or Sioux or combination. It took three days for you to die."

Bobbie asked, "Was I a male?"

"Not sure," Linda answered. "You held a prominent position. Your name was Mehahtoc. Time period of death was 1602. From Quebec...they held Christian belief." (She referred to the men who had killed Mehahtoc.)

We paused for a few moments, sitting silently to absorb all that Linda had just reported. I was a bit stunned. I knew Bobbie would be happy to hear confirmation that two spirit mediums had told her of the lifetime as a Native American that was tortured or, as Chip Coffey had said, crucified. Bobbie and I looked at each other solemnly.

Bobbie addressed Linda. "One of the things that came up in our phone reading were other past lives. Tell me more about the lifetime as a politician you told me about on the phone."

Linda responded immediately. "It feels like a hand or fingers or something like that. The reason it's there is you signed...I'm seeing finger bones. They have this part of your body there. It had something to do with slavery. You will find yourself in the Smithsonian Institute. You will find your hand or the bones of your hand. Or bones. Feels like a hand or fingers."

All my mind could conjure up was a black, withered hand, and I secretly questioned the authenticity of the information and Linda's ability. I admit I was skeptical. I wondered if she meant it more as a metaphor. Maybe the person had a hand in something with slavery, or there was actually a wax hand. I could not imagine the bones of his hand would be on display, and I silently doubted we'd discover anything.

"The reason your hand is there," Linda continued, "is that you signed some form of an important document, and for some reason, they have your hand. Not yours literally. It feels like a finger or hand. I'm not sure. I'm seeing finger bones and a ring? Something on finger bones...they have part of your body there. It's the Smithsonian. Definitely the Smithsonian. It has something to do with Africans coming to this country. It has to do with legalizing the right to own people. There had to be laws written that actually legalized owning people, so people could own and use these people. They couldn't just do it. They had to have something agreed upon that made it legal, and you wanted this to happen, so that's what you...you signed this.

You signed this into law. You had to do with making it legal. There could not be ramifications because there were several people from the church that were fighting this at the time. It was the Protestants who were saying this is not correct because they had just come from…OK, this is getting good. The people who were opposed to slavery because they left what they considered to be slavery to come here, so they were very much wanting freedom for all people, and yet the people that wanted the slaves for financial benefit would bypass him, so they had to have laws that overrode what this religious sect wanted."

Bobbie looked at me intently and said, "I want to explore this lifetime in Washington, DC." And so we began.

Bobbie continued to go into hypnosis effortlessly. I was no longer concerned she'd have performance anxiety from the cameras and lights. "Notice a long hallway with many doorways and find the door marked Washington, DC," I instructed.

"I found it," she whispered.

"Step inside and find yourself in a beautiful mist. At the count of one, the mist will disappear, and you'll find yourself in a scene, situation, or event that has everything to do with why you are here today. Three, two, one. Be there now, and when you're ready, tell me what is happening."

"There are buildings."

"Inside or out?"

"Outside."

"Day or night?"

"Day."

"Are you wearing anything on your feet?"

"Shoes…leather…man's…old-fashioned. Heavy…dark…charcoal…stockings," she continued, as she described her clothing. "I'm a *big* man." She emphasized the word *big*, and I wondered if she was referring to her height or weight.

"How old are you?"

"Forties to fifties…hair…weird…bald, but I have hair."

"Tell me about the scene you find yourself in."

"Capitol? Leaving office or meeting…satisfied…about money."

I was curious who of importance she was with and asked her, "Who is the most important person there?"

She surprised me with her quick, unabashed answer. "Why *me*, of course!" she answered, as though I were ignorant for asking. I silently laughed, hearing his arrogance. "More money."

"What is your name?"

"John…James…Bridger." She then began to spell it out letter by letter: "B-R-I-D-G-E-R. I'm a Royalist…very open area, not a big city…people… lots of people."

"Who do you work with?"

"I can't tell."

"Where are you?"

"Virginia…Roanoke…home, I think…in the meeting."

"At the count of one, you can hear everything being said. Three, two, one."

"I'm in a small room…small room with desks…people upset…I'm just listening to who's speaking," she said before pausing. "I think it's like Congress…I don't know…I'm standing back next to the wall. Observing. Yelling. Too much noise…*angry!*"

"Because?"

"I can't tell…hmm…British influences."

"How do you feel about the topic they are discussing?"

"Concerned."

"Because?"

"It affects my money."

"Because?"

"The outcome somehow." She paused again before adding, "I can't tell. It's about business…need to influence somehow…the outcome is important to me…somehow. Humph. "Something I paid for…wiry man…had influence."

"I'm going to snap my fingers, and you'll know his name." *Snap.*

"Douglas."

"What's his last name?" I asked.

"I can't tell." I snapped my fingers. "Chamberson."

"What is his role? What is he doing there?" I questioned.

"Persuading. Still yelling. I wish this nonsense would get over with! It's a waste of my time!" she said angrily. I could feel Bridger's impatience with those present in the meeting. "Damn *fools*!" Bridger was clearly visibly upset by the meeting.

"Who is the most important person in the room?" I asked once again.

"Me! I am!" she answered, obviously frustrated I asked such a stupid question.

"What year is it?"

"1765?...I don't know." I knew it couldn't be Congress if the year was correct, but it must have been some other governing group.

"Go now to the next significant event. Three, two, one. Be there now."

"I'm home. It's night...fireplace."

"Who do you live with?"

"A woman. My wife, I think. Ester. I know her...she puts up with me. She's so quiet, demure...children. She doesn't like what I do. There's a door. Fireplace is to the left. Dining room to the right. Old, quite comfortable, old-fashioned. Children younger...six, five maybe, one more...older. There's an upstairs kitchen in back."

"Do you have an office in your home?"

"There's a desk, chair, paperwork...it's organized. Humph. Pen...feather in a well. Books to left. Children." She smiled. "Hmmm. They're playing. I love my children. One boy, one girl, other one. I can't figure out. Apples and cinnamon cooking...smells *good*," she said, emphasizing her last word.

"What season is it?"

"Chilly."

"Go now to the next significant event."

"I'm in a carriage...with others...driver."

"Where are you going?"

"There are buildings...quaint...morning."

"Arrive at your destination."

"Office...walking into office. Not my office. The office is dark...inside. Hmmm. Somebody else's. I'm selling...talking...*impatient*!"

"Because?"

"It's taking too long!" she stammered, clearly irritated.

"What is taking too long?" I dared to ask.

"Don't know. I have to wait for other people. They have to choose... for or against. Land...something about land...Pennsylvania...Virginia... somewhere. Foreclosure...or something. Pompous ass! *Idiot!*" she said with annoyed authority.

"Move time forward, James."

"Regret...I hurt people. I just know I did. I'm older...much older...children grown."

"Go now to the most important day of who you were," I said, hoping to understand who James was.

"Recognition Day...outside...politics parade...Washington again. 1700s... seventeen...I don't know. I'm outside...lots of others...happy."

"What are they happy about?"

"Freedom! Freedom from the British! It's new...we're new...we're *new*."

"How do you feel?"

"Pride...and scared...lost old friends."

"Because?"

"Nations...England...new beginnings...scary business."

"How will it affect your business?"

"I don't know yet...fools...rejoicing," she said, sounding indignant and arrogant.

"What is your role?"

"I wanted the king to win...this messes things up. I was comfortable. Old. Fifties...cranky."

"Go now to the morning of the last day of your life."

"Old...I'm not feeling well."

"Looking back on your life, how would you describe it?"

"Incomplete. I could have done more. Influenced a nation or politics."

"How do people view you?"

"Mixed...control...builder of some kind."

"Go through the death scene and find yourself floating above and looking down."

"I'm alone," Bobbie said quietly.

"Times passes, and you have all the knowledge and all the wisdom. What did you want to learn on a soul level?"

"Tolerance."

"Did you learn it?"

Bobbie hesitated before she answered, "Eventually."

I emerged her from hypnosis. Bobbie turned to me and said with a doleful look on her face, "I was *not* a nice man. I was so arrogant. I saw the desk, the fountain pen. I died alone." Her eyes looked off to the side of me, as her mind drifted to the images she had seen in the regression. "The British were involved. I was a redcoat."

Bobbie complained of feeling dizzy and having some nausea after the session. I did a few exercises to ground her, but the feeling was still faint, and I couldn't figure out why. I asked if she was hungry.

Bobbie had agreed not to do any research that would compromise the integrity of her work. After she left the office, I quickly googled for information on a John or James Bridger and found nothing on him. Had we come to a dead end?

BOBBIE

Captain Joseph Bridger

At her next appointment, Bobbie said she had resisted the urge to explore Bridger or the meeting that he had attended or any other details. I chose not to tell her that I had researched John or James Bridger, only to find nothing on him. She said she had thought about the session and felt she was a British officer. "I'm not seeing the dates clearly. Kind of like with Jessica. Dates are floating all over. But it has to be the American Revolution, since redcoats were all over the place," she said, referring to what she had seen in her regression.

Once she was hypnotized, we began the regression. "Go back to your lifetime as a young John Bridger," I instructed. I wanted to see where his life began.

"England. My clothing is heavy. Hot. I'm standing on cobblestones."

"Tell me about your shoes."

"Black, buckle, loose...coat, black, church."

"Are you outside?"

"Yes. It's daytime. The air is crisp. It's Sunday. I'm in front of the church... standing on cobblestones. Circle pathways."

"What is the name of the church?"

"Church of England." She paused before adding, "Joseph. That's my name. Joseph. My family is proper." She had corrected her name to Joseph. I wondered if it would make a difference when we researched him.

"Turn around and notice your surroundings, Joseph," I requested.

"I'm in the country…beautiful."

"How old are you?"

"Seventeen."

"What is your last name?" I asked again to be certain.

"Bridger. I'm looking around. Church is old…beautiful…traditional… brick face, garden, quaint. Humph. We're late for church."

"Who are you with?"

"Mother…she's wearing a long, flowing dress…dark colors…conservative."

"What is the name of the town you live in?"

"I don't know." A long pause. "G…R…I don't know."

"That's OK. What happens next?"

"We're in the church. There's a sermon. I'm sitting on the left side, almost center, next to Father…bored. Huh! There's a woman…girl. I think I like her. I wish this was over with…the sermon."

"Move time forward, Joseph. Find your answers."

"I'm on a ship…in my twenties. In uniform, a young officer, red coat, embroidery on sleeves. Humph. I'm going to America. I feel it's about honor, duty." She paused before continuing, "Sad…family…ship of the line…oh…the sea."

"How many men are on board?"

"Seventy-two," she said without hesitation. "She's a third rate…(inaudible—boat?). Seventy-two *guns*, one hundred twelve men," she corrected herself.

"Are you a passenger?"

"I'm in the army, not the navy. Captain?"

"You are going to America because…?"

"Orders. Help establish colonies…first line of defense…against the French. We don't want the French there. They're in Canada…show of force to establish colonies."

"Where do you land once you arrive in America?"

"Hampton Roads. It's a disappointment…so primitive…rowing ashore… some town. Can't see town…" Her voice trailed off.

"What happens next?"

"I'm a paymaster. I hate the job. It's beneath me. I oversee pay...payment to troops. I'm extremely bored...not what I thought it'd be."

"What happens next?"

"I'm in the ranks. There are hundreds."

"Where are you?"

"Not sure...orders to crush the rebellion. Cowards! They place women on ramparts!" she said, clearly angry about the situation.

"Because?"

"So we cannot shill." I wondered if this was a word used in that time period for gunfire. I wrote it down phonetically. "We cannot fire!" she said, agitated.

"Move time gently ahead."

"They put a blaze to the town. Why? Such a waste...British, not my men, burned buildings. Jamestown...forced out of Jamestown...Governor. We came back. Captain...Colonel...Captain...I don't know. Company light infantry. 1600s. Indians. Some kind...people upset with them, though."

"Go to the next significant event."

"Martha! I think she's my daughter...such a baby," she said, smiling.

"Describe the scene you find yourself in."

"Home...relaxing at home...I hold her...and feed her."

"How old is she?"

"Young...five or six...comfortable home. I think it's in town somewhere."

"How old are you?"

"I'm forty or fifty...thereabouts. I own land. I'm arrogant." Her tone indicated she was surprised as she realized this.

"Because?"

"I'm important...with the council or something...county...something."

"Go to where you work, Joseph."

"I'm in a building...small table...feather quill...other men there. Isle of Wight. Virginia. North Carolina."

"Why are you important?"

"Something about a church…don't know…Church of England. Joseph. I think he's my son…irritating little boy…as a young man, stubborn!"

"Because?"

"His ways are not my ways."

"Because?"

"I don't know."

"Do you work with him?"

"No!"

"Go to the next important event."

"I can't…um…inside, light, alone in bed…head hurts. I'm much older… sixties maybe."

"Looking back on your life, Joseph, how would you describe it?"

"I feel sadness over Jamestown. We were run out."

"How did you feel?"

"Anger! Something about the church."

"I'm going to snap my fingers, and you'll know." *Snap.*

"Council member or board…Church of England."

"Where are you living?"

"Smithville…I don't know."

"Go to the morning of the last day of your life."

"Not feeling well. Isle of Wight…lived there. My head hurts…tired… proud of Joseph. He's not like me." (Bobbie was referencing Bridger's son by the same name.)

"Were you involved in slavery?"

"I don't know."

We needed more information. "Go back to the council," I instructed.

"Governor talking…humph…*pompous ass!*" she said, clearly incensed.

"Look around," I directed. "Tell me what is happening."

"Men…I'm in uniform. They're angry…at the governor…something about Indians."

"How do you feel about it?"

"There's nothing to be afraid of."

"Describe where you are."

"There's a large building…greenish…white trim…porch…like a town hall…small town. I think it's Jamestown…dirt road…in a clearing. Building is behind me…church in front…shop to right."

"Are there people present?"

"Yes. Man, white shirt, trousers, black, young, tri-corner (tricorne) hats."

"Any women?"

"Not in sight."

"Street signs?"

"No."

"Weather?"

"Summer or spring…sunny…inside ramparts. To left…ramparts or wall."

"How do you feel?"

"Anger, fear, and frustration. We're not doing enough…to protect."

"To protect whom?"

"The town…some gentlemen. Men of the trade…soldiers…redcoats… British…white trousers…leggings…they're accusing the governor of something. Baker…Bleaker…" she said, struggling to get the correct name. "Light brown coat, wig, trousers, leggings, cane! Some kind…" her voice trailed off.

"Go to the last day of your life, Joseph."

"My head hurt a long time. I could have done more. I hurt people sometimes…said mean things. I was angry…always angry…asleep…nightcap."

She went through the death scene on her own before saying, "I'm sorry for my arrogance…being ruthless and pompous. My wife, men…they respond. It's OK."

I emerged Bobbie.

"I have a bad headache and feel nausea again," she said. "I remember horses. Saddest part, and humiliating, is that we were about to attack the town rebels or something, but we retreated. We couldn't fire our guns because of the women on the ramparts." Bobbie drew a rough map of where everything was located in Jamestown, including the church, shop, town hall, and another building.

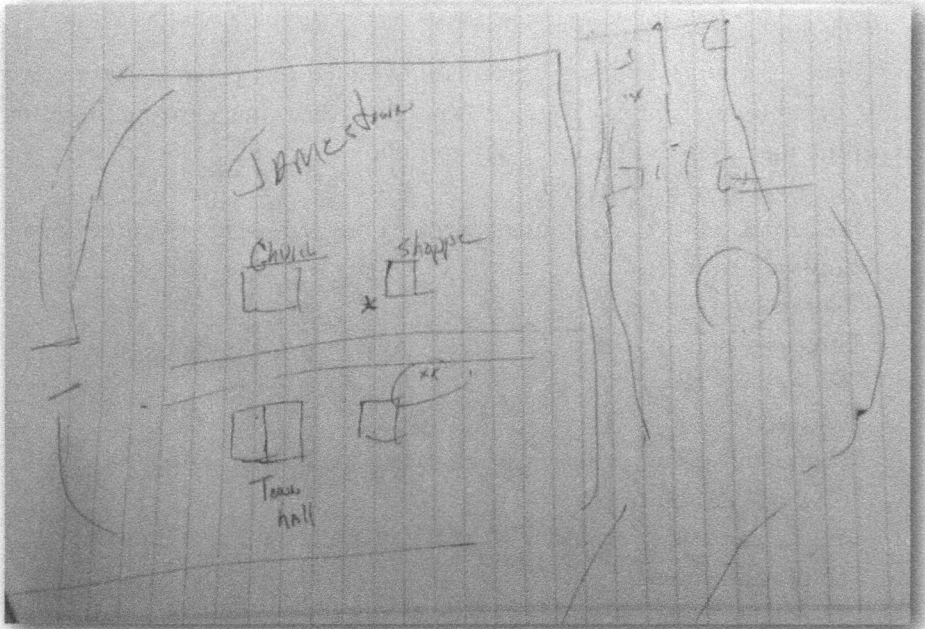

Courtesy of Bobbie
Map Bobbie drew of Jamestown

I could hardly wait to look up Joseph Bridger. Perhaps the new first name would give me different results than John Bridger. I was far from disappointed.

~

Colonel Joseph Bridger was born in 1628 in *Gloucester, England.* (During the regression, Bobbie had started to spell the name of where she was from with a *G* and said there was an *R*—the first and last letters of Gloucester.) He married *Hester* (I thought she said Ester during the regression) Pitt in 1654 before traveling to Virginia the same year. They had three sons and four daughters. One *son* was named *Joseph,* and a *daughter* was named Mary.

Bridger was a member of the Virginia House of Burgesses from 1657 to 1658 and again in 1663 as *Captain* Joseph Bridger and once more as Adjutant General of Virginia in 1676. The House of Burgesses was a group of wealthy landowners who grew and sold tobacco. They were the first assembly of elect-ed representatives of the English colonists in North America. I wondered if this could this be the legislative body that Bridger thought was like Congress. The first meeting of the House of Burgesses was held in *Jamestown, Virginia.*

He served as the co-acting governor of Virginia from 1684 to 1685. He was a *Royalist* who, until his death at the age of fifty-eight in 1686, served King Charles II of England. As a member of nearly every important com-mittee, Bridger was often named to deal with intercolonial problems and was influential in subjects pertaining to military defense. Bridger was one of the wealthiest and most prominent men in Colonial Virginia at the time.

At his death, he owned more than twelve thousand acres of land in Isle of Wight County alone, making him one of the ten largest landowners of his day in Virginia. He was the builder of Whitemarsh Plantation's twenty-one-room brick mansion—one of the two largest houses ever built in seventeenth-century Virginia.

My research revealed that the rebellion Bridger was involved in was Bacon's Rebellion in 1676, named for Colonel Nathaniel Bacon. (Bobbie had a hard time getting the name but said *Baker* or *Bleaker.*) It was the first rebel-lion in the American colonies, during which he supported Governor Berkeley. History reports that Bacon's forces outnumbered Berkeley's, and they *retreat-ed* across the river. Colonel Bridger was denounced in Bacon's proclamation, having fled to Virginia's eastern shore during the rebellion. However, he was promoted to general by his superiors after the rebellion. His son Joseph sided with Nathaniel Bacon, and for this he was disinherited by his father.

The discovery of tobacco started the plantation economy in Virginia and created a demand for cheap labor. The labor was done at first by poor white indentured servants and then by black slaves. Both slaves and indentured ser-vants joined in Bacon's Rebellion. The rebellion occurred in the midst of a fundamental shift in the labor force after planters decided to replace white indentured servants with more easily controlled enslaved Africans. Bacon's Rebellion was successful largely because he helped direct the people's fear and anger toward Indians and Governor Berkeley, who was considered to be a friend to the Indians. Colonists believed Berkeley was failing to defend the frontier against attacks by Native Indians. Bacon felt that Indians and whites could not peacefully live together. One of the results of the rebellion led to the introduction of the Indian Reservation system in 1677.

Colonel Bridger was said to be a man of strong emotions and given at times to angry outbursts. I found this statement especially interesting, as I had certainly witnessed these outbursts during Bobbie's regression. Bridger had used the term "ship of the line," describing the boat as "third rate" with "seventy-two guns." Knowing Bobbie had been in the navy, I asked her what those terms meant. "I don't know what it means. The size of the ship? They may have covered this in a history class of the navy in basic training, but that was nearly forty years ago, and I just don't remember." Bobbie told me she loved the navy. "I've never felt more at home or in life in general than when I was on a ship."

I googled third rate ships and discovered the "seventy-four" meant the ship carried seventy-four guns, and it was a type of two-decked ship referred to as *ship of the line.* Developed by the French navy in the 1740s, they spread to the British Royal Navy, where they were classed as *third rates.* I was surprised by this specific knowledge by Bridger, even if he was off by two guns. However, Bridger died in 1686. Over fifty years prior to the ship being developed. I began to wonder if we had stumbled onto knowledge from another lifetime.

I wrote to the Smithsonian Institute, asking if there was a finger, hand, or even bones, something to do with slavery and Joseph Bridger at the Smithsonian. My request was sent to the department of anthropology in the National Museum of Natural History and was answered promptly. The answer stunned me. The Smithsonian had conducted an analysis of Joseph Bridger's skeletal remains several years earlier. *The bones of Bridger had been sent to the Smithsonian,* except for one bone which remained for further testing.

Linda Farr was right! We found his bones at the Smithsonian! I was astonished.

Upon further investigation, I discovered the remains of Colonel Joseph Bridger were exhumed from the chancel of Historic Saint Luke's Church by famed forensic anthropologist Douglas Owsley and his team from the Smithsonian Institution. The primary reason his remains were taken to the Smithsonian was to research the possibility of a common cause of death among the wealthy during that time period by examining their bones. The event was filmed by the History Channel for the "Written in Bone: Life and Death in Colonial Chesapeake" exhibit at the National Museum of Natural History in Washington, DC, in 2007. However, there was another video, no longer accessible, that I watched, which showed Bridger's *finger bone* being the first bone exhumed.

Colonel Bridger's remains, originally buried in 1686 on his plantation, were moved several miles away to the Historic Saint Luke's Church in 1894, where he had lain until 2007, when he was moved to Washington, DC. He was returned from the Smithsonian by Alain Outlaw, husband of Merry Outlaw, a descendent of Colonel Bridger. Both are archeologists. All his bones except a femur bone, which as of this writing remains at the Smithsonian, were reinterred at Saint Luke's Church under a ledger stone in 2014.

They learned that Bridger most likely died from lead poisoning. Those of wealth (and he was one of the ten wealthiest Virginians of his time) drank from pewter, which had a very high lead content. When his remains were tested, his bone lead levels were 149 ppm—more than seven times the average level today. No doubt he suffered from the effects of lead poisoning, which include headaches, dizziness, and nausea. I had found the reason for the dizziness Bobbie felt during some of her regressions.

~

Bobbie reached out to the Smithsonian as well, which led her to contact Jean Tomes, the founder of the Bridger Family Association, a documented descendant of Joseph Bridger and a member of the Jamestowne Society. She is also the Virginia state president of the National Society of Daughters of Founders and Patriots of America. Bobbie began correspondence with Jean through e-mail, telling her she was creating a documentary, elements of which would include Jamestown and Joseph Bridger. They set up a phone appointment, during which Bobbie told Jean about the documentary, past life regression, hypnosis, that a subject who was regressed was discovered to have been Colonel Joseph Bridger, and that much of the information revealed in the regression had been validated through Internet research. Jean asked if the subject was a descendant of Bridger and was curious why Joseph Jr. had been disinherited. Jean was surprised when she learned Bridger was a female in this life, and when she kept pressing for more information on the subject, Bobbie admitted she was the subject. Jean became silent over the phone.

Bobbie told Jean I was a hypnotist specializing in past life regression and about my book *Angel Babies*. Jean then spoke to her much-loved daughter-in-law, who had lost a baby and subsequently read my book. Feeling safe or confident, I'm not sure which, Jean was open to hearing more about Bobbie's regression and her past life as Bridger.

Bobbie set up a conference call with Jean. Bobbie, Linda, and I sat in my office and put Jean on speaker phone. Jean spoke about her ninth great-grandfather Colonel Bridger, stating that everything she knew had been handed down as family lore. This is a transcript of Jean's conversation with us:

Jean: *In 1984 the bones of Bridger were moved from the farm to the church. Only one quarter of the bones were moved. They discovered this during the exhuming of his body. The family wanted to get DNA, which can only be attained from teeth. He had retained his teeth, which was unusual because wealthy people ate sugar and typically lost their teeth. During that time period, men were typically five feet three. He was six feet five to six feet seven. A giant of a man at the time. The bones were in a little brick vault. A finger bone was the first bone that was exhumed.*

Linda had thought there were fingers or bones at the Smithsonian. Bridger's finger was the first bone held. Linda had described to Jean that Bridger was very tall for that time period. You could hear Jean's excitement as she told us that the Smithsonian estimated him to be at least six feet seven inches tall. Bobbie had described Bridger as a big man. Further confirmations!

Jean: *His son Joseph married a girl whose brother worked with Bacon. Bacon kidnapped the wives of leading citizens and put them in a place on the front line.* (This must have been the ramparts Bobbie mentioned when Bridger was so angry they couldn't shoot because of the women.) *Hester was Bridger's wife's name. In Bridger's will, he described each room of his house. He had twenty-one rooms. Brick. It was the second-largest home in the region. The house burned two times. Every Christmas, the woman who lives in the house now says she hears foot-steps walking heavily up the stairs and assumes it is his spirit.*

Regarding slavery, he was a member of the House of Burgess from 1657 to 1673, and from 1673 to 1686, he was on the council of state and co-acting as governor of Virginia. He was paymaster for the British army, just as Bobbie had said. Bridger had two African slaves. This was at a time before slavery was as we think of it now. Late 1600s is when real slavery happened.

Jean was curious what Bridger looked like, as there were no drawings or paintings of him. Bobbie told Jean she had brought in a sketch artist to draw Bridger from Linda's description of what he looked like to her.

Courtesy of artist Lora Humphrey
Colonel Joseph Bridger

Linda said, "He had green eyes."

Sounding surprised, Jean said, "I have green eyes!"

"And he had a high forehead," Linda continued.

Jean added, "His skull was in twenty-four pieces, but we knew he had a high forehead."

"And he had black hair," Linda added.

"That's the Roman influence," Jean replied.

In a separate e-mail, Jean wrote:

This afternoon I was reading some books on-line about Colonial Virginia (what else?) and came across something that jumped right out at me...This is from "Southside Virginia Families," Vol. 1 by John Bennet Boddie. He did a fabulous job in these books. On page 18–19 in Vol. 1, above it states: 'When Bacon besieged Jamestown these ladies wearing white aprons were compelled to stand before the breastworks so they could be recognized by their husbands and Gov. Berkeley ceased his cannonade. Ann, wife of Col. Thomas Ballard, Mrs. Elizabeth Bacon, wife of Nathaniel Bacon Sr. (cousin of Nathanial Bacon Jr. the Rebel), Mrs. Angelica Bray, wife of Col. James Bray and Mrs. Elizabeth Page wife of Col. John Page. All were wives of members of the Council and were captured by Nathanial Bacon Jr. during the raid on Middle Plantation (home of the Governor.)' It did not mention Hester Bridger, wife of Gen. Joseph Bridger so they may have been at their home "Whitemarsh" at the time, which is across the James River from Jamestown or she may have been sent to the Eastern Shore of Virginia where Gov. Berkeley and Joseph Bridger finally went."

Further confirmation of the women being on the wall or ramparts, just as Bobbie had said.

In *The Tidewater Hearth*, John D. Bridgers, MD, wrote:

(Joseph Bridger)...came listed as 'Capt. Joseph Bridger.' There's no record as to how he received this military rank, but as we review the plethora and continuity of armed conflict, which marked English history of the day, it seems likely he could have enjoyed an army career as a young man.

He came sponsoring a fairly large group of other would-be pilgrims from Gloucester, so either by inheritance, venture or both he had obviously accrued some worth before he left for the colony.

When one brought others, mostly they came as indentured servants for a term of seven years to their sponsor, and, as well, the sponsor received an extra grant of 50 acres of land for each whose passage he had paid.

So he was set-up as a considerable landholder from the beginning...Joseph arrived in Virginia around 1650. Among those brought with him was the family of Thomas Pitt, his daughter, Hester, having married Joseph Bridger before the migrating group left Gloucester.

From the beginning Joseph was an officer in the Virginia militias, rising quickly to the rank of colonel...but after subsequent service in "Bacon's Rebellion" he was promoted to Adjutant General.

When General Bridger died in 1686 he names his two older sons and his daughters as his sole heirs. Completely cutting off his younger son, Capt. Joseph Bridger Jr., his will explained that he did not wish to further support his younger son in "his wild and profligate ways." (http://tk-jk.net/Bridgers/Shaggy/fog0000000027.html)

~

It had been exciting to be able to validate so many specifics with Jean and with our own research. Bobbie felt she had learned a lot about herself in her lifetime as Bridger. We had found, as Linda said, her lifetime as a politician, and we found her bones in the Smithsonian, which astonished us all.

BOBBIE

General Joseph Bridger

Bobbie internally and consciously struggled with being Bridger, a great and powerful man. Her conscious struggle regarding the credibility of the documentary and her internal struggle regarded reconciling herself as an important person (as Bridger), as in her current life she is "an average person who prefers to remain behind the scenes." She felt the internal struggle was a normal response, as some of the information was difficult to digest—perhaps as a defense mechanism of denial. "To this day I still have a little difficulty in knowing that I was Bridger, but I cannot deny what I saw, what I felt, and what I heard," she said.

Because of this struggle, she decided to move forward with another subject for the documentary. She hoped to find a compelling story other than that of Joseph Bridger while conveying a past life regression experience.

More than two years had passed since Bobbie's last regression to the life of Colonel Joseph Bridger. She had decided to use someone other than herself for her documentary, so her focus and commitment had been on those regressions and research. As if the universe had other plans, that story was not to be, and she returned to Bridger once again, still curious to see if she could discover more information about him. She told me her intuition told her to explore more. Admittedly, I wondered what more we could uncover through reliving her lifetime as Bridger that would benefit her, but Bobbie felt compelled to explore more about him.

Once she was in hypnosis, I guided her back to her lifetime as Bridger. Initially, much of the information she revealed was the same—in fact, exactly the same—as you would expect if the truth (or your truth) is being told. However, more details did emerge.

Bobbie continued to go into hypnosis easily and began reporting to me immediately. "I'm standing...ground...dirt...pants almost like suede... dark...green jacket."

"Notice your hands," I continued.

"Oh gawd. They're huge!" she said, pausing before she continued.

"Your hands will tell you how old you are. How old are you?"

"Thirty...forty. My hair is pulled back...ponytail...daytime...feel warm. I'm in Jamestown. People are doing their work...I'm angry!"

"Because?"

"I'm not hearing anything. I'm not getting reports!"

"What is your role?"

"Paymaster...feels bad...like a prison. I feel trouble."

"Go to the next important event."

"Yelling...people...men in town...angry. Trouble. Trouble with Indians. It is not the Indians that bother me..." Her sentence drifted off. "*Pompous ass!*" she exclaimed with vigor.

"Who?"

"Nathaniel. Nate. People working...but worried...chopping wood."

"What are you doing?"

"Visit with governor or someone important. He's assigned. He doesn't want to be there. He's afraid."

"I'm going to snap my fingers, and you'll know his name." *Snap.*

"Berkeley. Dressed...lace. Not a commoner."

"How long have you known him?"

"A while. He doesn't seem to have a backbone. It's warm. Late summer. We're here to meet people."

"What is your name?"

Her voice dropped significantly when she responded, "Joseph Bridger. General Joseph Bridger." She paused before continuing, "People are complaining about the Indians, but I've heard of no problems. Nate stirs up trouble. I'm not hearing anything. I'm not getting reports."

"Where are you?"

"In the chair against the wall…feel cramped. Nate trying to stir up trouble. Ten to fifteen people. I'm not part of Jamestown. Just visiting. Meeting. Close but not in town. Mmm. Rum tea or rum coffee? That's good," she said, seemingly enjoying the drink at hand. "They don't want to look at me. Nervous around me."

"Because?"

"I don't know. I'm bigger. Bigger than they are…and I have *no* patience. They're kicking us out. The governor and me."

"Colonel Bridger," I continued.

"*General* Bridger," she said sternly and in an intimidating manner, correcting me

"General Bridger," I corrected myself, feeling scolded. I noticed I sat up straight. "Move time forward to the next important event."

"My son. Angry at my son."

"Because…?"

"He loves a girl beneath him. Bacon…he'll never…young, strapping lad. He's a fool," she said, sputtering the words as though the whole idea was inconceivable.

"What's his name?"

"Joseph. We're arguing."

"Where are you?"

"House. He leaves angry. Defiant."

"Describe the house to me."

"Nice. I think brick or some wood…flowers outside at the edge. Large. It's an estate. No streets. No town. Marsh Estate. Three servants. I smell cinnamon and apple. Smells good!"

"How long have you lived there?"

"Five years. Ten maybe…lots of land. There's a tree out there…big tree. Makes me sad…so sad…a loss. Someone dear." She paused for a moment and then said in a deep voice of authority, "I'll not go there!"

I wondered what would get him so upset about the tree. "Is someone buried there?" I inquired.

"I'll not go there!" she said sternly, as though the topic or what was at the tree was strictly off limits.

"Go to the next important event, General Bridger."

"I'm governor! The governor left. He went to visit home. I'm acting... Virginia...South Carolina?"

"Walk over to your desk and notice what's on it."

"Proclamations. Hate the job. Dealing with these people. I was asked to be governor." She paused. "We get things done. Five to six years. He never came back."

"Go to the next important event now."

"I'm confused...everything...confused...angry...everything. Sixty? Fifty?"

"What happened to Nate?"

"Don't know. I have remorse. Joseph. I disowned him. He defied me," she said, before adding her physical conditions. "Weak. Dizzy. Home. Too sick to be governor. Feel old...unhappy...I want things a certain way. Now I'm old... sick."

"Go to the morning of the last day of your life as Bridger," I requested.

"Dark...early morning...vomiting...dizzy...a while...months...servants steal from me."

"Go through the death scene and find yourself floating above your body looking down."

"Old, frail. I look old. Unclean. In my bed."

After I had the information I needed on Bridger, I asked a wise and loving Being to come to Bobbie. Instead, her mother, whom she had lost several months earlier, came to her. She said she looked healthy again, and she felt great love from her. Bobbie sobbed at the enormous feeling of love and sight of her mother. It was a very powerful, tearful reunion. I gave her time to speak to her mother privately, and when she was done, I emerged her from hypnosis.

"Oh, my gawd!" Bobbie exclaimed, her eyes filled with tears. "I felt her presence and her love. She said, 'I love you, too.' Those words have a unique meaning," she whispered. "In her last year of life, I would always tell her 'I love you' each night before she went to bed. As if my mom knew the significance of those words and the meaning behind them, she would look at me and say, 'I love you, too.' There was such grief and sadness with her loss, and somehow I now feel a release."

Bobbie had been her mother's caretaker for ten years. She had dementia during her last two years of her life. I could see the change in Bobbie's face. She looked more serene after speaking to her mom. Although we learned a bit more about Bridger, perhaps this was the real reason for wanting a regression.

BOBBIE

Mehahtok

Bobbie returned a month later, and she was interested in attaining even more specifics of her lifetime as General Bridger. I reminded myself of the healing she had received with her mother and trusted her inner guidance. There was something more she needed to learn.

This time, I had her go to higher and higher states of awareness, "To a place where you can discover everything. At the count of one, you'll be back at a scene, situation, or event that has the most importance in your lifetime as General Bridger. Three, two, one. Be there now. Daytime or night time? Inside or out?"

"Daytime. Inside." By now Bobbie knew the type of questions I would ask and began reporting on everything she was seeing and experiencing. "Forties, trousers, long coat, maroon, light shine."

"Notice your hair."

"I think I'm wearing a wig!" she answered, sounding surprised.

"Are you alone or with others?"

"With Berkeley…taken a promotion."

"A promotion?"

"General…Admiral? A little girl…my little girl is there."

"What is her name?"

"Martha."

"How old is she?"

"Eight. Maybe nine."

"Where are you?"

"His office."

"How do you feel about Berkeley?"

"He's OK. He helps everyone. Very political. He likes my little girl."

"How long have you known him?"

"Years. Ten."

"Where is the office located?"

"Isle of Wight?"

"Let the scene unfold, and when you are ready, tell me what is happening."

"Spring day. He's happy," she said, with a big smile.

"Because?"

"He's amused by the girl. She's having fun."

"Do you live nearby?"

"No. I'm building a house close by. It's going to be a grand house. Big house. Twenty rooms."

"How many are in your family?"

"Three...four. Married...Hester. Ten years." I knew she hadn't done any research on Bridger in more than two years, but I recalled his wife's name was Hester.

"Where'd you meet?"

"Introduced. Smaller house. Dinner party."

"Where were you born?"

"England...Gloucester."

"What is your role?"

"Running the militia."

"Have you done this before?"

"No. Honored."

"Go to the next important event."

"Job promotion. On a boat. Several boats...military...cargo...men and horses...just off shore...we're going to Jamestown."

"Because?"

"Rebellion."

"How are you feeling?"

"Angry! Wasn't needed. I have no choice. I'm on a horse…it's *hot*. September. September. September. We're marching to Jamestown," Bobbie whispered.

"You and who else?"

"Militia…ragtag crew…hundreds. Five hundred."

"What is your purpose?"

"Rod out the rebels…arrest Bacon." I thought the use of the words *rod out* was interesting and wondered if that was an expression used during that time period.

"What does Bacon do?"

"He attacked the Indians and caused problems."

"Which Indians?"

She paused before she answered me. "Ssss…Swa…Swakanee?" She struggled, trying to pronounce the word, sounding unsure.

"Find your answers," I gently suggested and waited for her to respond.

"We form ranks. Sloppy ranks. Not professional soldiers. They're tradesmen and farmers. We advance. Outside town…crossing a field. We halt. Men are confused. They put women on the walls. Five or six. Forced to stand in front of…we can't shoot."

"Do you know or recognize the women?"

"They're affluent. Friends of families. One's crying. One is outraged," Bobbie said and then laughed. "She won't shut up! The others…don't know."

"Is Berkeley with you?"

"No."

"Because?"

"He trusts me."

"What happens next?"

"We talk terms. They shoot. Men break ranks. Ours. Some panic. They're angry and upset. Bacon burns the town. We take what's left."

"What was the purpose of burning the town?"

"Anger, spite. Untrusted person. Betrayed Berkeley," she responded.

"Where are you now?"

"Outside of Jamestown...men...restoring order...send a messenger to Berkeley. Rebels have been...town has been burned."

"Move time ahead now to eating a meal at your home."

"We're happy. Town is secure."

"What year is it?"

"1670s. Still hot! Ten to fifteen miles from town. Smell of burned woods. Whitemarsh. Road goes to manor. Large estate."

"Describe the front of the house."

"Brick...columns...majestic. I believe it's the biggest building in Virginia. Large table. I'm at head. Hester on other side...children...having pheasant. Martha...a young lady now. Joseph. Four others."

"Do you own any other homes?"

"We have other properties. Tobacco. I think one's in North Carolina."

"Who lives there?"

"Tenants...farmers."

"Do you have slaves?"

"Three...in the house. Others as well. Crops and stuff. Feel bad about slaves. Sign of wealth, but...I feel bad...they suffer. Doesn't feel right. Looking at the fields. Just tobacco."

"How many acres?"

"A lot. Thousands."

"Go now to the last month of your life."

"Weak...confused...don't know who I am sometimes...always sick. Hester...she's worried. Now it's bad."

"What does the doctor say?"

"None to be had."

"Does Hester share any of the same problems?"

"Some...not as bad."

"How do you pass?"

"Asleep."

"Float above your body and look down."

"Withered and old."

"What did you want to learn on a soul level as Joseph Bridger?"

"Justice."

I silently questioned why justice would be so important and thought Bobbie would want to know, too. "Find yourself going to an ancient building. Your guide will be waiting for you outside."

"I'm here."

"Now go in and find yourself in an ancient library with thousands upon thousands of books. Find yourself on a very long aisle. All of the books on this aisle are all about you. The ones closest to you have to do with your life as Bobbie. The ones further away have to do with other lifetimes and issues. Find the book titled *Justice*."

She paused for a few moments before saying, "I have it."

"Describe the book to me."

"Large...leather bound. Feather attached."

"I'd like you to take it to a desk. In a moment I'm going to have you open it, and it will open to the exact page that will help you understand your choice of wanting to learn justice in your life as Bridger. It may be a word, a feeling, or a scene that comes to life. Open the book now."

"Male. I'm being killed. They think I'm the devil. I don't understand. I'm upside down." Bobbie began moving and twisting her left hand and fingers.

"What is happening with your left hand?" I questioned.

"Rope...leather...trying to loosen," she answered.

"Are there others this is happening to?" I asked, wondering if she was in a group.

"Just me...they *stink!*" she said and crinkled her nose. "They wear skins... beards."

"Are they native to that area?"

"No."

"What color is your skin?"

"Red. Brownish. Their skin...white. Two men. They wanted me to show them something," she said, before pausing a few moments. "Like an animal... my arms are spread. Upside down. There are mountains and a valley."

"What are your last thoughts?"

"Why?" She sounded confused and sad. "My family...son...wife."

"Any negativity you've brought forward from that lifetime goes into the light for healing."

We had learned Bobbie's need for justice; her compassion toward Native Americans, which seemed to be apparent in her lifetime as Bridger; and the source of her anger. I emerged Bobbie from hypnosis. As she opened her eyes, I noticed they were extremely bloodshot. Much, much more than normal. Bloodshot eyes are a sign of being hypnotized, but I couldn't help but wonder how bloodshot one's eyes become if one were being held upside down for a long period of time. Bobbie said the torture went on for three days. She also said it felt like she had a hard time breathing upside down, and her lungs felt suffocated. "That feeling freaks me out, and I've had it in this life."

~

Bobbie was curious to validate some of the information in her regression. She discovered that, although Lewis and Clark discovered the Northwest Passage during the 1800s, the fur trade of the French Canadians began about 1560, when French fishermen brought home furs traded by the natives. The Blackfoot Indians were located in the Northwest United States and Canada. Frenchmen came to explore and trade specifically for furs in early 1600.

Bobbie's gut feeling of needing to return to her life as Bridger led her to Mehahtok and the lifetime Chip Coffee revealed as a Native American with a "unique crucifixion." It gave her a better understanding of her need for justice, as Linda Farr had said. Could it be that in Mehahtok's future life as General Bridger, this was the reason he had no problems or concerns with the Indians? Was the theme of justice playing out in both lifetimes?

In Bobbie's early years, she served in the navy. Later, she was an auxiliary police officer, and today she works behind the scenes as an advocate for veterans' medical care. Her blood pressure is often high from the stress of her job, dealing with the bureaucracy and political battles to get justice. Perhaps the theme of justice is still being played out in yet another way.

MARCELLA ZINNER

Psychic Reading of General Bridger

Bobbie asked local clairvoyant medium Marcella Zinner, one of only twenty-eight psychics certified by the Edgar Cayce Foundation, to my office to give her a reading.

Marcella had been given no information about the focus of the reading, only that Bobbie was doing a documentary about past life regression and how a medium could connect to a past life.

I asked Marcella to explain how she can read someone's past life when the person has reincarnated, and she explained it in this way: "I am able to shift out of my current awareness or consciousness and move into the subject or person at hand. I follow an energetic thread deep into the energy field of the person or situation. I feel, sense, clairvoyantly 'see,' and hear information. It comes through in an orderly or chronological manner, but I do not know or understand what the information means or how it is relevant. As this is all new to my energy field awareness; I am like a receiver of a variety of information. Usually, it comes quickly, and I have to relay it immediately as I don't hold a memory of what I say. It is very hard for me to repeat something. As I 'talk' or communicate the information more, awareness comes through and then leads to another thread and takes me deeper. I emotionally feel and 'see' the situation, so I am not entirely unaware. When I see or feel something unpleasant I react but do not hold it in my memory. It is as if I am there for a moment in time. I am in the energy imprint of the person's past life as if it is now, but only for a fleeting moment. If another question is asked of me or I sense something else, I can stay in that thread of energy until completion of the imprint. I use the client's energy field, travel through it into the past. I am shown an energy imprint, see it or feel it, which is very clear to me. I also hear clairaudient messages, which give me clarity or specific details. I ask what else I need to know silently to get more information. I believe I hear from a variety of guides and teachers in the higher realms. I access those who have the specific information I need. There is an energy shift for me when I access these energies. Most of the time, the pictures and senses and words come through one right after the other. A client's response enables them to associate and understand what it all means. Tapping into someone's past life is not any different for me than tapping into a current person or situation."

Bobbie wanted to discover further information, circumstances, other people, or details she might be able to validate from her lifetime as Colonel Bridger. Most importantly, she was interested in understanding Bridger's involvement with slavery.

Marcella knew Bobbie had experienced past life regressions with me, but we did not tell her anything else before giving her the name *Bridger* moments before her reading began.

"Can you tell me about Bridger and his involvement with slavery?" Bobbie asked.

Marcella took several breaths, closed her eyes briefly and then opened her eyes again, focusing straight ahead before she began to speak. "He's telling me it was pervasive. Trading. Money. Making money off of slaves and slave trade. A lot of that was illegal. They were captured and brought over illegally. This is where slavery actually started. It was initially made to look like they chose to come for housing and food because conditions were bad where they lived. This wasn't true. They were captured and chained. That's what was bothering him. He was part of that environment, so he tried to fit in. He tried to make it look legal. That enabled him to do what he did. To facilitate things, although he wasn't into power or status. This money wasn't able to be used. It wasn't good money. It was taken in exchange for people or slaves."

Bobbie asked Marcella, "Were they bribes?"

"Yes, it was not honest money. He couldn't do anything with it," Marcella responded.

"Did he have remorse about it?" Bobbie questioned.

"No, he didn't care. He said it wasn't about the money. He had more of a higher focus and purpose. He knew he had to play the game…with the culture and products of that culture in the power position he took on."

Bobbie asked, "Would he place himself in the category of being corrupt?"

"He's telling me no because he was constantly fighting against corruption, but he had to do it in a quiet, subdued way because nobody wanted to be shown as being corrupt. Because everybody was corrupt. He didn't feel he was corrupted…because he was doing things to try and right the wrong and go to a higher moral ground and a higher level of human respect. He was bribed, but he didn't feel he was corrupt. He was bribed because that is how business was done."

"So that was the norm at the time?" Bobbie asked.

"Yes. Yes. That's just doing business. He was very adamant saying he was not corrupt, but he was bribed," Marcella answered.

Bobbie gave a deep sigh. "I don't know if I want to know that."

"The documents are filed in the state of Virginia archives," Marcella added. "The finger was symbolic. He had his finger on the pulse of things. It's pointing to the truth that needs to be brought out."

Bobbie and I looked at each other, knowing Marcella had no knowledge of the finger bone. Yet here it was, coming up in a different way.

Bobbie proceeded to try and discover what more she could uncover about Bridger and his life through Marcella. "Does he feel like talking about Jamestown?"

"He said, 'Well, that can be boring.' I'm seeing horses. Lots of horses. There was horse trade. I would say it's stealing, but it was accepted, so they wouldn't have been called thieves. Wild horses. They justified taking them and moving them."

I asked Marcella, "What are his feelings about the Native Americans?"

"He's saying, 'Who are we to disrespect them? They were here first. It's their land. Their home.' I was seeing the slaves on boats."

"Did you see him on the boat?" Bobbie asked.

"On one, but not a slave boat," she answered.

We then played a small part of Bobbie's regression from her laptop computer for Marcella to see. She stopped playing the tape when Bridger said, "I'm angry. Wasn't needed. No choice."

"It wasn't needed," Bobbie said. "There was some kind of amphibious landing. It was the Bacon Rebellion. Was Bridger involved in this?"

We waited for Marcella to answer. "There was a fight. I guess a rebellion as you called it. So he had to stay on the ship for a little bit. Stay there and...I'm not sure what they were fighting over. It was like a faction felt one thing, and the other faction thought something else. It didn't make sense. He had to do what he had to do, so he was wanting to divert this because people were killed. But he had to...his position, his power of authority. Who he represented."

"In my regression," Bobbie began, pointing to her right arm, "I remember seeing this arm holding the reigns of my horse, and there was militia on the sides. Was he on a horse?"

Marcella answered, "He's explaining that when he was able to get off the ship, he was leading the militia. He had to get out of there. It was dangerous. He decided he needed to get the men out of there."

"Are you seeing this picture in your mind's eye?" I asked.

"Yes. There's smoke. The dwellings were burning," Marcella answered.

"Who was the leader of the other side?" I asked.

"They were an indistinct group. They weren't an army per se. A Franklin? He wanted all the power. He wasn't a trained soldier. Maybe it was Nathaniel," Marcella said, correcting the name she heard. "I'm kind of thinking he was from Britain...trying to get land back."

Bobbie added, "Nathaniel was Nathaniel Bacon. He was from the UK. He led the rebels, and he burnt the town. The feeling I got about him was that he was a pain in my backside."

Marcella tried to explain the situation further. "It was confusing. They didn't know who they were fighting. Nathaniel was trying to get control."

Bobbie played another clip of her regression for Marcella to see. We watched the segment of Bobbie as she whispered, "September, September, September," as Bridger.

Marcella interjected, "It was hot and rainy. Hurry up. Rushing."

The tape of Bobbie in the regression continued. "Militia. Hundreds. Five hundred."

"What is the purpose of going to Jamestown?" I asked.

"Rod out the rebels. Arrest Bacon," Bridger answered. (I had assumed *rod out* was perhaps a term used at that time that meant to draw out.)

"What did Bacon do?" I asked.

"Indians attacked. Indians caused problems," Bridger said.

Bobbie stopped the regression tape. She explained to Marcella that Bacon had retaliated on the wrong tribe of Native Americans.

Marcella continued with her reading. "He didn't consider Indians had human rights. He was kind of stupid. Bacon. He was ego driven."

"Do you have a name of the Indians?" I asked.

Marcella responded by saying, "S…"

We turned the regression tape on again. *"Did you ever come across Indians?" I asked.*

"On occasion. Peaceful."

"What happened in Jamestown?" I asked.

"We form ranks. Sloppy. Sloppy ranks. Unprofessional soldiers."

"Is there anyone else with you on horseback?"

"Lieutenant."

"Describe the scene as you come into town."

"We're outside town. We're crossing a field. We halt." There was a long pause before she continued. *"Men are confused. They put women on the walls."*

"Notice the women on the walls. How many are there?"

"Five. Maybe six?"

"What are they doing in front of the walls?"

"They are being forced to stand in front of the walls. We can't shoot!"

"Do you recognize any of them?

"They are affluent. They are friends of families."

"As the women stand there, what is their reaction?"

"One's crying. One is outraged. She won't shut up!" Bobbie chuckled. *"The others…don't know."*

"Do you know any of them personally?"

"I think so. Family of Berkeley."

Bobbie stopped the tape. "Does *Berkeley* sound familiar?" she asked Marcella.

"It feels like a person or a place? Is this a conference to communicate what happened?" Marcella responded.

I answered Marcella. "Berkeley was sent back to England to report on the rebellion."

"Is there a place Berkeley in Britain?" Marcella asked.

Bobbie responded, "There was a Governor Berkeley who was sent back to Britain."

I corrected Marcella several times as well, stating Berkeley was the person and the place was Britain.

Marcella repeated herself. "Berkeley. It was a place in Britain. It was a place."

Bobbie and I ignored Marcella's comment. We continued with the reading Marcella was giving on Bridger.

"Notice the militia, how they're dressed, if you would," I requested.

"Well, when I first saw them, they were just shabbily dressed, not necessarily in uniform, just shabbily dressed men."

"And can you move time forward, even half an hour or hour or so when you see a vision?"

"Uh-huh, yes," Marcella replied before her face grimaced. "It didn't go really well. Men were killed unnecessarily."

"Can you see the scene from above the men?" I asked.

"He was riding...trying to control and direct it. It was chaotic. They were trying to listen, but it was chaotic. And noisy. There was smoke. Musket smoke? Fires. They were burning the land...destroying. There were some dwellings. The horses were involved as well. Trying to get them contained. Oh. Ugh. It was awful! Then he was trying to get his men he was in charge of or responsible for to turn and go this way." She motioned with her hands. "Not hightail it, but diverted them...north of Jamestown a bit, to be safe...safer. West. West of Jamestown, because there was this certain faction of people who wanted to take control of the city. He was actually trying to divert that…or prevent that. He sort of did, actually, but, um, he had to get away, so there wouldn't be more people dying…there were horses dying. They are lying on the ground," Marcella said, with a look of distaste on her face.

"One of the things I picked up on during my regression," Bobbie began, "was exactly what you mentioned about the attire. That they were just kind of like, a ragtag group, there weren't, like, you know how you see rows and columns of British soldiers and stuff? This was not even close to it. I did pick up on the fact that brown and green was the color, colors that we wore, but I did also pick up on—I just have this horse's head, ears, white horse in my head, and you know, it was hot!"

"You were on a white horse?" I asked. I found it to be an interesting detail.

"Yeah," Bobbie replied.

Marcella added, "He was, but the others weren't. There weren't other white horses. He had a semblance of a uniform, but the others did not."

Bobbie continued, "And I had, you know, I think it was some kind of green and brown. It was some kind of symbolic color of militia or something. I don't know what it was. That's where we need to get a historian to kind of look at the military for the state of Virginia." Bobbie hesitated before she continued. "Umm…" I could see she was questioning internally how much to say to Marcella. "There was a battle. But it didn't go well. Where were the women?" Bobbie asked.

"They weren't there…fields and houses," Marcella initially responded, but as though she was getting more information, she added, "Well, there were women, but…some of them were cap…cap…captive."

"Can you see what happened to the women who were captive?" I asked.

"They kept them, but I keep getting pulled. They took them inland a bit."

Satisfied with the information Marcella had given us, Bobbie wanted to know about the tree that held such emotion for her. "I won't go there," she had said during the regression.

Bobbie looked at Marcella and asked, "What's his feeling about the tree?"

Marcella paused for a moment, as though she was hearing the information in her mind before she spoke. "The first word was *worship*. He worshipped the tree. It was a symbol of sacredness and strength and…doing the right thing and making sure that everything was in line the way it was supposed to be."

"Was this the tree on his property?" Bobbie asked.

"Well, yes. It's a tree on his property, but it was a symbol for him…to be strong and sturdy. Which he took seriously. It was more than a tree. It was a symbol of his life."

Bobbie wanted more specifics. "Was there any emotional context to it?"

"Well, yes, because it meant a lot to him. To remind him to stay sturdy, stay strong, stay the course. Do what was needed, no matter what."

Marcella paused, and Bobbie added, "I picked up a heavy sadness around that tree. I didn't want to go near that tree."

"It represents a lot of past sorrow for him."

"What about loved ones?" Bobbie inquired.

"Parents?" Marcella paused. "Was there a hanging in the tree? Ugh," she said, followed by a big sigh. "Feels like a male. That's why *a* tree and *the* tree are so profound in his life."

Bobbie confirmed what Marcella said. "There was a genuine sadness about that tree. I don't want to be near it."

"I keep getting pulled back to when he was young…a youngster. Ugh! He witnessed a hanging when he was young. It was so horrendous. It didn't seem fair. It was like he had to stay there and watch all this. He had to, but he didn't want to."

"What was the skin color of the person?"

"It was dark. He was African American. But he knew the person that was hung [sic]," she said, referring to young Bridger. "That did it for him for his whole life. That moved him into what he had to do to make wrong things right. It was wrong from his perspective. It shouldn't have happened. It propelled him into moving through his life to right what was wrong." My mind went to Mehahtoc.

The reading ended. Marcella had picked up and confirmed many facts, even though she had only a vague recollection of ever hearing about the Bacon Rebellion in a history class.

I began to research Marcella's comment about illegal slave trade. "This is where slavery actually started," Marcella had said. She was correct. Slavery in America began when the first African slaves were brought to the North American colony of Jamestown, Virginia, in 1619, to aid in the production of such lucrative crops as tobacco. European settlers in North America turned to African slaves as a cheaper, more plentiful labor source than indentured servants (who were mostly poorer Europeans). After 1619, when a Dutch ship brought twenty Africans ashore at the British colony of Jamestown, Virginia, slavery spread throughout the American colonies.

The status of the first Africans was similar to that of indentured servants, and some became landowners once they had fulfilled their years of servitude. In 1650 African Anthony Johnson is recorded as a freeman owning 250 acres of land. In 1654 an African by the name of John Casor became the first legally recognized slave in America. One year later, Bridger would arrive in Virginia.

According to the Colonial Williamsburg Foundation, the growth of the black population grew from three hundred in 1648 (seven years before Bridger arrived) to three thousand in 1680. Nearly one hundred years later, slavery exploded. Between the years of 1740 and 1775, the black population grew from sixty thousand to two hundred ten thousand.

In 1662, Virginia passed a law that even if the father is a freeborn Englishman, any children of an enslaved mother will follow her status and automatically become slaves. Undoubtedly, this law seemed to be designed to free whites from legal responsibility for their mixed race children. Some Blacks joined in Bacon's failed rebellion, and afterward were singled out for slavery.

Marcella had said it was made to look like it was a choice for the slaves to come to the New World and said to check documents filed in the state of Virginia archives. Not only was she aware they were in Virginia but, perhaps more importantly, that I could locate documents about Bridger's involvement in the archives. "The finger was symbolic. He had his finger on the pulse of things. It's pointing to the truth that needs to be brought out," she said.

As Marcella had suggested, I contacted the Library of Virginia archives department, and the reference librarian led me to the information that Bridger had represented the Isle of Wight from 1657 to 1658 and also in 1663 in the House of Burgesses. Bridger did not pass any laws regarding slavery during those years, although laws were passed in other years. His direct connection to slavery was unclear, and yet he was said to be on every important committee, so he certainly must have had a pulse on things.

I wrote the librarian again and asked what Bridger's connection was to slavery. In an email he said, *"I have read the entry on Joseph Bridger in the* Dictionary of Virginia Biography, *Volume 2, pages 224–226. The article does not mention Joseph Bridger bringing slaves to Virginia. However a 7 June 1666 land patent for Capt. Joseph Bridger for 7800 acres in the Isle of Wight County or Nansemond County mentions among the 156 persons transports, 9 Negroes."*

He wrote to me again and said:

After e-mailing you, I quizzed a colleague about the status of the transported Negroes who explained to me that at this time period they were likely indentured servants not slaves. The codification of a racial system began in 1639; the first description of Africans as slaves, however entered statute books only in 1659, and it was not until 1670 that Virginia ruled that the imported Africans were slaves for life. From the very beginning, moreover, some African Americans lived other than chattel. The record contains the names of men and women who lived as freeholders or owners of a notable amount of land. Large scale African slavery, according to historian Edmund Morgan, was instituted after 1680.

I then spoke to a representative at the Virginia Historical Society who told me that records from the 1600s were sparse and mostly had to do with land and money. Land was important because the production of tobacco was just beginning and thought to be how landowners would acquire wealth. I couldn't find out what truth Bridger had wanted to come out, unless it was that he wasn't involved in slavery to the degree we expected. And if that is the case, it would explain why it never came up in Bobbie's regressions.

As a result of Bacon's Rebellion, where there was unity between poor whites and blacks fighting together, Virginia instituted a system of racial slavery and phased out indentured servitude. Landowners began to hold Africans against their will, refusing to free them after their period of indenture. This process expanded into racial slavery in the 1700s.

Marcella was able to pick up on many important facts of Bridger's life, as follows:

* Marcella mentioned the name *Nathaniel* as being part of the opposition.
* Marcella said Nathaniel was from Britain.
* Marcella said Nathaniel burned down the town (Jamestown).
* When I asked Marcella if she knew the name of the Indian tribe, she could only say the letter *S*. I learned Bacon had attacked the Susquehanaugs, which was the wrong tribe. Perhaps this is also the tribe Bobbie was trying to pronounce when she said *Swakanee*.
* Marcella was adamant that Berkeley was both a person and a place. I had explained to her, rather confidently, that Berkeley was the name, and England was the place. I was certain I was right, repeating myself several times. Marcella repeated herself about Berkeley being both a person and a place. I then searched the Internet for Berkeley, England, and discovered there *is* a city Berkeley located in Gloucestershire County. Berkeley Castle, located in Berkeley, has been in the Berkeley family since the twelfth century. Marcella was correct. Berkeley was a place and a person. (Interestingly, Gloucestershire is the same county Bridger lived in as a child.)
* Marcella said the people in the rebellion were shabbily dressed men. She was right again.
* Marcella knew the rebellion was in Virginia and that the women were put in front of walls or ramparts, as Bobbie called them.
* Marcella had given Bobbie a new understanding of why the tree, where young Bridger had witnessed a hanging of someone he knew, was so powerful. It was the reason Bridger had so firmly stated in the regression, "I'll not go there." It all made sense to Bobbie.

~

Berkeley authorized a five-hundred-man army to fight the Indians and appointed Bridger to organize it, but because Berkeley was dealing with the Indians for their valuable furs, the army never marched against them. As a result, the farmers, feeling vulnerable, became rebellious and sided with Bacon. Bacon did not think kindly of Bridger for his continued loyalty to England.

During a phone conversation with Jean Tomes, she told me they had discovered a large amount of money hidden in the ground throughout the farm. She said this was money Bridger had brought from England. She also said he was not involved in slavery.

I sent a copy of the sketch of Bridger to Jean, who responded by saying, "I have a picture on my desk of my mother who was a Bridger. The forehead was so much like Mother it gave me cold chills. The sketch looked just as I thought he would look."

Bobbie's past life regressions gave her new insight. She wrote to me, sharing her new understanding: "I started looking at my past lives and realized there is more to this universe than what we know and that the anchors of organized religions and science bind us to such a narrow view. Now I can no longer accept the traditional thinking as Gospel but only look at it as a baseline to explore from...to others I would say—'It's ok to explore the unknown so long as you harm none, you make a positive difference and that you do so with love in your heart.' The unknown only remains unknown till you take the journey. All that just from these few past life experiences and a phone call with Chip Coffey."

Bobbie's past life regression experiences led her down an uncharted path that she wasn't sure she completely believed was possible. She had discovered two of the lifetimes Chip Coffey had told her about: as an abused woman in the 1800s whose last thought was "never again" and as a male Native American "crucified" in an unusual way. Spirit medium Linda Farr told her about her lifetime in Washington, DC, as a politician and stated Bobbie would find her finger or bones in the Smithsonian. And she did! When spirit medium Marcella Zinner gave Bobbie a reading, she confirmed many specifics of what Bobbie had experienced in her regression during the Bacon Rebellion.

Bobbie had satisfied her curiosity about the link between a psychic reading and a past life regression. What she had never anticipated, however, was finding specific historical facts to validate many of the memories from her regressions. She didn't expect to discover she had been co-acting governor of the state of Virginia in the 1600s or that she would speak to descendants of the man she was in that lifetime, General Joseph Bridger. Nor did she expect to find the feeling of injustice that she did as Mehahtok, which was perhaps the source of her internal anger and desire for justice. She did not expect she would experience healing of the deep grief she had felt after her mother passed. She didn't expect to discover the love of a mother for her child as Jessica or that, out of desperation, she had become a prostitute in the Old West. Nor did she expect to find her killer. And finally, she didn't expect the physical healing that occurred as a result of learning how Jessica had died. As of this writing, nearly five years after her regression, Bobbie's stomach issues have never returned.

~

I spoke to Jean again as I was confirming details for this book. She put me in touch with Bill Carrell III, an attorney, ninth-removed grandson of Joseph Bridger, and the author of *The Landed and Personal Estate of General Joseph Bridger*. I viewed Bill as an expert on his great-grandfather. When I called him and introduced myself, I began by saying, "*General* Joseph Bridger. Although nearly all of my research refers to him as *Colonel*, he made it very clear he was a general and wants to be addressed as such."

"Finally! Yes! I've been trying to get that changed! I agree!" Bill said excitedly. We spoke for nearly two hours. He quizzed me on how I knew certain information regarding Bridger, and I assured him I had done extensive research on him, but to please correct me if I had anything wrong. Finally, Bill asked if he could speak to Bobbie directly. It was quite moving for me to introduce Bobbie to General Joseph Bridger's great-grandson. They, too, spoke for hours on the phone. Bobbie is planning a trip to Williamsburg to see Saint Luke's and Smithville. Bill said he will meet her there. He wants to meet her and show her around.

SOUL EXPLORATION

This is not a scientific study, but rather a collection of past life regressions that I found especially intriguing. Each of the past lives you have read about were included to show how past life regression helped heal my clients or gave them greater insight into themselves. Some clients came to me to discover who they were in a previous life, while others came for clinical hypnosis and spontaneously regressed to another life, even though reincarnation was not part of their belief system.

Ginny was one of those clients. Her fear of heights that "only happens when I'm in control" brought her to her life as a French colonel, sitting on his horse on a high cliff while looking down, unable to help as he witnessed twenty-five thousand of his men being slaughtered. She learned it wasn't the height itself that caused the fear, but what she was experiencing emotionally while at a height.

In Sunny's regression as Marisha, she learned her sister today was her mother in an ancient time in Saudi Arabia, a time when she was taken and killed. The regression somehow healed her sister's daily panic attacks and deep grief for a daughter she had lost fourteen years earlier. Although Sunny's sister didn't know about her regression (or believe in reincarnation), she had healed simply by Sunny's experiencing her Saudi life. Could it be that her sister had such an extended, deep grief because her soul remembered the loss of her child in an ancient time? Had something much deeper happened on a soul level that helped to heal her sister, as her guide Eli had said would happen?

Other clients were open to reincarnation but expected to regress to a time in their current lives, as was the case of teenage Sarah, who found herself at the early age of three needing to feel and heal an old wound with her father that cleared a path for her to have relationships with males. As she uncovered the cause of her problem, she was able to discover where it had originated so that she could recover. An unexpected bonus was her spontaneous regression to another life, where she was made fun of for playing sports in her life as Elizabeth. By doing so she cleared her block to fully participate in sports. Most surprising was that once she remembered how she had been shot in the chest as Elizabeth, her chronic asthma healed.

Bill came to understand his attachment to his ex-wife when he saw her as his wife in his life as Louis. This understanding allowed Bill to let go of her. In his life as Fred Colton, he learned where his deathly fear of snakes had begun when he died from a poisonous snake bite. It also explained his birthmark that resembled a small cut Fred's son had made to get the poison out before going for help. Bill no longer walks in fear while cautiously looking for a snake on his hikes.

Pat healed her chronic throat clearing once she remembered she had died from smoke inhalation in a barn fire as the small child Carly. In another regression her chronic fingernail biting since early childhood (due to the stress of living with her mother) healed when she learned her mother was her wife whom she could never please in her African American lifetime. This had carried into her current life, and in the knowing of the circumstances, Pat was able to release it. Her nails are now healthy.

Bobbie's stomach problems were resolved once she remembered being stabbed and killed by a member of the infamous Bender family in her life as Jessica, the lifetime Chip Coffey had told her about in a reading, a life that ended with a feeling of "never again." She also discovered for the first time the deep love for a child. Childless in her current life, the love for a child was a feeling she had not experienced as Bobbie.

In Diane's story, you met Mary Lincoln, but others were famous in their own right as well: Ginny as the harpsichordist Marchand and as General Claude Louis Hector, Duke of Villars and Bobbie as General Joseph Bridger, a co-acting governor of Virginia involved in the Bacon Rebellion.

Martha's past lives explained her difficulty with motherhood and healed her relationships with her daughter, mother-in-law, and sister-in-law. Her soul exploration led her to discover her lives as a monk and a mistress, a general and a slave, a sea captain and a Native American.

Linda learned where her fear of doctors and water came from with her discovery of Lilly's time in a mental institution and suicide by drowning. She realized her off-the-cuff statement "If you put water in my face, I go *insane*" was eerily accurate.

Ginny's life as Julia taught us the importance and choice of having Down Syndrome, as she simply wanted to love and be loved. As Elsie Gruenwald, we learned how her last thoughts before being gassed at Auschwitz (feeling it would have been easier if she had never loved or been loved) had resulted in her current life, in which she could unlearn that thought.

Remembering our previous lives enables us to better understand our fears and to start to heal any unseen wounds. Are you curious about your past lives? Do you wonder who you have been or what countries or time periods you have lived in? Perhaps your interest has more to do with people in your life and their connection to you from a time long ago.

Past life regression can help you:

* Overcome fears or phobias
* Better understand your current life and the "theme" you are working on
* Develop better relationships by understanding previous life connections
* Become aware of attitudes that might hold you back in some way
* Understand your talents and abilities and bring them to this life, if appropriate
* Remove blocks to being all you want to be
* Get a sense of being eternal and lose your fear of death and dying
* Heal yourself on an emotional, mental, and physical level

Here are some important points to consider for your soul journey:

When you look for a past life hypnotist/regressionist, it's important that you feel safe with whomever you choose. Be certain he or she is experienced. Trust your intuition.

Allow yourself to be hypnotized. Relax and let go. If you get too caught up in your thoughts, you can block the process:

"I don't think I'm hypnotized" thought: Trust that you are hypnotized. Remember that it doesn't feel as weird as you may think because it's a natural state you go into and out of throughout the day.

"I'm making this up" thought: If you think you are making it up, consider this normal. It's your conscious mind getting in the way. Then give yourself permission to continue making it up, and see how the story unfolds. Don't be concerned about what part of your experience is your imagination, fantasy, or metaphor. Allow your imagination to soar. Color outside the lines. Let it happen.

Imagery and symbolism are the languages of the subconscious. Tell your analytical mind to sit in the corner and watch silently. You can analyze it later, but for now just let the information come. Remember, imagination is the gateway to the soul.

"I knew I couldn't do this" thought: Don't judge what you are experiencing. If you are too anticipatory or try too hard, you'll block having an experience, so get out of your own way. Relax, let go, and take those beautiful, nice, deep breaths. The more you let go, the more the information will come to you. It may come as a feeling, a thought, a sensing, or a knowing instead of seeing something. The more you do this, the more successful you will be.

WHAT YOU CAN EXPECT IN A PAST LIFE REGRESSION:

Regardless of your belief about reincarnation, you can still experience and heal from a past life regression, even if you think of it as a metaphor, a psychodrama of the mind, or even something that you made up.

You may not see in your mind's eye during a regression but instead feel or somehow know what is happening. That's OK. There is no right or wrong. However you receive the information is perfect for you.

A past life regression may feel like the present instead of the past. You may be "in" a different body or looking at a scene in which, in a few moments, you "know" who you are. You may feel like you are reliving the experience, or you may watch it unfold in front of you.

If you find yourself in a scene that is unpleasant, your hypnotist can have you float above the scene and look at it without emotion or put it on a movie screen, move time forward, or use other techniques. It's about finding out what happened. Know that even if you go through the death scene, you don't die. Instead, you discover that a part of you still lives and is aware of everything. People lose their fear of death once they experience a past life and realize this.

You are eternal. You exist beyond all limits, beyond your body and your mind. You are immortal. Life is continuous. We don't die when our bodies die. We are spiritual beings.

We are all energy, and energy never dies. The soul itself is an energy, and without it our human bodies cease to function. If our body is the car, it won't move without gasoline. Your soul is the gasoline.

You may feel great emotion and cry. They are healing tears. Give them permission to flow. Feel it to heal it.

You may become unaware of your physical body.

You may not get answers to every question that is asked by your hypnotist. That's OK. You aren't doing it wrong; it may be that the information isn't important. Remember, too, that the information you get is coming from *your* perspective. In the big scheme of things, the year, your name, or the name of the town where you live doesn't matter. Let go of expectations and agendas. Sometimes you get what you need, not what you want or think you'll get.

Some people want their soul's evolution revealed to them in a few hours. Past life regression is not a drive-through at a fast food restaurant. Knowledge comes as you are ready and able to accept it. All will be revealed to you when you are ready to receive the information. Trust your inner wisdom to take you where you need to go to help you heal and grow the most. Whatever happens, happens. Whatever you experience is perfect for you.

Unlike a dream that you often quickly forget, regressions can be remembered for a very long time, especially if the lifetime is profound. Only 1 percent or fewer of regressed people go so deep they don't remember anything. More information and answers may come to you after the regression through dreams, while daydreaming, while driving, and in other ways.

Not all the information that comes through a past life regression may be 100 percent correct, as it is still going through the human mind. But if you look at a regression in its totality, the information revealed is compelling. And ultimately, it's the healing and insight that make the difference.

I never know where the soul of a client will take him or her to heal, but I always trust it. There is a part of you that remembers *everything*. Ask to discover what will help you heal and grow the most, and then let your deeper wisdom take you there.

Those with scientific minds and a "prove it" attitude should remember that true science begins with observation. Keep an open mind. Galileo was imprisoned when he shared his findings that Earth and other planets revolved around the sun. Charges were brought against him by the Inquisition (the legal body of the Catholic Church) when most people of the time believed Earth was the center of the universe. He was accused of being a heretic at a time when most were put to death, as his findings were opposed to Church teachings. He recanted, but when he published a book in 1633 stating his original findings, he was accused of heresy and sentenced to life imprisonment. After a thirteen-year investigation by the Roman Catholic Church, he was exonerated in 1992, 350 years later. It can take a long time to open minds.

Many thought the world was flat until Ferdinand Magellan sailed around the world. Electricity has always been available to us, yet it has only been in the last 150 years that we've figured out how to use it. Until recently we thought there were only three dimensions; however, in an article published in *The Proceedings of the National Academy of Sciences* (March 2014), scientists achieved a quantum entanglement with a minimum of 103 dimensions with only two particles. They said the states could include being dead, alive, or in 101 other states simultaneously and entangled in a way that what happens to one immediately affects the other. What we understand to be our truths now can and will change. What will our truths be next?

Past life exploration will enlighten you as to who you really are and your soul's history. It's an in-depth soul study to help you realize and understand that you are eternal. Life is continuous. You exist beyond all limits, beyond your body and your mind. Your soul remembers everything and is rich with wisdom and scars from past lives. Discover your innermost ancient truth about who you really are, and become your own soul explorer.

RECOMMENDED READING

Beyond the Ashes: Cases of Reincarnation from the Holocaust
by Rabbie Yonassan Gershom and John Rossner

Children's Past Lives
by Carol Bowman

Coming Back: A Psychiatrist Explores Past-Life Journeys
by Dr. Raymond Moody

Destiny of Souls
Journey of Souls
by Michael Newton, PhD

Many Lives, Many Masters
Messages from the Masters
Only Love Is Real
Same Soul, Many Bodies
Through Time into Healing
by Brian Weiss, MD

Miracles Happen
by Brian Weiss, MD and Amy Weiss

Other Lives, Other Selves
    by Roger Woolger, PhD

Reincarnation: The Missing Link in Christianity
    by Elizabeth Clare Prophet and Erin L. Prophet

Soul Agreements
    by Dick Sutphen and Tara Sutphen

There Is a River
    by Thomas Sugrue

Twenty Cases Suggestive of Reincarnation
    by Ian Stevenson, PhD

You Were Born to Be Together
    by Dick Sutphen

ABOUT THE AUTHOR

Patricia S. McGivern worked in the corporate world for almost twenty years and might still be there were it not for a personal tragedy. Events leading from her unborn baby's miscarriage ignited McGivern's interest in reincarnation.

Now a certified hypnotist with both the International Board for Regression Therapy and the National Guild of Hypnotists, McGivern is in private practice. Trained by Brian Weiss, MD, she specializes in past life regressions.

McGivern is the author of *Angel Babies: Messages from Miscarried and Other Lost Babies* and a recipient of the Editor's Choice Award. *Angel Babies* explores spiritual communication with early-loss babies and is based on McGivern's own spiritual experiences.

www.PatriciaMcGivern.com

www.ingramcontent.com/pod-product-compliance
Lightning Source LLC
Chambersburg PA
CBHW021615270326
41931CB00008B/707